TIME CAPSULE/1932

TIME CAPSULE/1932

A HISTORY OF THE YEAR CONDENSED FROM THE PAGES OF TIME

TIME-LIFE BOOKS, NEW YORK

TIME / **1932**

EDITOR *Henry R. Luce*
MANAGING EDITOR *John S. Martin*
ASSOCIATES *John Shaw Billings,
Laird S. Goldsborough, Myron Weiss*
WEEKLY CONTRIBUTORS *Elizabeth Armstrong,
Carlton J. Balliett Jr., Noel F. Busch,
Washington Dodge II, Mary Fraser, Albert L. Furth,
Allen Grover, David W. Hulburd, E. D. Kennedy,
T. S. Matthews, Frank Norris, Ralph D. Paine Jr.,
Francis deN. Schroeder, Cecilia A. Schwind,
Charles Wertenbaker, S. J. Woolf*

EDITOR *Maitland A. Edey*
EXECUTIVE EDITOR *Jerry Korn*
TEXT DIRECTOR *Martin Mann*
ART DIRECTOR *Sheldon Cotler*
CHIEF OF RESEARCH *Beatrice T. Dobie*

SERIES EDITOR *John Dille*
ASSISTANT *Richard Oulahan*
RESEARCHER *Louise Samuels*
DESIGNER *Arnold Holeywell*
ASSISTANT DESIGNER *John Woods*
COPYREADER *Rosemarie Conefrey*

PUBLISHER *Rhett Austell*

COVER ILLUSTRATION *Lou Lomonaco*

EVENTS OF THE YEAR

Editors' Note

This was the year in which the Great Depression hit bottom. In late July the U.S. Army had to be called out to disperse a mob of bonus marchers from the nation's Capitol. The financial world, groggy from three years of falling stock prices, bank closings and corporate failures, was further shaken by the sudden collapse of two great empires—one controlled by Chicago utilities magnate Samuel Insull, the other by the "Swedish Match King," Ivar Kreuger. The nation was also shocked by the kidnap and murder of its favorite hero's son, Charles A. Lindbergh Jr. But there was less depressing news as well. Sparked by the hitting of Babe Ruth and Lou Gehrig, the New York Yankees won the World Series from the Chicago Cubs. And the U.S. enjoyed playing host to a warm and fascinating visitor from abroad, German scientist Albert Einstein, who said, "Nice people, those Americans."

■

TIME CAPSULE/1932 is one of a series of volumes, each adapted and condensed from a year's contents of TIME, the Weekly Newsmagazine. The words, except for a few connecting passages, are those of the magazine itself, and therefore reflect the flavor, the attitudes and the state of knowledge of the day—sometimes innocent, sometimes opinionated, sometimes prescient. The book is divided, like the magazine, into departments, and is organized so that each department forms a chronological chapter for the entire year. The dates in the margin are the issue dates of the magazine.

NATIONAL AFFAIRS

The Presidency

In 1932 Herbert Hoover was in his third year in the White House and the Great Depression was at its worst. There were 12,000,000 U.S. unemployed, and in June, 20,000 of them, all veterans, marched on Washington, demanding immediate payment of their World War I military service bonuses. Hoover rejected the demand. He also turned down numerous proposals for sweeping federal aid programs, though he made one major effort to restore the nation's economy through the Reconstruction Finance Corporation, set up to make urgently needed loans to business. Hoover's political career was destined to end in November, when Franklin D. Roosevelt defeated him by 7,000,000 votes.

JAN. 4 **CHRISTMAS SHOPPING:** This year Hard Times, more as an example than as a necessity, made a difference even at the White House. The President & Mrs. Hoover frowned down costly gifts, decided all presents should be inexpensive. Three days before Christmas, Mr. Hoover with his sons and daughter-in-law went shopping for the children, pushed their way like ordinary persons through the Washington store crowds. At a toy department the President picked out a gasoline filling station and a war tank. Mr. Hoover was fascinated with a miniature electric range, bought it and some toy cooking utensils. As usual on Christmas morning the President got down on the floor to play with his grandchildren's toys.

ARMS, MEN & A WOMAN: President Hoover went boldly forward last week with his plans for U.S. participation in the League of Nations' general disarmament conference at Geneva Feb. 2. He refused to let world rumors to the effect that the meeting was predestined to failure daunt his hopes. He tossed tradition to the winds and reaped a loud round of public applause when he named a woman to the delegation. She was

Miss Mary Emma ("May") Woolley, 68-year-old president of Mount Holyoke College. The President chose her because "the whole question of disarmament is and has been of profound interest to the women of the United States." A large, florid woman, Miss Woolley dresses in somber clothes, wears low-heeled shoes, believes "no lady would smoke." Declared Delegate Woolley last week:

"I've long been interested in the substitution of international understanding for international brute force. There are many reasons why women are on the side of world understanding. One is what may be called the biological argument. 'Only a woman knows what a man costs.'"

CANDIDATE: "To those who have inquired of me whether or JAN. 25 not the President would be a candidate for re-election, I have replied that of course he was a candidate. The friends of the President feel that he ought to be renominated." Postmaster General Walter Folger Brown, most politically-minded member of the Cabinet, was talking to newsmen in the lobby of the White House offices. He had just emerged from a long heart-to-heart talk with President Hoover. Now for the first formal time, he was announcing the obvious: Herbert Hoover would stand for another four years in the White House.

The White House has left its scars of service on the President. His hair is greyer. His shoulders seem to droop in discouragement. The lines about his eyes have cut in deeper and those about his mouth have hardened. The round baby-pink face of the 1920s has grown firmer, more mature. To strangers he may appear a beaten man but his friends marvel at his fortitude and lack of bitterness. Thin-skinned, he has learned to shrug off criticism with a philosophy described as "almost oriental in its calm." No longer do his fingers drum a nervous tattoo on his chair arm or his eyes rove the floor. He talks in a low, steady, less querulous voice. His words are weighed with patient resignation.

ACTION: All week long President Hoover kept prodding his FEB. 1 newly constituted Reconstruction Finance Corporation forward into action. The President had signed the bill setting up the new agency within a few minutes after it reached the White House—"Herbert" with one pen and "Hoover" with another. Then he praised the "patriotism" of Congress.

About Washington there was a great hustle and bustle to get R.F.C. operating. Congress sped through an initial appropriation of $500,000,000 as working capital. Chairman Eugene Meyer received 2,500 letters asking for jobs, inquiring about loans.

Japan, which had overrun Manchuria in September 1931, moved into China proper and occupied the city of Shanghai in late January 1932. The U.S., concerned with the protection of its interests in the occupied zones, suddenly found itself facing a crisis in the Far East.

FEB. 8 **STEAMING ORDERS:** With the Far Eastern sky flaming as red as the sunburst of the Japanese flag, President Hoover, looking worn and worried, summoned Secretaries Henry L. Stimson of State, Col. Patrick J. Hurley of War and Charles Francis Adams of the Navy for a White House Council. With them hurried General Douglas MacArthur, Chief of Staff, and other officers. The President and his advisers hunched over maps of China, talked in low voices. Before President Hoover was a request from U.S. Consul General Edwin Sheddan Cunningham at Shanghai for more protection for U.S. citizens there.

When his decision had been made, the President told an anxious nation:

"Directions have been given to send to Shanghai the 31st Regiment, together with 400 Marines [later increased to 600] on the transport *Chaumont* leaving tomorrow. The cruiser *Houston* and six destroyers left Manila this morning for Shanghai."

FEB. 22 **SORE HANDS:** After White House receptions at which he shakes thousands of hands, President Hoover goes directly upstairs where is waiting for him a basin of antiseptic diluted in hot water. Into this the President plunges his red swollen hand to relieve the ache. Last week the White House secretariat announced that the President would hold no more receptions, shake no more hands. "To greet so many visitors," said a spokesman, "presents too great a task for the President at a time when official demands occupy every waking hour."

CROONER: Two years ago when Hubert Prior Vallée was in APRIL 4 Washington a White House secretary suggested to President Hoover that it would be good publicity and politics for him to receive the crooner. The President, before consenting, was reported to have replied rather irritably: "Who *is* Rudy Vallée?" Last week Crooner Vallée was back at the White House. In the President's office the following talk occurred (according to Vallée):

President: Are you still pleasing people with your songs?

Crooner: I hope so.

President: Well, if you can sing a song that would make people forget their troubles and the Depression, I'll give you a medal.

PRO BONO POLITICO: Last week the Congressional tide for APRIL 11 paying off the Soldier Bonus at once and in full continued to rise. At the Capitol *pro bono publico* became *pro bono politico.* In the House 167 members were said to be ready to support Bonus legislation, more than enough to force a roll-call vote. Somewhere in the House background was said to be a colossal petition signed by two million veterans calling for Bonus cash. The Ways & Means Committee set next week to begin hearings on Bonus legislation. House leaders warned that further cash payments would hopelessly unbalance the Budget but declared themselves impotent to check a House once stampeded by the "soldier vote."

President Hoover bestirred himself early and started beating back the Bonus tide before it reached its legislative flood. In a sharp emphatic voice, he read a statement to the Press:

"Informal polls of the House have created apprehension in the country that a further bonus bill for $2,000,000,000 will be passed. I am absolutely opposed to any such legislation. Such action would undo every effort that is being made to reduce Government expenditures and balance the budget."

Congressman Wright Patman of Texas is the House's loudest advocate of full Bonus payments. He proposes that the two billion dollars be raised by straight currency inflation, that is, the issuance of unsecured paper money. Said he of the Hoover statement: "The millions released by the Reconstruction Finance Corp. went to the big boys by way of New York. The millions involved in the full payment bill will go to the little fellows, in every nook and corner of the nation."

APRIL 18 **ROCKABYE HOOVER:**

Rockabye, Hoover, on the tree top,
When the wind blows, the market will drop,
When the boom breaks, the prices will fall,
Down will come Hoover, Curtis and all.

With such songs President Hoover heard himself and Vice President Charles Curtis burlesqued by Washington correspondents at their Gridiron Club dinner last week. As usual, he "enjoyed it."

MAY 2 **DRY VISIT:** A bevy of Dry women laid down the law to President Hoover at the White House last week. They represented the Women's National Committee for Law Enforcement. Mrs. Henry W. Peabody, who marched them into the executive offices, is so Dry she moved out of Massachusetts when that State went Wet.

President Hoover shook hands with his callers, stood silently before his desk while Mrs. Peabody took the floor. She read him quotations from his own past speeches and remarks in which he endorsed Prohibition. She demanded more rigid enforcement. She suggested that U.S. Ambassadors be ordered to stop drinking abroad. President Hoover smiled, said nothing.

MAY 30 **"A FEARFUL PRICE":** Taking time out at his trout-fishing camp on Virginia's Rapidan River President Hoover called a stenographer and dictated a 2,500-word letter to Herbert Samuel Crocker, president of the American Society of Civil Engineers, ardent advocate of a big public works program.

"The back of the Depression," the President wrote, "cannot be broken by any single government undertaking. That can only be done with the co-operation of business, banking, industry and agriculture in conjunction with the government. We cannot squander ourselves into prosperity. What is needed is the return of confidence and a capital market through which credit will flow in the thousand rills with its result of employment and increased prices. Such a program as the huge Federal loans for 'public works' is a fearful price to pay in putting a few thousand men temporarily at work."

SHOCK & ANGER: Shocked and angered was the President JUNE 6 when Speaker of the House John Nance Garner brought out *his* relief program: a billion increase in R.F.C.'s funds for public construction by States and private enterprise; another billion-odd from the Treasury for Federal undertakings; 100 million more to be handled by the President as an emergency fund. No sooner had the Garner bill been laid before the House than irate President Hoover addressed the nation in the strongest language he had used since taking office:

"An examination of only one group of these proposals— that is, proposed authorizations for new postoffices—shows a list of about 2,300 such buildings, at a total cost of about $150,000,000. The Post Office Department informs me that the interest and upkeep of these buildings would amount to $14,000,000 per annum, whereas the upkeep and rent of buildings at present in use amounts to less than $3,000,000.

"I am advised by the engineers that the amount of labor required to complete a group of $400,000,000 of these works would amount to only 100,000 men for one year, because they are in large degree mechanical jobs. This is not unemployment relief. It is the most gigantic pork barrel ever proposed to the American Congress. It is an unexampled raid on the public treasury. Our nation was not founded on the pork barrel, and it has not become great by political log-rolling!"

Back snapped Speaker Garner: "It would be just as logical to refer to the Reconstruction Finance Corporation act as a 'pork barrel' for the banks, insurance companies, railroads and financial institutions of the country. The Democrats did not expect to receive real co-operation from the President in any manner benefiting the masses."

"I SHALL LABOR": One noon last week President Hoover JUNE 27 flipped on his White House radio and sat down to listen to his renomination in Chicago. By long distance telephone he had bossed the Republican Convention as completely as if he had stood up on the Stadium rostrum and shouted his orders directly at the delegates. At his dictation every event moved according to schedule, the renomination was hardly more than a perfunctory anticlimax.

JULY 11 **FAVORITE CANDIDATE:** President Hoover was not surprised. For months he had had a hunch that the Democrats would pick Governor Franklin D. Roosevelt to run against him. Mr. Roosevelt was his favorite candidate, the one he was told he could most easily beat. All aglow from a game of medicine ball the President sat on the South Lawn of the White House with his fruit & coffee and listened to the balloting. His advisers assured him the country was conservative and that Governor Roosevelt could be defeated.

JULY 25 **PAY CUT:** President Hoover cut his own salary from $75,000 per year to $60,000. This was his contribution to the Government's economy campaign, voluntary because Congress lacks Constitutional power to reduce his pay.

AUG. 8 **FOR PAT & WEEGEE:** Washington dog licenses Nos. 1 and 2 were ceremoniously carried to the White House by Collector of Taxes Chatham Moore Towers, handed to the President. He put No. 1 on Pat, his German shepherd, No. 2 on Weegee, his Norwegian elkhound.

In midsummer the President was called on to deal with the Bonus Marchers, an angry mob of unemployed veterans who had descended on the Capitol and were getting out of hand. For the full Bonus March story, see page 29.

AUG. 8 **RIOTS:** After the first open clash between the 20,000 Bonus Marchers and the Washington police, the three District of Columbia Commissioners asked for Federal help in ousting the veterans from the city. President Hoover was lunching when they called to ask him for Federal troops. "Tell them to put their request in writing," said the President. They wrote:

"A serious riot occurred. This area contains thousands of brickbats and these were used by the rioters in their attack upon the police. It will be impossible to maintain law & order except by the free use of firearms which will make the situation a dangerous one. The presence of Federal troops will result in far less violence and bloodshed."

Without declaring martial law (he did not have to because Washington is Federal territory), President Hoover ordered Secretary of War Hurley to call out the Army. Secretary Hurley passed the command along to handsome, well-tailored General Douglas MacArthur, Chief of Staff, in the following crisp dispatch:

"You will have United States troops proceed immediately to the scene of the disorder. Surround the affected area and clear it without delay. Any women and children should be accorded every consideration and kindness. Use all humanity consistent with the execution of this order."

Six minutes later MacArthur's troops were on the march.

"UNDEFEATED AND UNAFRAID": To accept his first nomi- AUG. 22 nation for the Presidency four years ago, Herbert Clark Hoover had crossed the continent to his Palo Alto home, addressed 70,000 persons in the Stanford Stadium. It was a day bright with sunshine and political good fortune. Nominee Hoover expatiated statistically upon the country's prosperity, pointed to the vanishing poorhouse, promised, with God's help, to "banish poverty from this nation."

Last week it was a leaner, graver man who accepted his second nomination a few blocks from the White House. In his shoulders was a perceptible droop of fatigue. Plain were the marks of three of the worst years any peacetime President has had to endure.

Before accepting the nomination, President Hoover gave a lawn party to 500 important G.O. Partisans at the White House. Beneath striped awnings on the South grounds were tables piled with a buffet luncheon—potato and chicken salad, cold cuts, sandwiches, iced tea and lemonade, six kinds of ice cream. President Hoover moved informally among his guests, eating a little here, a little there.

That evening the President went to the D.A.R.'s Constitution Hall to deliver a speech opening his campaign for re-election. Some 4,000 admiring friends sat before him; countless millions listened over the largest political radio hook-up ever attempted (160 stations).

"In accepting the great honor you have brought me," the President began in his plodding, somewhat mournful voice, "I desire to speak so simply and so plainly that every man and woman who may hear or read my words cannot misunderstand.

"The past three years have been a time of unparalleled economic calamity. We met the situation with the most gigantic program of economic defense and counterattack ever evolved in the history of the Republic. Our measures have repelled these attacks of fear and panic. We have maintained the financial integrity of our government. As a nation *we are undefeated and unafraid.*"

AUG. 29 **FISH, FUN, FILMS:** President Hoover last week spent only one full working day at his White House desk. The first three days he was aboard the *U.S.S. Sequoia,* fishing in Chesapeake Bay. The last three were passed at the Rapidan camp in Virginia. It was the President's first real fun in months.

At the camp President Hoover put in a hard 90 minutes with newsreel photographers and "still" cameramen. For three years the Hoover retreat has not been violated by the prying eyes of the Press. But this is a campaign year; presidential candidates must be popularized. The President became a patient performer in their hands. He put on rubber boots, waded in his favorite pool, cast his fly again & again. The photographers' cries for "more action" scared the trout away but the presidential fly whisked neatly to & fro, caught no trees or brushes. Then the President propped a book open on his knee, played with his dogs, strolled about. Mrs. Hoover brought out her knitting. Changing to riding breeches, the President had his horse Billy brought up from the Marine Corps corral, rode it at a walk up & down the mountain trails while shutters clucked, cranks whirled.

SEPT. 12 **ELECTIONEERING:** The White House elevator broke down. Into the White House grounds drove a repair truck. On the front of it was a plate: "Repeal the 18th Amendment." On the rear a sign read: "Vote for Roosevelt."

OCT. 3 **NOT "ECKONOMICS":** Amid the aroma of cigar smoke President Hoover was talking to big, burly Christopher Morley, poet and writer, in the Lincoln Study. Inquisitive about the President's reading habits Mr. Morley had been invited as an overnight White House guest. Last week's *Saturday Review of Literature* published his White House findings. Reported Reporter Morley:

"The President is a good man. He pronounces *economics* correctly, with a long *e*. Beware of statesmen who call it *eck-onomics*. He does not care for wildcat literature. He sank his shafts deep into the solid ore of Balzac, Brontë, Cooper, Dickens, Dumas, George Eliot, Bret Harte, Hawthorne, Howells, Kipling, Meredith, Scott, Stevenson, Thackeray, Mark Twain. There is nothing austerely highbrow in his choice: he enjoyed the same thrillers you and I were reared on. Among late American novelists his favorites seem to be Tarkington, Edith Wharton, Willa Cather, Zane Grey."

Mr. Morley was struck by the fact that Mrs. Hoover at the dinner table called her husband "Daddy" and that granulated sugar was served with the after-dinner coffee.

"GIVE!": President Hoover started a six-week nationwide cam- OCT. 24 paign to raise millions of dollars locally for local relief. A non-Government enterprise, this cash drive constitutes the backbone of the President's program for getting the country through the winter. Having promised in his stump speech at Cleveland that no "deserving" citizen shall starve, President Hoover appealed by radio to "the great heart of the American people." He spoke of "a wealth of human sympathy" and "the precious warmth of a friendly hand." He concluded:

"Let me say no richer blessing can fill your own hearts than the consciousness on some bleak winter's evening that your generosity has lighted a fire upon some family's hearth that otherwise would be black and cold and has spread some family table with food where otherwise children would be wanting. I wish my last word to you to be the word GIVE!"

HOMING HOOVER: *Snip-snip-snip-snip.* Herbert Hoover was NOV. 14 cutting up into paragraphs a rough draft of a campaign speech. His scissors made the only sound in the quiet of the Lincoln Study. Over a large table he spread out his cuttings. He picked up a paragraph on balancing the Budget and a paragraph on Democratic extravagance, pinned them together. Likewise joined were paragraphs on New Zealand butter and tariff protection, on Democratic campaign tactics. Thus the separate paragraphs were being woven together into an oratorical tapestry when an aide knocked on the study door, told the President it was nearly train time. Into a big envelope the loose paragraphs were swept. Out of the study and out of the White House marched the President to start for Palo Alto on his first trip home in four years.

As his train skirted Chicago his boosters turned out with placards: "Hoover or Hell." At Springfield he laid a wreath on Lincoln's tomb. The President pictured himself standing in Lincoln's shoes when the latter reviewed the retreat of the Union arms. He recalled the Democratic clamor for immediate cessation of hostilities. He continued:

"Lincoln was renominated but the country was profoundly disheartened. Then as now the resources of the nation were mobilized and organized. Today our opponents are declaring, in words strangely reminiscent of those used by their predecessors 68 years ago, that the struggle of this Administration against the Depression has been a failure. So again today, as in the midst of a great war, they call for a change of leadership. The nation in 1864 refused to be swerved from its course. It declined emphatically to turn aside to untried policies. The same alternatives are before the people today. My fellow citizens, can we doubt what that choice will be?"

In a driving rainstorm the Hoover special rolled into St. Louis 20 minutes late. The President looked thoroughly exhausted. His voice kept running downhill into a mumble. Turning north the President traveled into Illinois and Wisconsin. At Beloit one Henry Vance was arrested as he was caught pulling up spikes out of Chicago & Northwestern tracks over which the Hoover special was shortly to pass. Between station and hotel at St. Paul President Hoover was booed by street crowds. Declared an oldtime White House secret service man: "I've been traveling with Presidents since Theodore Roosevelt and never before have I seen one actually booed, with men running out into the street to thumb their noses at him. It's not a pretty sight." Then, with one last radio plea on election eve from Elko, Nev. Herbert Hoover closed the most desperate campaign this century by a President seeking re-election.

*With the nation in such financial plight there was mounting pub-
lic pressure for reopening the question of repayment of French
and British war debts to the U.S., which with interest amounted
to a total of $17.9 billion. In July 1931—when a total of $15.4
billion was still owed the U.S.—President Hoover declared a
one-year moratorium on the debts, and Congress forbade any
cancellation or reduction.*

DEFEAT & DEBTS: Two days after his defeat by Franklin NOV. 21
Roosevelt, President Hoover was resting himself at his Palo
Alto home when suddenly War Debts came crashing back
into the headlines.

In Washington, Sir Ronald Lindsay, British Ambassador,
called upon Secretary of State Stimson, left a note which
said: "His Majesty's Government ask for a suspension of
the payments due from them." A French note delivered next
day at the State Department suavely echoed the request "that
suspension of payments may be granted in order that the
study of the present serious problems now under discussion
may be continued in the necessary atmosphere of mutual
trust."

In substance Britain and France wanted two things from
the U.S.: 1) a conference to reduce their debts; 2) another
moratorium pending such reduction.

When this news was flashed across the continent, President
Hoover ordered out his special train a day in advance, started
back to Washington at top speed. Before he left California,
he dispatched a momentous telegram to President-elect
Roosevelt at Albany.

After giving his successor the gist of the British note, he
declared:

"I am loath to proceed with recommendations to the Congress until I can have an opportunity to confer with you personally. I understand that you are planning to come through
Washington and I hope you will find it convenient to stop off
long enough for me to advise with you."

Governor Roosevelt was sick abed with a head cold in the
Executive Mansion at Albany. To President Hoover's invitation he replied:

"I shall call you on the telephone as soon as the time of

my departure for the South has been determined. You and I can go over the whole situation. My kindest regards."

Never before in U.S. history have a President-reject and President-elect sat down together in the White House before inauguration to discuss grave matters of state.

DEC. 5 **PRESIDENTS, ELECT & REJECT:** "The Governor of New York!" cried the White House usher as President-elect Roosevelt hobbled out of the White House elevator from the basement and turned to the left into the Red Room. President Hoover and Secretary of the Treasury Ogden Mills got up.

"Mr. President," said Governor Roosevelt extending his hand.

"Governor, I'm glad to see you again," replied the President as they shook hands.

Professor Raymond Moley, on whose arm the President-elect had been leaning, was introduced. The men settled themselves in red chairs around a small mahogany table. President Hoover lighted a cigar, Governor Roosevelt a cigaret. Down from their gilt frames gazed Jefferson, Madison, Adams and Grant upon the first White House meeting of a President-reject and a President-elect.

While an ornate mantel clock ticked off the fateful minutes, War Debts, World Economics and Disarmament were soberly discussed behind closed doors. President Hoover did most of the talking.

The situation: Britain, France and Belgium had asked the U.S. to reconsider their War Debts. Pending reconsideration they wanted their Dec. 15 payments suspended. Only Congress has the power to grant either request but from the President some sort of national leadership was expected. President Hoover favored another commission to negotiate with the debtor powers, hear their arguments. Complicating factors were the proposed World Economic Conference and the moribund Disarmament Conference at Geneva. Governor Roosevelt listened to this long recital in silence, nodded his head in comprehension if not agreement, promised nothing. He repeated what he had said in accepting President Hoover's invitation: that, as he was not yet President, he could not be asked to accept presidential responsibility.

Then while the White House secretariat was issuing a curt

communiqué reporting "progress," Governor Roosevelt drove to the Mayflower Hotel. There he ordered and consumed tea & cinnamon toast while dressing to dine with Washington correspondents at the National Press Club.

FAREWELL MESSAGE: As required by the Constitution, President Hoover last week sent to Congress his farewell message on the State of the Union. Its undertone was that of the campaign; the principles it preached were those which the U.S. electorate had rejected for a "new deal." The President might be defeated but he was convinced he was still right. Excerpts: DEC. 12

¶ Union—"Our country is at peace. Education and Science have made further advances. The public health is at its highest known level. There should be no hunger or suffering from cold."

¶ Depression—"Continued constructive policies promoting the economic recovery must be the paramount duty. Confidence in the future."

¶ The Budget "must be balanced."

¶ Taxation—"Further revenue is necessary."

¶ Reorganization—"I shall issue executive orders in a few days grouping or consolidating over 50 agencies. A host of interested persons will at once protest."

¶ The U.S. Banking System "has failed to meet this great emergency. A solution should be found now."

¶ Europe—"We must co-operate for organized world recovery. Successful result from a world economic conference would bring courage and stability which will reflect into every home in our land."

¶ War Debts—"We do not approve of suspension of the Dec. 15 payments."

¶ Principles—"Ours is a government consciously dedicated to a faith in the inviolable sanctity of the individual human spirit. We have builded a system of individualism. The background of our American system is that we should allow free play of social and economic forces. Social and economic solutions will not avail unless they conform with the traditions of our race, deeply grooved in their sentiments through a century and a half of struggle for ideals of life rooted in religion and fed from purely spiritual springs."

The Congress

The 72nd Congress, elected in the middle of Hoover's term, was largely antagonistic toward his programs. The Senate had a Republican majority of one seat, but included several progressive Republicans like William E. Borah, George W. Norris and Hiram Johnson who repudiated the Administration. The President was left with no effective majority. In the House of Representatives, the Democrats, with a majority of six, repeatedly thwarted the President.

JAN. 4 **RELIEF AFTER RECESS:** After two weeks of work, Congress last week scattered for two weeks of rest. President Hoover had tried to induce Congress to forego its usual holiday and legislate economic relief but the leaders told him that not a corporal's guard, much less a quorum, could be kept in Washington to work through Christmas and New Year's Day.

With its holiday adjournment Congress did not shut up shop altogether. Relief legislation requested by the President had to be made ready by committees. Announced the President: "Leaders of both houses assure me that the Reconstruction Finance Corp. will be the first to receive consideration and that it has sufficient support to be passed by Congress."

The R.F.C. would receive as primary capital $500,000,000 from the Treasury and then issue and sell $1,500,000,000 in Government-backed debentures. These two billions of assets would be lent to hard-hit industries able to get credit nowhere else.

JAN. 25 **ARKANSAS GOES FIRST:** One cold drizzly day last week Democratic Arkansas did what no other State in the Union has ever done before. It elected a woman to the U.S. Senate. She is Hattie Wyett Caraway, the small, steady-eyed, straight-mouthed widow of Senator Thaddeus Horatius Caraway. Already sitting in the chamber by appointment of Governor Parnell, Mrs. Caraway did not bother to return to Arkansas to campaign against two feeble independents. So poverty-pinched was the election that it entirely lacked a Republican candidate. Unlike her late husband, the Lady from Arkansas sits quietly in her rear-row Senate seat, is no floor-pacer, no caustic interjector. She has sat for four weeks without delivering her maiden speech.

IMPEACH MELLON: "Mr. Speaker, I rise to a question of constitutional privilege. On my own responsibility as a Member of this House I impeach Andrew William Mellon, Secretary of the Treasury of the United States, for high crimes and misdemeanors."

Before a silent House of Representatives stood Wright Patman, a pink-cheeked, curly-headed young Democratic Congressman from Texas repeating an ancient and awful parliamentary ritual. A legislative neophyte in his second term, this rather personable impeacher, aged 38, comes from the northeastern corner of his State, where hillbillies corner their rabbits in hollow logs and take Levi Garrett snuff (between lower lip and teeth) with their politics. Like many of his neighbors, Congressman Patman is a "hard-shelled" Baptist, frowning upon music, dancing, cards. A good rabble-rouser, with a quick twangy tongue, he was elected to Congress in 1928, refused to be suppressed with other obscure newcomers. Insistently he demanded that the Government cash its soldier bonus certificates in full. Secretary Mellon tut-tutted him as a wild young man. But Congressman Patman kept harping away on his issue until he had started a backfire among the veteran vote that was stopped only when Congress, over the President's veto, raised the loan value of bonus certificates to 50%. In that fight was born his dogged antagonism for Mr. Mellon which culminated in impeachment proceedings.

Congressman Patman spent two days trying to make out a *prima facie* case that Mr. Mellon's services violated a statute of 1789, which provided: "No person appointed to the office of Secretary of the Treasury shall directly or indirectly be concerned or interested in carrying on the business of trade or commerce or be owner in whole or in part of any sea vessel."

The prosecuting argument: Mr. Mellon is a heavy stockholder in Aluminum Co. of America; *ergo* he is in trade. Gulf Oil Corp. owns seagoing tankers; Mr. Mellon is a large stockholder in Gulf Oil; *ergo* he is an owner of sea vessels. Under him the Treasury has issued a publication which recommends the use of more aluminum in the current public buildings pro-

President Hoover's hair is greyer, but friends marvel at his fortitude. Page 10. *Wright Patman frowns on dancing and Treasury Secretary Mellon.*

gram, thus drumming up trade for Aluminum Co. He has caused "millions" of dollars in taxes to be refunded to Aluminum Co. and Gulf Oil, "thousands" of dollars to himself.

The defense argument: Mr. Mellon owns only about 15% of Aluminum Co. He controls no corporation. He owns no bank stock. Stock ownership does not constitute "trade or commerce." Mr. Mellon personally owns no sea vessel. He never passes on tax refunds. He was allowed a refund of $91,000 on his taxes but was also assessed an additional $209,000, making a net tax loss of $118,000. [A month later Mellon left the Treasury and was appointed U.S. Ambassador to Great Britain. The impeachment charges were dropped.]

MAY 9 **LAST HEFFLE:** Most Senators thought they had heard the final heffling of James Thomas ("Tom-Tom") Heflin, their hulking colleague for a decade, when on March 4, 1931 the 71st Congress was silenced. As the Capitol's double doors closed on his flapping broadcloth coattails, they believed that his creamy vest, his lush black tie, his florid face and droning voice had passed forever from the scene. Had Alabama not repudiated him in 1930, electing John Hollis Bankhead in his place? Those who supposed they were through with heffling were mistaken. Last week, in full oldtime regalia, "Tom-Tom" Heflin was back upon the Senate floor, smashing a hamlike fist into a pink palm, ranting and roaring as of old, crying, "My God, Senators, think of that!"

Democrat Heflin contested the election of Senator Bankhead, claimed it had been stolen from him. For months he haunted the Capitol corridors while a Senate Committee investigated his charges. As a final courtesy he was extended the extraordinary privilege of addressing the Senate as a private citizen on why he should be seated over Mr. Bankhead. Given two hours, he took five hours, twelve minutes. His speech filled 27 pages in the *Congressional Record,* cost the Government $1,000 to print.

He quoted Jesus Christ, Pontius Pilate, Byron, Bryan and a man named Bugg. He told funny stories (the widow at her husband's funeral who was so surprised at the preacher's eulogy that she sent her son up to look into the coffin to see if the dead man really was his "pa").

"Alabama!" he heffled in conclusion. "I'd give my life to protect its good name and honor. I'm fighting for the factory girls, the farmers, the schoolteachers and the boys who go down into the bowels of the earth to dig for coal and iron. I'll fight on & on & on. . . ."

The Senate was unimpressed. It voted (64-to-18) to seat Mr. Bankhead. Flushed, crushed, Citizen Heflin gave the chamber one last lingering look, marched defiantly out. Democrats were gathering around Senator Bankhead with congratulations. Not one bade "Tom-Tom" Heflin good-bye. The 18 Senators who had voted for him were all Republicans.

BRAVERY IN THE HOUSE: One day last week the Senate Rules DEC. 26 Committee dismissed as an "unfortunate incident" the invasion of the Senate Press Gallery by a veteran Senate employe with a loaded revolver. Sixty-six minutes later a pale, pinched young man stood up in the House gallery, slung one leg over the railing, brandished a .38 caliber revolver and shouted at the top of his lungs:

"I demand 20 minutes to address the House. Whoever tries to stop me will die. Is that understood? I want to be heard."

Twenty feet below on the floor the House was taking a teller vote on a minor appropriation amendment. At the gallery gunner's outcry the hundred members present were seized with honest panic. Most of them sprinted for the safety of the cloakrooms. Others ducked under tables. A few sat petrified in their seats.

One Representative who did not lose his head was Minnesota's "lame duck" Melvin Joseph Maas, an overseas aviator with the Marine Corps during the War. Stocky & brave, Representative Maas marched across the floor to a spot directly under the armed intruder and called up:

"All right, son, you can have the floor and make your speech. But you can't do it with that gun in your hand. Come on, drop it down to me."

The youth stared down dully.

"Throw me your gun, that's a good fellow," coaxed Representative Maas. The revolver, loaded and cocked, plunked down into the Minnesotan's open hand. Simultaneously New York's stocky little Fiorello La Guardia, also a wartime aviator, who had dashed directly to the gallery, helped capture the young man from behind. Representatives sneaked sheepishly back to the floor from the cloakrooms. The teller vote was resumed. The *Congressional Record* made no mention of the interruption.

The youth told police he was Marlin Kemmerer, 25, of Allentown, Pa. where he works in the sporting goods department of a Sears, Roebuck store. His friends described him as an expert marksman. Before hospitalizing him for mental observation, police found two sticks of dynamite in his rooming house, a ten-page speech in his pocket. Said he: "You need a gun these days to get the right to make a speech."

"I IMPEACH. . . .": One afternoon last week Representative Louis Thomas McFadden, rambunctious Pennsylvania Republican, planted himself in the House well, squared his stocky shoulders, spoke these words:

"On my own responsibility as a member of the House of Representatives, I impeach Herbert Hoover, President of the United States, for high crimes and misdemeanors and offer the following resolution."

The House, shocked as if by electricity, sat bolt upright. For 20 seconds there was a stunned silence. Not since 1868 when lame Thaddeus Stevens made charges against Andrew Johnson had the awful ritual of impeachment been uttered in the House against a U.S. President. An excited buzzing broke

Tom Heflin departs the Senate, flushed, crushed and unwept.

Rep. McFadden is a Democrat, a Republican, a Dry and a maverick.

loose as Representative McFadden passed his resolution to the clerk on the rostrum and took a seat on the front-row bench. Beneath his red hair his face looked pale and drawn. No man in the House hates President Hoover more intensely than he. Last session he accused him of treason in granting the Debt Moratorium. He has fought the Hoover financial policy at every turn. Now he had pulled his grievances together into 24 impeachment counts which the House quickly recognized as "old stuff." Above the members' resentful babble only phrases of the McFadden resolution as read by the clerk could be heard:

"Herbert Hoover . . . unlawfully usurped legislative powers . . . a policy inimical to the welfare of the United States . . . unlawfully dissipated financial resources . . . injured the credit and financial standing. . . . He did appoint one Andrew W. Mellon Ambassador while a resolution for the impeachment of the said Mellon was being heard. . . . Treated with contumely the veterans . . . sent a military force heavily armed against homeless, hungry, sick, ragged and defenseless men, women and children and drove them out by force of fire and sword. . . ."

When the clerk finished reading, North Carolina's Edward William Pou, senior House Democrat, declared: "Mr. Speaker, I move to lay the resolution on the table." A great cheer went up as the Democratic majority, party politics aside, massed in defense of the Republican President.

The impeachment resolution was "laid on the table" (*i.e.* defeated) by the overwhelming vote of 361-to-8. Seven Democrats voted for it. Rarely before had a U.S. President received such a thumping big non-partisan vote of confidence from the House.

Impeacher McFadden, denounced and condemned by all Republicans for his "contemptible gesture" against his President, was re-elected last month on the Republican, Democratic and Prohibition tickets from his district in northeastern Pennsylvania.

Veterans

One of the most poignant stories of the Depression years concerned the Bonus Marchers, a ragtag army of unemployed veterans of World War I who marched on Washington and camped on the city's outskirts for two tense months in a futile attempt to win immediate payment of $2 billion as a war-service "Bonus."

JUNE 13 **B.E.F.:** Bivouacked in shelters at Anacostia Park, in vacant stores, in charity institutions, some 2,500 jobless War veterans announced last week that they would stay in Washington "until 1945 if necessary" to get an immediate cash settlement of the bonus. While most of the B.E.F. ("Bonus Expeditionary Force") eked out a meager existence from day to day on Mulligan stews and coffee, their leaders began to lobby. By the end of the week 145 Congressmen (the requisite number) had signed a petition to force a House vote on the Patman bill for immediate Bonus cashing.

General Pelham Glassford, chief of District of Columbia police, had almost exhausted his funds for feeding the B.E.F. and announced that the B.E.F. would be transported on trucks to points 50 mi. from the city. Meanwhile the march on Washington continued to swell in all parts of the land.

¶ Two hundred Cleveland Police manhandled members of a mob of 900 marchers who had clogged the Pennsylvania Rail-

road's yards for 24 hours trying to board freight trains.
¶ At Aberdeen, Md. a B. & O. engine was cut loose from a string of freight cars when 400 veterans clambered into empty coal gondolas.
¶ Five hundred Texans, starting each day's march with prayer, passed through San Antonio.
¶ A hundred men left Muncie, Ind. with $60 between them.
¶ At Council Bluffs, Iowa, 250 San Franciscans got their first meal in 24 hours.
¶ The Michigan Central allowed a Detroit contingent to ride in coal cars.

BONUS CITY: Last week the House of Representatives surren- JUNE 20
dered to the siege of the Bonus Expeditionary force en-camped near the Capitol. It voted (226-to-175) to take up the bill by Texas' Wright Patman for immediate cashing of Adjusted Service Compensation certificates at a cost of $2,400,-000,000 in printing-press money. This first test of the Bonus boosters' strength indicated that the House would probably pass the Patman bill and send it to the Senate. In that body 56 Senators—a majority—were said to be lined up against the Bonus. But even should the measure get by Congress an insurmountable veto awaited it at the White House.

Largely ignorant of legislative processes, the B.E.F. bivou-acked some 15,000 strong on the Anacostia mudflats, was delirious with delight at its House victory. Its tattered person-nel whooped and pranced about among their crude shelters. Most of them had left hungry wives and children behind. They had gone to Washington because, long jobless, they had nothing better to do.

Now, in camp with their wartime fellows again, they seemed to have revived the old ganging spirit of Army days as an es-cape from reality. They convinced themselves that they were there to right some vague wrong—a wrong somehow bound up in the fact that the Government had opened its Treasury to banks, railroads and the like but closed it to needy indi-viduals.

The discipline at "Bonus City" continued good, despite the fears of alarmed Washingtonians. Crude shelters were built from old lumber, packing boxes and scrap tin, and thatched with old straw. Several hundred secondhand Army tents were provided. Streets were laid out. Latrines were dug. Regular formations were held daily. Campers were organized for field sports to keep them out of mischief. Newcomers were required to register after proving that they were bona fide veterans with honorable discharge papers. A military morale permeated the whole encampment, with no larking out of bounds.

Over Bonus City hung the constant threat of pestilence. Flies swarmed. Garbage lay half buried. The men bathed in the Eastern Branch (Potomac), virtually an open sewer. The air reeked with filthy smells. Scabies broke out. Public health officers declared conditions were "frightful," warned of a "terrible epidemic" which might suddenly fan out from the camp across the city and country.

To feed the B.E.F. costs about 7¢ per day per man. Father Charles Coughlin, radio priest of Detroit, forwarded $5,000. About $2,500 was raised by exhibition boxing matches. Hometown friends loaded trucks with free supplies and started them to Washington.

JUNE 27 **BONUS BEATEN:** The House passed the Patman Bonus bill (209-to-176) and the B.E.F. turned its attention to the less friendly Senate. From their Anacostia camp tattered veterans marched by thousands to the Capitol. They packed into the Senate galleries. They flopped down in corridors to nap. They swarmed over the wide Capitol steps. They sprawled on the grass. They sang and joked. By dusk there were close to 10,000 of them in & around the Capitol. Shortly after 8 p.m. their comrades in the Senate Chamber flashed out the news— "Bonus beaten 62-to-18."

The B.E.F. was stunned with disappointment. A bewildered murmur that rose to a roar swept the crowd. Then suddenly, starting from nowhere, they began to sing "America" until the night sky seemed to tremble with their resolute voices. Later in small groups they drifted back to their crazy shacks and shelters on the mudflats.

What would these idle, ragged men, ghosts of the A.E.F. do next? Their commander said they would "dig in for the winter" and stay "till hell freezes." Red agitators began to work within the ranks. One general fear was that homeward-bound veterans, hungry, penniless, desperate, would form roving bands which would prey upon the countryside.

"TO HELL WITH CIVIL LAW!": The stews were thin, the rain JULY 11 cold, the sun hot and politics rampant in the camps of the Bonus Expeditionary Force at Washington last week. Four radical veterans were caught selling Communist propaganda, turned over to police. The veterans' food supply had reached lowest ebb. The Red Cross provided 9,000 lb. of flour, but that did not go far to fill the stomachs of nearly 20,000 men, among whom twelve cases of dysentery were discovered.

BREAK UP?: For the past six weeks Pelham Glassford, super- JULY 18 intendent of the District of Columbia police, has served as the Government's grinning, good-natured host to the Bonus Expeditionary Force. The next youngest Army Brigadier in France, he understood these tattered, jobless, hungry veterans who had marched by thousands upon Washington. Altogether General Glassford gave Washington and the country a remarkable demonstration of mob management without benefit of tear gas, riot club or machine gun.

Last week Superintendent Glassford thought he was about to be relieved of most of his charges when the Government at last moved to send them home. Taking his first official notice of the B.E.F., President Hoover recommended to Congress a $100,000 appropriation to send the men home, feed them on the way. House & Senate acted promptly. Each veteran was to be advanced the price of a cut-rate railroad ticket, allowed 75¢ per day for food during the journey. No gift, the advance was to be deducted in each case from the final payment of the veteran's bonus certificate.

NO MAN'S LAND: The Capitol plaza was No Man's Land last JULY 25 week. Some 700 ragged, hungry veterans arrived from the Pacific Coast to join the siege of Congress by the Bonus Expeditionary Force. At their head was a thin, leathery roofer from Los Angeles named Roy Robertson. Behind his head was a steel brace from which a strap was fastened under his chin. While serving in the Navy he had fallen from a hammock, permanently injured his spine. His disability in no way diminished his capacity to stage one of the grittiest demonstrations of the Depression.

Roy Robertson believed that the B.E.F. had blundered badly when it encamped at Anacostia, four miles from the Capitol. His strategy was close and continuous picketing to keep the Bonus issue squarely under Congressional noses. The first night in Washington his band flopped down on the plaza lawn, slept on newspapers after police confiscated their bedding. Next morning they trooped to the House Office Building to wash & shave. Soon thereafter Commander Robertson started them on a slow, shuffling march around the plaza that was to last four days, three nights.

Roy Robertson was injured in the war, but now he leads a gritty show.   *General MacArthur: "It was a bad looking mob." Page 37.*

Back & forth behind a soiled U.S. flag filed his men on the far side of the black expanse of asphalt. Food was served them afoot, including 1,000 sandwiches contributed by Mrs. Evelyn Walsh McLean. Shoes came off, blistered feet padded doggedly on the hot pavement. After the first all-night march exhaustion threatened to break the line. Robertson detailed relays to keep the demonstration going. Those off duty squatted on the low stone coping where indulgent police allowed them to doze.

Such persistent picketing gave Congress a touch of nerves. Vice President Curtis had the Marines called. From the Navy Yard 60 Marines arrived by trolley with rifles & bayonets. The marchers guffawed at this turnout. Ten minutes later the Marines were on their way back to barracks. "I'm fed up with hysterical meddlers!" snorted General Pelham Glassford, whose amiable discipline has kept the B.E.F. in good order for eight weeks.

Robertson, worn to a frazzle from sleeplessness, keeled over three times on the street. To him General Glassford said: "You certainly have got guts. Give yourself a break."

On what promised to be the last day of the session the B.E.F.'s regional commander, Walter Waters, led thousands of his men to the Capitol to protest adjournment. Barred from the plaza by a thin line of police, the veterans were at first good-natured and docile. Suddenly the front rank spotted Commander Waters boldly striding across the forbidden plaza toward the Capitol. The packed mass stirred forward, broke the police barrier. With one tumultuous rush thousands surged across the plaza after their leader.

Alert to the emergency General Glassford bobbed up on a bandstand near the Capitol's main steps. Commander Waters was arrested, clapped into the Capitol. Bellowed General Glassford to the rampant B.E.F.: "I don't want any trouble, but we'll have it if you don't get back."

"We want Waters!" thundered the veterans, now almost a mob. "Turn him loose or we'll go in and get him."

Spectators and newsmen shrank back in fear of what might happen if these angry thousands turned violent. The plaza remained uncleared. Dangerous tension was broken when a buxom, yellow-haired woman leaped to the stand. She was Marotta Arsonis, a New York trained nurse who had befriended the B.E.F. Seizing a megaphone, she yelled: "Be calm, men! Be calm! Let's sing." She tuned up with "America."

But the veterans had their own song. Across the plaza rolled:

> *My bonus lies over the ocean*
> *Oh, bring back my bonus to me.*

With its own music the sullen temper of the crowd melted. Commander Waters was released, went back to the Capitol to announce to his followers: "I've got permission for you to use these center steps. We're going to stay here until I see Hoover."

Thus the B.E.F. took No Man's Land and the Capitol steps, only to be defeated and driven back, not by police clubs and riot guns, but by the adjournment of a determined Congress. Gradually the veterans drifted back to the Anacostia mudflats.

AUG. 8 **BATTLE OF WASHINGTON:** When War came in 1917, William Hushka, 22-year-old Lithuanian, sold his St. Louis butcher shop, gave the proceeds to his wife, joined the Army. Honorably discharged in 1919, he drifted to Chicago, worked as a butcher, seemed unable to hold a steady job. Long jobless, in June he joined a band of veterans marching to Washington. Last week William Hushka's Bonus of $528 suddenly became payable in full when a police bullet drilled him dead in the worst public disorder the capital has known in years.

The trouble started when the U.S. Treasury moved to repossess Government property on the south side of Pennsylvania Avenue, three blocks west of the Capitol. General Glassford had persuaded Walter W. Waters, the B.E.F.'s curly-headed commander, to evacuate his men on the promise of new quarters elsewhere. Treasury agents arrived at 10 a.m. to clear the buildings. But most of the veterans refused to leave. Police helped the Federal men do their job. Hundreds of veterans swelled to thousands as men flocked from other B.E.F. camps to the scene to watch the eviction. By noon the buildings had been practically cleared when a trio of veterans carrying a U.S. flag tried to march back in. Police blocked them. Somebody tossed a brick. "There's a fight!" went up the cry. More bricks flew.

"Give the cops hell!" a veteran shouted. His massed companions pressed in upon the police, now flailing with their clubs. One policeman had his head bashed in. Veterans trampled him. Blood streamed down others' faces. Veterans swung scrap iron, hunks of concrete, old boards. General Glassford rushed into the mêlée, was knocked flat by a brick.

"Be peaceful, men! Be calm!" shouted General Glassford. "Let's not throw any more bricks. You've probably killed one of my best officers."

"Hell, that's nothing," a veteran flung back. "Lots of us were killed in France."

Meanwhile hot-headed veterans had seeped back into their old quarters to tussle with police. Two officers were cornered on the second floor. "Let's get 'em!" someone shouted. The

The battle of Washington. The chief of police, knocked flat by a brick, cries out, "Be peaceful, men!" But men die, in one of the Capital's worst days.

policemen pulled their revolvers. A half dozen shots banged out. William Hushka keeled over with a bullet in his heart. Two other veterans were wounded. One of them died later.

The street fighting gradually subsided. General Glassford withdrew his forces. The B.E.F. cooled off. Commander Waters nervously declared: "The men got out of control. There's nothing I can do."

But there was something the three District of Columbia Commissioners governing the city could do and they did it. They persuaded President Hoover to act, and soon cavalry and infantry to the number of 1,000 men began moving into Washington for an encounter with the B.E.F. In their wake came five small tanks, a fleet of trucks. Bayonets glittered in the sun, equipment clanked over the pavement as the force marched slowly up Pennsylvania Avenue. Reaching the "affected area" (4:45 p.m.) troopers rode straight into the hooting, booing ranks of the B.E.F. Veterans scrambled out of the way of swinging sabers, trampling hoofs. Steel-helmeted infantrymen with drawn revolvers advanced 20 abreast. Behind them came others with rifles lowered, bayonets prodding. Suddenly tear gas bombs began to pop on the street. The soldiers put on their masks, pushed slowly on while the heavy grey fumes cut great gaps in the retreating throng of veterans.

The unarmed B.E.F. did not give the troopers a real fight.

They were too stunned and surprised that men wearing their old uniform should be turned against them. Here & there veterans would toss back gas bombs with half-forgotten skill, kick the troopers' horses, throw a few bricks. But resistance was wholly unorganized.

General Douglas MacArthur [Chief of Staff of the U.S. Army] directed the military operation, tears streaming down his cheeks, not from emotion but from the fumes of the bombs. When his cavalry rode down a group of veterans with a U.S. flag, a spectator sang out: "The American flag means nothing to me after this." General MacArthur snapped: "Put that man under arrest if he opens his mouth again."

The rout of the B.E.F. from Pennsylvania Avenue broke its back. But the military was not yet through. It "gassed" small scattered camps in the vicinity of the Capitol, shoved out their occupants, left smoking ruins behind. By 9 p.m. the troopers had advanced to the bridge beyond which lay Bonus City. The camp commander rushed out waving a white shirt for a truce, asked for time to evacuate the several hundred women and children. He got an hour's grace.

As the infantry moved into Bonus City (10:14 p.m.) gassing each shack and shanty, veterans by the thousands trudged off into the night. Some carried their belongings wrapped in bundles on their backs. A few sang old war songs. Women carried babies in their arms. Huts and lean-tos were set afire, partly by the departing veterans, partly by the soldiers. By midnight Bonus City, once the home of 10,000 jobless hungry men & women, was a field of roaring bonfires. President Hoover could see its fiery glow on the Eastern sky from his White House window. At dawn the place was a charred & blackened ruin. The B.E.F. was gone.

The next day President Hoover expressed his indignation: "A challenge to the authority of the United States Government has been met, swiftly and firmly. Government cannot be coerced by mob rule."

General MacArthur observed that the B.E.F. "was a bad looking mob animated by the essence of revolution." A week's delay by the President, he thought, "would have threatened the institution of our Government."

When the troops were withdrawn, Secretary of War Hurley exulted: "It was a great victory. Mac [General MacArthur] did a great job. He is the man of the hour. (A thoughtful pause.) But I must not make any heroes just now."

B.E.F.'s END: With troops, tanks and tear gas President Hoover succeeded in driving the Bonus Expeditionary Force out of Washington fortnight ago. But that did not break up the tatterdemalion army and scatter it home. With diplomacy replacing armed force, the rest of the job was accomplished last week by the combined efforts of Daniel Willard, president of Baltimore & Ohio R.R. and "Eddie" McCloskey, scrappy little Mayor of Johnstown, Pa. AUG. 15

Impetuous Mayor McCloskey, onetime prize-fighter, had invited B.E.F. leaders to Johnstown to reorganize their forces retreating from Washington. His invitation was also accepted by the B.E.F. rank & file. Almost overnight an encampment of some 8,000 men, women & children sprang up in an amusement park on the outskirts of town. It teemed with filth and flies. There was little or no food. One good storm would have devastated its pup tents, lean-tos and bough huts. As a camp, it made the Anacostia bivouac look like a regular Army post. Mayor McCloskey realized he and his city were in a serious predicament.

To Johnstown's alarmed citizens went the Baltimore & Ohio chief of police, direct from Mr. Willard, on a mysterious mission. Mr. Willard, it was gathered, had seen President Hoover. The B. & O. would provide trains to move the B.E.F. westward. Somehow the Federal Government would foot the bill. One noon a citizens committee called on Mayor McCloskey, told him of the B. & O.'s offer, induced him to use his hard-boiled political oratory to get the B.E.F. to entrain. He could, he was assured, take all public credit for arranging the evacuation. Johnstownians feared that the Bonus Marchers would never accept the B. & O.'s offer if they knew it had been inspired by Washington.

Next day Mayor McCloskey hustled out to Camp McCloskey, popped one heckler in the jaw, exclaimed:

"God sent you here and I'm sending you away. I want to tell you mugs something. I can lick anybody in this damned outfit. If you don't think so, just start something. You'll ride the cushions home and there'll be food for you. I'm giving you guys a break. I won't call in any troopers to massacre you.

I'll put you to hell out myself. I'll knock the teeth out of anybody who hangs around here."

The B.E.F. understood such talk. That night the first B. & O. train rolled west carrying 800 veterans, their wives and children. Next day two more chuffed off from the siding near the camp. With a brass band the Mayor was there to shake hands, kiss babies, distribute small change. The evacuation was well under way after ramshackle cars were given a free tank of gasoline and $1 to start them over the mountains.

The Great Depression

Individual tragedies, less dramatic than the Bonus March, but affecting far more people, continued throughout the Depression. At the end of one of the worst summers in American history, TIME *collected a week's sampling.*

SEPT. 19   **DESTITUTION:** In Manhattan last week Subway Motorman Fred Floodgate had shut off his power and was coasting his north-bound express into the West 110th Street station when he caught a blurred glimpse of a slim, blonde woman poised on the edge of the platform. The next instant there was a downward flutter of a black-and-tan dress. Motorman Floodgate's hand stiffened on the emergency brake control. Clamped wheels shrieked. The train slid 50 ft. before stopping. Ten minutes later police gathered from the tracks the bloody remains of Elsie Green, 38. Her purse on the platform contained 55¢. A clerk, long jobless, she had died in a manner favored by many a New York suicide brought on by the Great Depression.

Also, last week, the following happened:

¶ In Kansas City Dan McLaughlin, 75, weary wayfarer from Texas, knocked at the door of the General Hospital, said he had a pain in his stomach. Doctors found he needed food, sent him on to the Helping Hand. There he cut his wrists, was carried back to the hospital. Said he to the doctors: "You didn't want me yesterday. Now maybe you'll take me this way. I've no job, no folks—nobody left. Why should I care?"

¶ In Boston Dr. Towneley Thorndike French, 57, graduate of the Harvard Medical School, murdered his wife "because I was tired of living in abject poverty." Six weeks ago Mrs. French was discharged as an elevator operator.

¶ At Babylon, L.I. police found May Hardy, 38, trained nurse, starving in a maple grove on a private estate. For two weeks, she had slept on a bundle of old rags and papers. She was penniless.

¶ At Mahwah, N.J. Norman Falconer, 55, murdered his wife, killed himself. His explanation: "My brain just cracked. I have had many financial worries. I am terribly sorry."

¶ Near Los Angeles Mrs. Edna Porter Killian, 35, clubwoman, murdered her rancher husband Howard, killed herself because she was worried over finances. The Killians, both graduates of the University of California, were prominent among the landed gentry around El Monte.

¶ In Oskaloosa, Iowa, Mrs. Myrtle Crump, 41, jobless school-teacher, prepared to spend a second winter with her two children in a tented hole in the ground.

¶ In Manhattan a desperate mother abandoned her two-month-old baby in an automobile parked in the night glare of Broadway. Her note: "His name is Billie. I have tried to keep him but I can't keep myself. I am a young widow almost starving. . . ."

¶ At Flushing, L.I. William Henry Joseph Tubbs, 32, jobless & penniless, was ordered from his wife's parents' home when a bad check charge was about to overtake him. Before he disappeared, he killed his six-year-old son asleep in a crib.

¶ In Boston Clarence R. Heath, 47, branch manager of Colonial Life Insurance Co., took cyanide of potassium, died in a hotel room. Reason: "Business Reverses."

¶ In Milwaukee Ignatz Rewolinski, 250-lb. policeman, was pushed through a window of a county food station, slightly cut, when a noonday breadline began to riot. Arrests: 13.

HOOVERCARTS: In Wayne County, N.C., a depressed farmer OCT. 10 cut off the rear end of his disused automobile, fastened shafts to the axle, backed in a mule, went riding. Other farmers, unable to buy 23¢ gasoline with 7¢ cotton or $5 tires with 11¢ tobacco, did the same. Soon the roads of eastern North Carolina were overrun with similar vehicles pulled by mules, horses, oxen, goats or a pair of husky boys. North Carolinians, many of whom had been Hoovercrats in 1928, transposed two letters of the term, called their conveyances Hoovercarts. Signs on the carts proclaimed: WE'LL GET THERE REGARDLESS OF HOOVER AND THIS AIN'T NO BULL.

Investigations

An investigation into New York City affairs, which had begun in March 1931, revealed that James J. Walker, the city's dapper and popular mayor, was involved in corrupt financial manipulations. The resulting scandal would ultimately cost him his job and provide a difficult political test for presidential candidate Franklin D. Roosevelt.

MAY 30 **SCANDALS OF NEW YORK:** After a year of skunk-flushing in New York City's political woods, Counsel Samuel Seabury of the State Legislature's investigation into municipal corruption last week bayed resoundingly on the trail of a fox. Never before had the chase come so close to slick little Mayor James John ("Jimmy") Walker.

Inquisitor Seabury first gave tongue last fortnight by revealing that the Mayor had been given $26,535 worth of bonds by a broker for whom it was in the Mayor's power to do a potent favor. The broker's name was Joseph A. Sisto. His firm issued the securities of Parmelee Transportation Co. which owns the city's biggest taxi fleet (2,300 cars). Broker Sisto met the Mayor at Atlantic City in the summer of 1929. The following autumn he sent his gift, made "in admiration," around to the City Hall. Later he spoke to the Mayor of the need of municipal taxi regulation to curb low-rate "taxicab racketeers." The next year Mayor Walker pushed through legislation creating a Board of Taxicab Control.

The Sisto revelation brought no immediate surge of public indignation against foxy Mayor Walker. The public seemed interested not so much in what Mayor Walker had done—$26,535 seemed small potatoes for a man of his parts—as in if and how he would elude punishment. After Inquisitor Seabury had further showed last week that the promoters of a bus company had bought Mayor Walker a $10,000 letter of credit, later extended by $3,000, the chase approached its most exciting stage—Walker on the stand in his own defense.

As a prelude to his defense, Mayor Walker went to Brooklyn to speak before the Women's Division of the Flatbush Democratic Club. On his way to the rostrum, roundly cheered, he stopped to kiss Mrs. Alfred Emanuel Smith, Club Leader Mary F. O'Malley and his sister. "Any man that cannot take it," said he, "does not belong in politics."

HIS HONOR'S HONOR: "Mr. Mayor, would you be good enough JUNE 6 to take the stand?"

Responding to this long-awaited invitation in the New York County Court House last week, the slick incumbent of "the third biggest job in the U.S." glanced alertly about him to orient friend & foe, shot his broad, lopsided campaign smile, sat down jauntily to defend himself against gravest suspicions of his official conduct.

Mayor Walker did not have to look far to discover his chief foe. Leaning casually against the rail of the Press box was the committee's counsel, grey-haired Samuel Seabury, pontifical, bland, courteous, smiling, maddening. For this moment Inquisitor Seabury had patiently labored for 14 months, relentlessly cutting his way through the city's political jungle, confident that he would come at last to its heart—the Mayor's office in City Hall. At stake were not only His Honor's honor, but His Honor's job and perhaps his liberty as well.

Inquisitor Seabury, following up testimony he had previously wrung from the Mayor's associates, conducted his inquiry into the major channels:

1) Buses—Why did the Mayor sponsor a franchise for Equitable Coach Co. when a competing company had promised to operate more buses at a lower fare and posted a substantial guarantee? And why did the Mayor buy securities in an abortive attempt to finance Equitable?

His Honor evaded any direct answer to the first question, jocularly wisecracking that the *best* offer the city ever had for a bus line came from a Long Island hay & feed firm *(Laughter)*.

To the second question the Mayor said: "I never owned a

share. I never profited one penny off any share of that stock."
But after the Mayor left the stand, Park Commissioner Walter
R. Herrick "remembered distinctly" buying 300 shares of
Interstate stock on the Mayor's behalf.

2) Taxis—Why did the Mayor accept $26,535 worth of
bonds from Broker Joseph A. Sisto, whose firm was interested in Parmelee Transportation (Checker Cab) securities? Was
it chance that the Mayor legislated into being the Board of
Taxicab Control?

Mayor Walker admitted that he had "many kind friends"
who did him unsolicited favors, but denied that the gift had
any connection with the establishment of the Board of Taxicab Control.

3) Fugitive—Why had one Russell T. Sherwood, a financial
agent of the Mayor's, fled the city ten months ago when sub-
penaed by the Committee? How had he managed to bank
$700,000 in five years on a salary which had never exceeded
$10,000? Why did he share a lock box with Mayor Walker?

His Honor was at a loss to explain Fugitive Sherwood's
disappearance. If the $700,000 was inferred to belong partly
to him, Mayor Walker said he "hoped the [Inquisitor] proves
it is mine. I'd try and collect it" (Laughter). The lock box, he
explained, had been shared when Mayor Walker was in the
State Senate and practiced law in a firm for which Sherwood
was accountant. It had been used by the Mayor as a reposi-
tory for papers relating to a law case.

If Inquisitor Seabury had failed to make the Mayor hang
himself on the witness stand, he had certainly brought out the
suspicious nature of the Mayor's business affairs, and he had
put on record a number of sworn statements by the Mayor
which could be checked up on. Whether or not it was His
Honor, someone had lied on the stand. There would be further investigations, the Inquisitor indicated, before his findings reached their ultimate destination, the Governor's desk
at Albany.

JUNE 13 **WALKER TO ROOSEVELT:** The Legislative Committee investigating New York City scandals abruptly ceased investigating
last week. Counsel Samuel Seabury left the case against Mayor
James Walker with a broad hint that it was now up to Governor Franklin D. Roosevelt to act.

During the four final days of his inquiry Counsel Seabury brought forth evidence to show that ten of the bonds which Joseph A. Sisto gave the Mayor three years ago were convertible bonds of a firm which sold the city $43,500 worth of traffic lights for Fifth Avenue last year.

As a result of this last finding, Counsel Seabury thrust the boldest forensic stroke of his inquiry: "I say the Mayor of this city cannot buy stock or hold stock in a company that has city contracts. It is ground for removal, and it is so provided in Section 1,533 of the City Charter."

"MALICE & SLANDER": Last week in Albany Governor Roosevelt was presented with a 27,000-word document wherein slick little James John ("Jimmy") Walker hotly defended his right to remain Mayor of New York. Replying to the ouster charges filed by Counsel Samuel Seabury, Mayor Walker opened his defense with an attack. He charged that Republicans had instigated the inquiry "to divert public attention from the dreadful condition of affairs throughout the nation." He accused Mr. Seabury of "malice, slander, rancorous ill-will," of conducting a "man hunt," and wound up his "solemn emphatic denial" of all wrongdoing with: AUG. 8

"Since the day of my birth I have lived my life in the open. Whatever shortcomings I have are known to everyone—but disloyalty to my native city, official dishonesty or corruption, form no part of these shortcomings."

The country waited to see how Governor Roosevelt would deal with Tammany, of which the natty little New York Mayor is the popular symbol. If he removed him from office, he might lose New York State in the Presidential election. If he did not, Republicans would charge him with truckling to a corrupt political machine.

"ATTABOY, JIMMY!": "Attaboy, Jimmy! You show 'em! Jimmy! Good luck, Jimmy! Get in there and fight, Jimmy!" AUG. 22

The friendly farewells of some 5,000 raucous New Yorkers echoed in the Grand Central Station last week as their saucy little Mayor entrained for Albany. A few hostile boos were silenced by cheers and police fists. With the Mayor, as usual when he is in a tight place politically, was his plump little wife, Janet Allen Walker, carrying her white poodle Togo. "My place," she said, "is beside my husband. If the worst comes, we can go to my Iowa farm."

Three hours later when the Mayor left his private car at Albany, a 30-piece band blared "For He's a Jolly Good Fellow." A salute of 21 aerial bombs banged out. Against the sunset sky, banners marked "Walker for Governor" fluttered before the Mayor, who acknowledged the demonstration by shaking his own hands over his head like a pugilist entering the ring.

But inside the Executive Chamber at Albany where the Mayor of New York was on trial for his official life, there had been no cheers, no applause, no bands, no roses, no hippo-droming. The great cherry-paneled room was solemnly hushed. Governor Roosevelt, as judge & jury, sat behind a huge flat-topped desk, flanked by legal aides. Before him, looking small and subdued was "Jimmy" Walker. To one side sat elderly Samuel Seabury, a faint smile on his wide, calm face.

Sweeping defense objections aside, Governor Roosevelt proceeded to examine Mayor Walker on the Seabury charges. Roosevelt confined himself mostly to the Mayor's own testimony, poking him on weak spots in his explanations. The Mayor wriggled painfully when, for example, the Governor took up the $26,000 in bonds the Mayor had received from J. A. Sisto & Co., brokers, as profits from a speculative pool in Cosden Oil Stock:

Governor Roosevelt: Practically what happened was they said to you, "We'll put you into the Cosden pool. It won't cost you anything." Now how many shares did you think you were getting?

Mayor Walker (flustered): I don't know that—er-er—if I did know—but I—my understanding was—in view—there were no questions asked. If I'd never heard of it again, it would have been all right—I mean there was—er-er—no definite agreement. It was one of those things amongst gentlemen.

AUG. 29 **LOGIC:** After five racking days of examination at the firm hands of Governor Roosevelt, a very perturbed and anxious "Jimmy" Walker last week fled to the courts in an attempt to hold his job as Mayor of New York. Governor Roosevelt had not yet actually removed him; but the Mayor, his counsel and most observers realized that his defense has not helped his case. The Mayor's wriggling and squirming under the Governor's pointed questions had made an unfavorable impression. Refusing to dismiss the charges without hearing more witnesses, the Governor had exploded that he was "fed up" with the niggling tactics of the Mayor's counsel.

Many of the Mayor's friends were dismayed at his strategy. They felt that to seek political asylum in the courts was not meeting the issues "on the facts." As for Governor Roosevelt, most spectators had only praise for the direct and fearless way he had handled the Walker examination. He behaved as if he had no thought of its political consequences. A Walker removal now would thunder across the land until election day as proof positive that Governor Roosevelt is no "Tammany man."

Mayor Jimmy Walker. He wiggles and wiggles till FDR is fed up.

Governor Roosevelt. By risking political danger he makes political hay.

WALKER OUT: Until last week nobody considered "Jimmy" SEPT. 12 Walker a quitter. But when it became apparent that Governor Roosevelt was on the verge of removing the Mayor, Walker defense attorneys fled to court for a restraining order. The Mayor complained that the Governor was not giving him a fair hearing.

Followed a four-day hiatus, due to the death of the Mayor's younger brother George. The Mayor was put to bed with a case of "nervous exhaustion." He could not attend the wake. At the interment in Long Island City the Mayor looked wan and hollow-cheeked.

Two hours later he shook off sleuthing reporters and disappeared alone in his $17,000 nickel-trimmed Duesenberg. At 10 p.m. he returned in high spirits to his Mayfair apartment on Park Avenue.

Reporters in the lobby asked him how he felt. "Great!" he grinned.

"How about going to Albany tomorrow for the hearings?" was the next question.

Mayor Walker thumbed his nose northward in the direction of Albany.

"Are you going to resign?"

"Get down to City Hall. There's a statement there for you." The Mayor went up to his apartment, took a cold shower, went to bed.

At City Hall 20 minutes later newsmen were handed the following from the Mayor to the City Clerk: "I hereby resign as Mayor of the City of New York, the resignation to take effect immediately." Even then hundreds of thousands of citizens refused to think the worst of him and Radio Crooner Morton Downey was among the first to rush to his flower-filled apartment where he was lolling around in blue silk pajamas and assure him that, even out of office, he was still "the greatest fellow on earth."

Politics

FEB. 1 **COURAGEOUS CANDIDATE:** The idealism of Woodrow Wilson appealed to New York State Senator Franklin Roosevelt. He traveled to Trenton, interviewed Governor Wilson, returned to start booming him for President. When Wilson won in 1912, he made the pleasant young man from Hyde Park his Assistant Secretary of the Navy. When War came, Assistant Secretary Roosevelt worked harder than ever to make a good name for himself. He bought up all the supplies he could lay his hands on, helped build the submarine chasing "mosquito fleet."

In 1920 the Democratic party nominated Roosevelt for the Vice Presidency at its San Francisco convention after Alfred Emanuel Smith had seconded his name. With Presidential Nominee James Cox, he campaigned strenuously about the country, took his inevitable defeat with good grace.

In August 1921 Roosevelt and his family embarked on Publisher Van Lear Black's yacht for their summer home at Campobello Island, N.B. Shortly after they arrived, Mr. Roosevelt caught a chill stamping out a forest fire. A cross-country run and a cold plunge in the Bay of Fundy seemed to help things, but when he got home he sat in his wet bathing suit to read his mail. He took another chill. Next morning he was down with infantile paralysis. Months later he arose to find his legs quite dead.

This sudden calamity he met with supreme courage and cheer. He continued his law practice, developed a wide personal correspondence among eminent Democrats throughout the land.

In 1924 Mr. Roosevelt came out of political retirement to advance the presidential candidacy of Al Smith. John W. Davis got the nomination, but Mr. Roosevelt's efforts did not pass unnoticed. Four years later he was again chosen to nominate his "Happy Warrior." But in 1928 "Al" needed a good strong name at the head of the New York Democratic ticket to help pull the state for his national ticket. Mr. Roosevelt was swimming at Warm Springs when Nominee Smith telephoned from New York that he must run for Governor. In the election that followed New York went for Hoover, but Mr. Roosevelt squeaked through to victory with a 25,000-vote majority. After two years as Governor, he was renominated and won a whacking victory with 725,001 votes to spare. His success in this second election was widely interpreted as his qualification for the Presidency.

"UNTHINKER" v. "DEMAGOG": It is always fair weather when the Democrats get together. It is seldom fair when they part. The feast that they held last week in Washington to commemorate Thomas Jefferson's birth was looked forward to as the last big Democratic function before the Chicago convention, the full dress parade to present a united front to the G.O.P. But it wound up in a fierce intra-party disturbance. APRIL 25

Notably absent was Franklin Delano Roosevelt. At the last moment he wired that he had to remain in Albany to attend to the public welfare. This emphasis on official duty was well understood by the dining Democrats. They well knew that Mr. Roosevelt well knew that a Jefferson Day dinner is no place for a Democrat who has already almost run away with the next presidential nomination.

The meeting began with speeches in sweetest harmony. But when Alfred E. Smith, still the Democrats' titular leader, arose to speak, something electric passed through the room. Everyone knew that the Messrs. Smith and Roosevelt, once closest friends, were friends no longer. And everyone knew that even Mr. Roosevelt's friends had been upset by a radio speech he had just delivered to the nation.

That speech had had for its theme the "forgotten man" at the bottom of the economic heap. Mr. Roosevelt had belabored the Hoover Administration for relieving only the top crust, the big banks and corporations. He had mocked "shallow thinkers" who had no idea how to help the farmer. Addressing himself to the proposed program of large Federal expenditures on public works—a program urged by Mr. Smith —Governor Roosevelt had declared: "It is the habit of the unthinking to turn in times like this to the illusions of economic magic. Let us admit frankly it would be only a stopgap."

Flushed and forthright, Mr. Smith now exploded his retort with no disguise except the omission of Mr. Roosevelt's proper name: "This country is sick and tired of listening to political campaign orators who tell us what is the matter with us. It is a perfectly easy thing to say we must restore the purchasing power of the farmer. Of course we must. But how are we going to do it? Exception to a program of public works was recently taken by a prominent Democrat on the theory that it is a stopgap. Who ever said it was anything else? This is no time for demagogs. I will take off my coat and vest and fight to the end against any candidate who persists in any demagogic appeal to the masses of the working people of this country to destroy themselves by setting class against class and rich against poor!"

The Smith-Roosevelt feud was thus put squarely out in the open where the G.O.P. could view it with undisguised delight.

"CHOCK": Last week the Roosevelt bandwagon trundled into MAY 9
Massachusetts. There for the first time its progress was halted.
Governor Roosevelt had been warned to keep out of the primary in Massachusetts on the ground that the State was still
as fiercely loyal to Alfred Emanuel Smith as it was four years
ago. In what was really his first serious fight for the nomination, Roosevelt took a terrible beating in Massachusetts. He
lost every single one of the State's 36 convention votes and an
incalculable amount of national prestige. The popular Smith
margin was 3-to-1.

After the primary, newshawks flocked to see Mr. Smith in
his high Manhattan office, asked him what the vote meant. He
explained: "It ought to put a chock under the bandwagon and
stop people from jumping on it, in the theory there's nowhere
else to go."

AGAIN "CHOCK": The Roosevelt bandwagon last week ran MAY 16
into John Nance Garner, onetime cowboy, in California.
Again the bandwagon was "chocked." The New York Governor's friends stopped claiming victory in Chicago on the first
ballot. Some 600,000 Democrats had turned out for the voting, compared with 250,000 in 1928. Speaker Garner carried
the State with a 60,000-vote lead over Governor Roosevelt,
who ran about 30,000 votes ahead of Alfred E. Smith.

SCOREBOARD: Eight States plumped for Franklin Delano MAY 30
Roosevelt last week. They were Oregon, Nevada, Tennessee,
Vermont, South Carolina, Kansas, New Mexico, Montana.
The Roosevelt total of "sure votes" at Chicago thus rose to
412. To Alfred Emanuel Smith last week went Connecticut
and New Jersey. Total Smith vote: 100. A majority of 578
is required to control the convention.

AGAIN, THOMAS: Dearly would Socialist Norman Thomas
like to be the eighth Ohioan, the third Princetonian to sit in
the White House. Last week, at the Socialist National Convention in Milwaukee, he got his second chance with his
second nomination. Candidate Thomas keynoted his campaign thus: "Not merely or chiefly the Democratic or Republican parties, but the capitalist system behind them stands
exposed in all its brutal stupidity. Its doom is written in its

own failures. The choice now confronting the world is between Socialism and catastrophe!"

JUNE 20 **"GIVE US AL":** The Roosevelt camp received another setback last week when the 25 potent Scripps-Howard papers throughout the land frontpaged an editorial entitled "Give Us Alfred E. Smith." Excerpts:

"Herbert Hoover and Franklin Roosevelt possess in common one dominating trait. Faced in a pinch with political consequences, they yield. Between the two it is a tossup. Between Roosevelt and the White House there now stands a man endowed in the very highest degree with those qualities which both Hoover and Roosevelt lack and which the country so sorely needs. That man is Alfred E. Smith. As Roosevelt generalizes, Smith is specific. As Roosevelt loves to delay, Smith loves action. Irresolution is ingrained in one; boldness in the other. In Franklin Roosevelt we have another Hoover. The election of either Hoover or Roosevelt would be a blow from which this nation would not recover in a generation."

JUNE 27 **NOMINATION:** Joseph Scott, premier orator of Pasadena, who has two tremendous eyebrows and two sons in the Catholic priesthood, stood up to renominate his friend Herbert Hoover.

"Why," cried he, "stand frozen with fear and trembling like the slaves of old? Why not remember the inheritance which is ours and stretch forth strong arms and stout hearts and be worthy of our patrimony? We have an illustrious example of such a spirit—the spirit of one who, through the last long grueling four years, has stood at the helm as the captain of our ship of state and has steered the vessel safely through fog and hurricane, and passed the terrors of the lee shore. This homespun American, HERBERT HOOVER."

Organized pandemonium broke loose. Each delegate had been given a small U.S. flag and a noisemaking gadget. High above the rostrum a flag fell from the illuminated portrait of the President. Delegate Louis B. Mayer, partner in Metro-Goldwyn-Mayer, was there in person to project ghostly slides of President Hoover on screens at each end of the hall.

The nomination of "this man Hoover" was seconded by eight orators, none of whom rose to the forensic heights of Chicago's Negro politician, Roscoe Conklin Simmons, who declared: "Not long ago I stood before the tomb of Lincoln. I sought a word from him for times of trouble and for the struggle that often almost overcomes me. He seemed to say: 'Go and speak to those who still gather in my name. And if you see him, speak to Hoover for me and say that his road is the one I traveled. Say that it is the path cleared for those who can walk alone toward these immortal fields where you sought and found me.'"

SPONTANEOUS CONFUSION: If there is any distinction between JULY 4 the Democratic and Republican Parties it is that the Democrats indulge in spontaneity. Democrats are the People—noisy, emotional, opinionated. In conventions assembled they generate an atmosphere where almost anything can happen.

Such an atmosphere last week pervaded the opening of the Democratic national convention at the Chicago Stadium. The first fight scheduled for the convention was on the permanent chairmanship. Originally picked to preside was Jouett Shouse, able chief at the Washington headquarters. Roosevelt was supposed to have sanctioned him. Then it was announced that Governor Roosevelt's man for the chair was Montana's grey-grim Senator Thomas J. Walsh. Mr. Shouse had been ditched, it was explained, because he did not favor the Roosevelt candidacy. Quickly the anti-Roosevelt battalions charged that Governor Roosevelt was guilty of bad faith. Al Smith vehemently declared: "A principle is at stake—the principle of keeping your word."

Intensifying the bitterness of the whole contest was an attack on Governor Roosevelt by Boss Frank Hague of Jersey City, field marshal for the Smith forces. Excerpts: "Governor Roosevelt, if nominated, has no chance of winning in November. He cannot carry a single State east of the Mississippi."

THE HOTEL DEAL: James Aloysius Farley, convention man- JULY 11 ager for Franklin Delano Roosevelt, looked wilted and broken when he clumped into his hotel suite last Friday morning after an all-night session. In those dragging hours a sullen minority had blocked, if not beaten, his candidate's nomination. Manager Farley dropped into a chair and groaned.

For four years Jim Farley had been building the Governor of New York up for the Presidency. He had arrived in Chicago with a clear majority of delegates. He had confidently predicted victory for Governor Roosevelt on the first ballot. Yet since dawn three ballots had come & gone and the Roosevelt nomination was unharvested. Jim Farley's plans had been stalled by the stubborn enmity of Alfred Emanuel Smith. Also the California and Texas forces of Speaker Garner had lined up with Smith on every convention vote so far.

During that dismal afternoon Louis McHenry Howe, the New York Governor's personal secretary and political eyes & ears, was waiting in Room 1502 when a little group marched in. Speaker Garner, they reported, was ready to drop his candidacy for first place on the ticket, provided he was given second place. Reaching for the telephone, Howe called Governor Roosevelt in Albany to confirm the deal. The Governor would be delighted to have Speaker Garner on the ticket with him. Mr. Howe informed Jim Farley of their candidate's prospective victory. Mr. Farley, who chews gum when happy, chewed gum happily. All that remained now was to notify Missouri, Illinois and Ohio to drop their favorite sons and get on the bandwagon.

THE DEAL GOES THROUGH: The night session of the convention was a perfunctory ratification of the Congress Hotel Deal. During the fourth ballot, with 682 delegates for Roosevelt and 190 for Smith, Mr. William Gibbs McAdoo arose to announce:

"California came here to nominate a President. When any man comes into this convention with popular will behind him to the extent of almost 700 votes. . . ."

Suddenly the rabble in the galleries sensed what was coming. They hooted, hissed, booed. "This convention wants to know," shrilled Mr. McAdoo above the din, "if this is the kind of hospitality Chicago accords its guests. I intend to say what I propose to say here tonight without regard to what the galleries or anybody else thinks. California casts 44 votes for Franklin D. Roosevelt."

This brought other States running henlike to the winner. The Roosevelt vote mounted to 945. Manager Farley was almost delirious. "What did I tell you! What did I tell you!" he kept babbling.

But Nominee Roosevelt was not the unanimous choice of

the convention. To a bitter, impractical end the Smith irreconcilables cast their 190 votes for their own candidate. In his hotel room Mr. Smith snapped off his radio, began packing up to leave town. Defeat went hard with him.

Next day Manager Farley executed his end of the "deal" when he secured Speaker Garner's nomination of the Vice Presidency by acclamation. Then from the Stadium he sped to the Chicago airport where Nominee Roosevelt was arriving from Albany.

ARMCHAIR: A great armchair beside a radio in the Executive Mansion at Albany held the Governor of New York most of last week. Franklin Delano Roosevelt, his lame legs stretched out before him, official duties forgotten, leaned back and listened happily. At his feet was his Scotch terrier, Megs. Nearby hovered his wife. His 77-year-old mother knitted silently. Sons Elliott, 21, and John, 16, paced about in nervous excitement.

"Oh, boy! Oh, golly," exclaimed young John, a fifth former at Groton, as Missouri joined the Roosevelt bandwagon. When the result was announced Nominee Roosevelt hobbled out to the ballroom to greet the Press. Mrs. Eleanor Roosevelt, pinning up the long sleeves of her green chiffon dress, went into the kitchen to cook eggs and frankfurters for "the boys."

Meanwhile the radio was booming back to Albany the nominee's message to the convention:

"I thank you. It is customary to hold formal notification ceremonies some weeks after the convention. This involves great expense. Instead may I ask the convention to remain in session tomorrow that I may appear before you and be notified at that time?"

The convention assented.

"A NEW DEAL": At the airport in the oldtime Capone stronghold of Cicero, Ill., 10,000 people waited to greet Nominee Roosevelt. In the crush his glasses were knocked from his nose. Helped up to the convention platform, the nominee rested his weight on his hands on the rostrum, delivered an address which he put together on the flight from Albany. Excerpts:

"Throughout the nation men and women, forgotten in the

Boss Frank Hague: "Roosevelt has no chance in November." Page 52.

Texan John Garner swings to FDR, says thoughtfully, "Politics is funny."

political philosophy of the Government, look to us here for guidance and for more equitable opportunity to share in the distribution of national wealth. I pledge myself to a new deal for the American people. This is more than a political campaign. It is a call to arms."

"POLITICS IS FUNNY": One evening last week Speaker John Nance Garner nervously paced the roof garden of the Washington Hotel, in which he makes his home. He had just released his Texas and California delgates at the Chicago convention to throw the Presidential nomination to Governor Roosevelt. Alfred E. Smith had tried to talk with him over long distance but the Speaker had refused to take the call. As he walked up & down alone, his cigar made a nasturtium-colored spot in the darkness.

"Mr. Speaker," asked a voice at his elbow, "you've gone to Roosevelt?"

"That's right, son. I'm a little older than you are, son, and politics is funny."

AUG. 8 **WHISPERS:** A Republican "whispering campaign" against lame Governor Roosevelt's physical condition similar to the 1928 "whispering campaign" against Mr. Smith's religion was alleged and denounced over the radio last week by Chairman

James Farley of the Democratic National Committee. Said he: "The Governor's lameness, which is steadily getting better, has no more effect on his general condition than if he had a glass eye or was prematurely bald. Governor Roosevelt might be handicapped in a footrace but in no other way need he fear comparison with his adversary."

MAINE QUAKE: Up to last week President Hoover had refused SEPT. 26 to appear conscious that he had a man named Franklin Delano Roosevelt running against him. Declining to take the stump, he appeared to set the Presidency above partisanship. Instead of advertising his adversary by hand-to-hand combat, he advertised his relief program by intense activity at the White House.

Then, in an election for governor and congressional seats, Maine went Democratic. In Washington it was instantly apparent that the foundations of the White House had been jarred, the President's campaign plans knocked to bits.

G.O.P. strategists trooped to the White House in the wake of the Maine returns and spent long gloomy hours with the President. He was told that he must revamp his personal campaign, get out to the country, make speeches, meet the Roosevelt challenge.

President Hoover was reluctant to change his tactics. He hates campaigning and crowds. Besides, he thinks it would be undignified to get out and hump himself for office like any ordinary politician. The President finally consented to make three October speeches—two in the Midwest, one in the East. Beyond that he would not go, even for another four years in the White House.

What caused Maine's voters to elect dapper, wisecracking Louis Jefferson Brann as its fourth Democratic Governor since the Civil War and send two Wet Democrats out of three to Congress? A variety of causes evidently combined. In low lobster and potato prices Maine is resentfully aware of hard times. Hoover relief is slow reaching its rocky shores, its little towns and farms. A majority of the 235,000 voters wanted a Change.

INCREDIBLE KINGFISH: The Roosevelt campaign was by no OCT. 3 means being carried along by the nominee alone. Already on the stump or itching to take it was an assorted chorus of vociferous henchmen the like of which was nowhere to be seen on the G.O.P. battlefront. In New Orleans curly-headed, loose-jawed, incredible Senator Huey Pierce ("Kingfish") Long champed impatiently to take to the hustings and raise his strident voice.

A frequent boast of this onetime lard drummer is: "I can sell anybody anything." He "sold" himself as both Governor and Senator to the Louisiana electorate. He "sold" them Oscar Kelly ("O.K.") Allen as his successor in the governorship. Now he is ready to join in "selling" Governor Roosevelt to the nation.

Last fortnight Huey Long attended a New Orleans dinner and announced:

"I'm leaving State politics for good. I've done all I can for Louisiana; now I want to help the rest of the country. The liberal element is running all over the world and they'll soon be in power in America. When they are, we'll put an end to multi-millionaires and bring back prosperity."

Packing a revolver in his pocket (he hates fist fights), he climbed into his limousine in front of his $60,000 Audubon Drive home, set out for Baton Rouge. There he marched into Governor Allen's office in the skyscraping State Capitol on the river bluff, sat down in Governor Allen's chair, began to give Governor Allen his political orders. Governor Allen is thoroughly accustomed to being thus bossed. One day during the last legislative session, Senator Long called out roughly: "Oscar, go get me those goddam bills we was talking about." Embarrassed, Governor Allen pretended not to hear. Huey Long howled: "God-dam you, Oscar, I can break you as easy as I made you! Get those goddam bills and get 'em on the jump." Governor Allen got them on the jump.

During his four-year rule in Louisiana energetic Huey Long has reduced property assessments 20%. He distributed 600,-000 free school books. At his free night schools 175,000 illiterates over 21 learned to read & write. Senator Long is responsible for 2,500 mi. of new paved roads, 6,000 mi. of new gravel roads. Thanks to him, twelve new bridges are about to span Louisiana rivers.

These accomplishments have not silenced many a Louisianan who views the Long record with utmost alarm. The

"Kingfish's" critics point out that he has raised the State's indebtedness from $11,000,000 to more than $100,000,000. The public payrolls have been loaded down with his fawning followers. Under him New Orleans has slipped from second to fifth among U.S. ports. Prisons are so overcrowded that last week Governor Allen had to release hundreds of offenders to save money. The gasoline tax has been upped from 2¢ to 6¢. A 4¢ tax is imposed on 15¢ cigarets. Enemies of Huey Long vehemently declare that his tax program has definitely hurt Louisiana business.

"There may be smarter men than me but they ain't in Louisiana," Huey Long likes to brag. Impervious to insult, he knows the trick of playing politics in its rawest, crudest form and he plays it with a vim, dash and audacity that stagger men with public sensibilities.

The night the Legislature passed his drop-a-crop cotton bill, he sent out for a cotton nightshirt. Near midnight he had himself photographed in it signing the bill. "Now I can take this damned thing off!" he exploded afterwards as he climbed back into his silk pajamas.

AT SUMNICK'S PLACE: Last week Farmer Gus Sumnick had OCT. 10 important company for midday dinner at his 1,200-acre place near Waterloo, Neb. Twenty-eight miles out from Omaha drove no less a person than Franklin Delano Roosevelt, trailed by a hundred automobiles full of family & friends.

Sun-bronzed Farmer Sumnick, coatless and with suspenders over his blue shirt, greeted Governor Roosevelt on the elm-shaded lawn before his house. He introduced his wife, his eleven sons and daughters.

"We're Republicans," said Farmer Sumnick to his guest, "but we've got eleven votes for you in our family and we'd have two more if the youngsters were of voting age. At the price quoted when Hoover was inaugurated the 30,000 bushels of corn I'm now harvesting would be worth $28,500 in Omaha. But instead it's worth only $8,100. And my 350 hogs at the price when Hoover became President would be worth $4,120, but at this year's prices would bring only $1,015. If Hoover and his Farm Board had kept their hands off, I'd be from $75,000 to $85,000 better off today than I am after four years of Hoover."

OCT. 17   **OUT STEPS HOOVER:** Out of the White House where he was buried in work, into the Midwest where he was born in want, a harassed and long-suffering President last week carried his case for re-election. Since his renomination he had left the burden of his campaign to non-elective Cabinet members who could not ask for votes in their own right. All their warm words failed to bring to life the silent, remote figure in Washington. Now, barely a month before the election and with the political tide running against him, he at last took the stump in his own behalf. As he crossed the line into his native Iowa, he thawed to the welcome of friends, recalled the old swimming hole of his childhood, greeted his old schoolmarm.

OCT. 24   **COOLIDGE PITCHES IN:** Calvin Coolidge and Herbert Hoover were never good warm friends during the five years one was President and the other Secretary of Commerce. President Coolidge had a trick of shoveling unpleasant Government jobs off on Hoover and then stepping harshly on his ego. But Calvin Coolidge puts the Republican party above personal feelings. Last week he emerged from retirement to make his campaign contribution in Manhattan's Madison Square Garden. G.O. Partisans counted on the magic of his name to pack the Garden and its environs with 50,000 persons. When only about 15,000 actually attended, ushers were sent out upon the streets to coax passers-by in to fill empty seats. The only living ex-President got a two-minute ovation which he cut short by holding up his watch after the din had wasted $340 worth of paid radio time. Then, as of old, his voice went twanging out across the land from 52 broadcasting stations.

Said Coolidge: "The charge is made that the Republican party does not show any solicitude for the common run of people but is interested only in promoting the interests of a few favored individuals and corporations. All this is a question of method. The Republican party believes in encouraging business in order that the benefits from such business may minister to the welfare of the ordinary run of people."

OCT. 31   **BITTER BOOS:** When the Hoover special drew into hungry Detroit a raucous, disrespectful din arose from 500 out-of-workers. Bonuseers and disgruntled citizens massed about the station. For 25 minutes the President stuck to the safety of his private car. When he finally emerged, he got a bitter booing. Before his eyes waggled placards: "We Want Bonus," "Down With Hoover," "Hoover—Baloney & Apple Sauce." During the 20-minute drive to the Olympic Arena he was jeered and derided by sidewalk throngs. Inside the hall he was among 20,000 friends yelling and stamping their welcome. On the platform with him was Hoover supporter Henry Ford.

President Hoover made campaign history at Detroit by mentioning his Democratic opponent by name for the first time. He read a letter from Governor Roosevelt to one Lowe Shearon, a Manhattan "forgotten man," which he said had been widely circulated among the jobless. The letter: "I believe in the inherent right of every citizen to employment at a living wage and I pledge my support to whatever measures I may deem necessary for inaugurating self-liquidating public works to provide employment for all surplus labor at all times."

Hotly the President declared: "This is a promise no government could fulfill. It is utterly wrong to delude suffering men and women with such assurances. I ask you whether or not such frivolous promises and dreams should be held out to suffering unemployed people. Is this the 'New Deal'?"

Aglow with satisfaction, President Hoover returned to the station. There Henry Ford's private car was cut into the presidential special just ahead of the Hoover car. On the journey back to Washington where he and his wife were White House guests, Mr. Ford urged the President to extend his campaign, go to California if necessary.

"WE WANT BEER!": Putting on what he called his "fighting OCT. 31 clothes" (dark grey sack suit), Governor Roosevelt last week traveled far, spoke often on his second campaign trip to "look, listen and learn." At Indianapolis 100,000 people packed Monument Circle to hear and see the Democratic nominee on a hotel balcony. Cried he: "This is not a campaign but a crusade!" G.O. Partisans looked on glumly while the crowd roared. "We want beer!" yelled St. Louis crowds. Governor Roosevelt promised it to them. Atlanta gave Roosevelt the kind of welcome it used to give Bobby Jones.

WITHOUT GLOVES: "Nonsense . . . misstatements . . . prattle NOV. 7 . . . untruths . . . defamation . . . ignorance . . . calumnies."

With such wrathful words did Herbert Clark Hoover last week characterize Franklin Delano Roosevelt, his public promises and the Democratic campaign in his behalf. On his fourth sortie the Republican President, fighting without gloves for his political life, traveled to doubtful Indiana. Gone was the Quaker's restraint. Gone was the aloofness. At Indianapolis his audience whooped "Atta boy, Herbie!"

Indianapolis finale:

"My countrymen! The fundamental issue that will fix the national direction for 100 years to come is whether we shall go on in fidelity to American traditions or whether we shall turn to innovations. I propose to go on in faith and loyalty to the traditions of our race, to build upon the foundations our fathers have laid over 150 years."

President Hoover journeyed back to Washington where he caught his breath over Sunday. Then the President brought his Eastern campaign to a climax in a mass meeting in Manhattan's Madison Square Garden where a capacity crowd of 22,000 gave him a 16-minute ovation.

Roosevelt and Al Smith (with Jim Farley in center) call off their feud. Says Smith: "If we were a couple of Frenchmen, we'd kiss each other."

FRIENDS AGAIN: Traveling west through Massachusetts from Boston, Al Smith was hailed like a conquering hero as he campaigned for the Roosevelt-Garner ticket. At every stop huge crowds clustered about his car. At Worcester one ardent friend snatched a cigar butt out of his hand, carried it off amid much scuffling as a souvenir.

In Albany Citizen Smith was invited by Governor Roosevelt to the Executive Mansion where he had lived for eight years. For an hour and a half they sat together in the study, smoking and talking. Reporters were called to behold this complete reconciliation.

Press: Can we call this an old-fashioned "Frank-and-Al get-together?"

Smith: Go as far as you like. If we were a couple of Frenchmen, we'd kiss each other. As it is we have to rely on a handshake.

ELECTION EVE: "We'll carry the country!" exclaimed Vice NOV. 14 President Charles Curtis last week as he swung into Kansas to close his solitary nationwide campaign for re-election.

ELECTION EVE (CONT'D.): "We'll carry the country!" exclaimed Vice Presidential Nominee John Nance Garner last week as he swung his feet off his desk in the Capitol and started back to Uvalde, Tex. to vote.

THE THIRTY-SECOND: Franklin Delano Roosevelt, his face relaxed in the easy grin that he had flashed at millions of his countrymen from the back platform of his campaigning trains, was easing himself down the steps of the old Hyde Park town hall. He had just voted for himself for 32nd President of the U.S. A motorcade stood waiting. At the swift pace which he always prefers, the Governor of New York and next President of the country was swept down the Hudson to Manhattan. On the way he stopped for luck at a firehouse—he had done that in 1928, to telephone his daughter, while being elected Governor. Then the motorcade rushed on.

Meantime throughout the length & breadth of the land, some 40,000,000 citizens were proceeding in quiet, orderly fashion to cast their ballots in the memorable Depression election of 1932. That most of them were marking "Roosevelt" instead of "Hoover" the former had at no time any doubt.

At his headquarters in the Biltmore that night the outer rooms were festive to the point of turbulence, but Roosevelt, sitting at a long table in an inner room, was not available to all comers. Jack Dempsey got in for a moment. But Franklin Roosevelt continued to concentrate on the returns. He wore a dark blue suit and blue tie. His Phi Beta Kappa key gleamed on his gold watch chain.

President Hoover's message conceding the election, dispatched from Palo Alto at 9:17 p.m. Pacific time, said: "I congratulate you on the opportunity that has come to you to be of service to the country and I wish for you a most successful administration." In Washington, the chief of the U.S. Secret Service ordered two of his best men to proceed at once to New York and take up their duty of guarding the person of the 32nd President.

Returning from the Biltmore to his town house on E. 65th St., Franklin Delano Roosevelt ate some ham & eggs and went to bed.

"I have work to do on the State Budget," was his parting word to the Press. "That will keep me busy for the next few days. I'm not President yet."

PRESIDENT REJECT: Toward dusk, in the big house on the Palo Alto hill, the guests and a host deeply dejected but keeping a brave front, watched the slow pile-up of the electoral total against Herbert Hoover. There was no mistaking the full significance of the landslide. Hoover's defeat was the worst any President had had in a straight two-party campaign since Lincoln beat General McClellan 212 to 21.

Floodlights on the roof lighted the faces of several hundred Stanford students who now were massing around the house. "SISS—BOOM—AH. . . . HOOVER!!" roared the students.

The President and Mrs. Hoover walked out to the terrace. "All I can do is thank you for this demonstration of fine loyalty," he said, and there were tears in his eyes.

NOV. 21 **WHAT TO EXPECT:** "We not only got a new deal and a new dealer but a practically new deck of cards. It is, however, the same game. The players change but the game not at all."

So wrote shrewd, able Frank Richardson Kent last week in the Baltimore *Sun* on the election of Franklin Delano Roosevelt. In his campaign President-elect Roosevelt had exhibited himself as a smart politician, and no smart politician who wants to stay in power suddenly and violently revolutionizes the game's rules on the first deal.

The Thirty-Second President emerged from the campaign fog as a vigorous well-intentioned gentleman of good birth and breeding who had large hopes for improving his country by ordinary political processes. If he lacked crusading convictions, he was at least free from his predecessor's stubborn pride of opinion. He had a Congress overwhelmingly friendly in which to work his will. The country seemed ready and waiting for him to lead. Never before were the possibilities better for a Democratic Administration to get things done.

Women

END OF A PRINCESS: After pausing for two weeks at the door SEPT. 5 of a bedroom in Chicago's Drake Hotel, last week Death came, as it must to all women, to Edith Rockefeller McCormick. Once she was called the world's richest woman. But cancer makes no distinctions. Two years ago she had a growth removed from her breast. Another appeared in her liver. When she moved to the Drake from her mansion on Lake Shore Drive in June, she and her doctors knew the end was near.

Beside her in the last two weeks, during which her indomitable rallies amazed every one, were her onetime husband, Harold Fowler McCormick, their three living children, and her brother John D. Rockefeller Jr. They had all come to her after years of an estrangement that was more of her making than theirs. A chief cause of the estrangement was also in devoted attendance—the plump little Swiss named Edwin D. Krenn with whom she had shared her last eleven years. Her brother John did not wait for the end. Itching painfully with an attack of shingles, he rejoined their father, John Davison Rockefeller, in the East. Long estranged too, and querulously jealous of his own health at 93, Father Rockefeller had not gone to see her at all. "He travels only between Florida and his home," John D. Jr. explained. In her last days, with the flesh fallen from her face and the death mask showing, Edith Rockefeller had come to resemble her father closely.

As near to royalty as it is possible to come in the U.S. was

Edith Rockefeller when, in 1895, she married that most handsome and eligible of contemporary Princetonians, Harold McCormick. The newspapers called her the Princess of Standard Oil. He was the Prince of International Harvester. The first two years of their life together were spent in the quiet little river town of Council Bluffs, Iowa, and it was not until the McCormicks moved to Chicago that her imperiousness began to assert itself and the strange things that happen to the very rich began to happen to her.

New, lusty Chicago loved display. Edith McCormick fed her guests off Napoleonic gold plate. She brought grand opera to Chicago, spent $5,000,000 keeping it alive. When her eldest son died of scarlet fever she donated the John McCormick Institution for Infectious Diseases. The scarlet fever germ was isolated there.

In 1911 Chicago heard she had had a nervous breakdown. With her husband she went to Switzerland. In Zurich she became a pupil of Psychologist Carl Jung, conceived the notion that her mission was to teach psychoanalysis. To practice humility she scrubbed the floor of her hotel. She took 99 patients, one of whom was her small, plump gardener, Edwin D. Krenn. Krenn returned with her to the U.S. in 1921. When she landed she announced that her husband was coming by another boat.

But Harold McCormick had spied Singer Ganna Walska on the other boat. When Mr. McCormick reached Chicago he announced to the Press: "Mr. & Mrs. McCormick are not living under the same roof." Edith Rockefeller divorced him on grounds of desertion. Later Harold McCormick married Walska.

Back in the Lake Shore mansion, Mrs. McCormick never spent a night out of it until she went to a hospital in 1930. No guest ever spent a night in it. She became more imperious, more eccentric. She practiced astrology, celebrated Christmas on December 15. She believed in reincarnation, decided she had been King Tutankhamen's child-wife Anknesenpaaten. "Then they opened the mummy chamber and when I saw the pictures of it, I knew. There was my little chair."

She developed phobias, kept six detectives in the house. She feared water, seldom bathed. Like Anknesenpaaten, she was not buried. Her body was put in a receiving vault, next to that of her son John, which had been there for 31 years, the cemetery people never having had any instructions on what to do with it.

Crime

SNATCHERS ON SOURLAND MT.: The last person known to MARCH have seen 20-month-old Charles Augustus Lindbergh Jr. was his nurse, a dark-haired, light-footed little Scotch girl of 26 named Betty Gow. Nurse Gow immigrated to the U.S. in 1928, has been in the Lindberghs' employ over a year. At approximately 8:30 o'clock one evening last week she went to his nursery. It is on the second floor, southeast corner of the home which Col. & Mrs. Lindbergh completed last autumn three miles north of Hopewell, N.J., ten miles north of Princeton, on a wild, lonely stretch of high ground called Sourland Mt. Nurse Gow tucked Charles Augustus, who had been ailing with a cold, into his crib and went down to the servants' quarters.

At 8:30 Col. Lindbergh returned from New York by motor. He ate dinner and afterward took a seat in his living room directly under one of the nursery's three windows, all of which were closed but none of which was locked.

At 10 o'clock Nurse Gow went to the nursery. The baby was not in his crib. She hurried downstairs and notified the parents. All three ran back upstairs. The first thing they did was to inspect the floor to see if the child had crawled somewhere. He had not. One more look around the room disclosed muddy footprints, an open windowscreen and a note on the sill below. Exact contents of the note have never been revealed, but if it warned against police intervention, Col. Lindbergh brusquely disregarded the warning.

The Hopewell police arrived not later than 10:30, for by 10:50 a teletyped message went humming through the length of the State with the news that the first-born of the nation's No. 1 hero had been kidnapped.

Instantly an impregnable wall was thrown around New Jersey's borders as city police and State troopers of New York, New Jersey and Pennsylvania began stopping cars at all bridgeheads, ferries, and at the mouth of the Holland Tunnel. By morning a gigantic posse of police, troopers, U.S. Department of Justice operatives, Coast Guardsmen, American Legionaires, civilians was combing an area from Boston to Baltimore. There had never been such an intensive search party since Booth shot Lincoln.

Object of the search was the most famous child on earth, whose birth, and, up to last week, whose life were jealously guarded secrets. So successfully did his parents keep his name and face out of the Press that ignorant gossip whispered that he might be defective. Only four photographs of Charles Augustus had ever been made public, one of them snapped surreptitiously last summer in Maine when his parents were flying to China. Now there issued forth from Col. Lindbergh's private collection cinema films by the score. These went broadcast through the land while enormous headlines splashed the child's name across every U.S. front page day after day.

President Ortiz Rubio of Mexico ordered his army to watch the border for the kidnappers. School children prayed. Herbert Hoover spurred Government sleuths from a Cabinet meeting. In Chicago, more precisely in Cook County jail where he is waiting a last appeal against an eleven-year Federal sentence, "Scarface Al" Capone interested himself in the Lindbergh case. Offering a $10,000 reward for the baby's safe return, he indignantly remarked:

"It's the most outrageous thing I ever heard of! I know how Mrs. Capone and I would feel. If I were out of jail I could be of real assistance."

Clues: At the end of the first six days, Anne Morrow Lindbergh, who expects another child, and her harassed husband had no more evidence as to who had snatched their child than was established in the preliminary examination of their estate. But there were several tangible pieces of evidence connected with the crime:

¶ A well-made ladder of three seven-foot sections. Footprints indicated that it had been leaned up against the nursery window, then taken 60 feet away and abandoned.

¶ A chisel, probably intended for prying open the nursery window.

¶ A note, not made public.

¶ Footprints, large enough to be a man's but muffled by burlap or moccasins, traceable toward the main road which bounds the eastern edge of the 350-acre estate. Other footprints, small enough to be a woman's, joined them a short distance from the house.

¶ A farmer's testimony that he saw a parked car on the road which runs down the south side of the estate, at 7:30 on the evening of the abduction.

¶ The remarkably narrow time limit within which the kidnapping probably took place: 8:30 when Nurse Gow says she last saw the child and 9:15 when Col. Lindbergh sat down under the nursery window.

A small, rheumatic terrier was in the house but did not bark while the child was being taken. There was a floodlight system on the grounds but it was not in use. These facts led some guessers to imagine that the person or persons who took the child knew the grounds, knew the house plan, knew the child's routine, possibly knew the child himself, since he made no outcry.

Meantime the frantic Lindberghs were making stronger and stronger efforts to get in touch with the kidnappers. Messages were sent over the radio and to the Press begging the kidnapper to communicate. In their most desperate move, Col. & Mrs. Lindbergh descended to the underworld. On the fourth night following their baby's disappearance they issued a signed statement, photostated copies of which were published in the nation's Press, as follows:

"If the kidnappers of our child are unwilling to deal direct, we fully authorize 'Salvy' Spitale and Irving Bitz to act as our go-betweens. We will also follow any other method suggested by the kidnappers that we can be sure will bring the return of our child."

"Salvy" Spitale was an obscure figure. The Press itself did not know much about him save that he made some of his money out of restaurants, was regarded as trustworthy by a number of gangsters and had Irving Bitz for a right-hand man. Go-Between Spitale thereupon disappeared from his usual haunts, and while everyone was wondering where he would bob up next, up he bobbed at a Madison Square Garden hockey game in Manhattan.

"I'm kinda sorry I got mixed up in this," said he. "Papers are printing pictures of my children and dragging my family into the story. My policy of avoiding publicity has been knocked for a row of milk bottles."

In Trenton, New Jersey's Governor A. Harry Moore remarked to newshawks: "Personally, I think if you all laid off for a few weeks we might get somewhere."

PRECAUTION: In the New York *Times* two days after the kidnapping, appeared an advertisement for a home ventilating system with a picture of a sleeping child, and these words: "Protect YOUR BABY. Dangers of open nursery windows are gone once you've installed an Airgard. Windows remain sealed tight—LOCKED."

MARCH 21   **FACTS & FANTASY:** The cold wind which, on the night of March 1, banged shutters and rattled windows at the lonely New Jersey home of Col. Charles Augustus Lindbergh, had died down last week. But still the curly-headed baby for whom all police and all good citizens of the nation were on anxious lookout, was a lost child.

The strain told on the bereaved mother. Physicians attended her, but still she was seen with her mother and sister going about her robbed house, managing, helping, hoping. At Hopewell, where the Press kept constant contact with the State police, new factual developments were only a thin trickle amid the welter of rumor, false report and fantasy which piled up from day to day.

Facts—It was announced that the original ransom demand was found some hours after the child's disappearance was discovered, and not, as originally reported, when Col. & Mrs. Lindbergh first rushed with Nurse Betty Gow into the nursery. And both parents were not downstairs when Nurse Gow found the crib empty. Mrs. Lindbergh was on the second floor taking a bath. Learning that Mrs. Lindbergh did not have the baby, Nurse Gow went downstairs to see if the child was with his father.

Fantasy—The New York *American* discovered an old "amazon" in the hills behind the Lindbergh home who intimated that applejack distillers had snatched the child to scare the Lindberghs out of the neighborhood. A mysterious trespasser was arrested outside a nearby deserted shack wherein a clean new diaper had been found.

As the case entered its second week, Col. Lindbergh began taking it more & more into his own hands. But the emissaries which he had appointed—two metropolitan 'leggers named Salvatore Spitale and Irving Bitz—turned up in Brooklyn's Federal Court last week, charged with landing liquor from a boat. It was evident that they had not been able to accomplish much toward the Lindbergh babe's return.

ON SOURLAND MOUNTAIN (CONT'D.): If Charles Augustus APRIL 4 Lindbergh Jr. was alive, he became 21 months old last week, the fourth week since he was snatched from his crib on Sourland Mountain near Hopewell, N.J. The State of New Jersey had already spent $50,000 searching for him. It had cost Columbia Broadcasting System alone $40,000 to keep the public informed of developments.

RANSOM: APRIL 18

CONFIDENTIAL NOTE TO EDITORS: NOT FOR PUBLICATION.

THE TREASURY DEPARTMENT HAS ASKED ALL BANKS IN THE COUNTRY TO BE ON THE LOOKOUT FOR A SERIES OF FIVE, TEN AND TWENTY DOLLAR BILLS, WHICH ARE NOT COUNTERFEIT BUT WHICH BEAR RECORDED NUMBERS. THE UNITED PRESS HAD BEEN ASKED BY COLONEL LINDBERGH NOT TO GIVE THIS STORY PUBLICATION BECAUSE IT WOULD SERIOUSLY INTERFERE WITH THE WORK THE FAMILY IS DOING TO RECOVER THE CHILD. NEEDLESS TO SAY THE DEDUCTIONS TO BE DRAWN FROM THIS SITUATION ARE OBVIOUS AND RUMORS TO THE EFFECT THAT THE BABY IS HOME ARE ERRONEOUS.

> (signed) R. J. BENDER,
> GENERAL NEWS MANAGER
> UNITED PRESS

This bulletin was issued last Saturday morning at the personal request of Col. Lindbergh, in an effort to stop publication of reports that he had been victimized either by the abductors of his son or by impostors.

The story was soon confirmed by Col. H. Norman Schwarzkopf of the New Jersey State Police on Col. Lindbergh's behalf: "A ransom of $50,000 was paid to the kidnappers, properly identified as such, upon their agreement to notify Col. Lindbergh as to the exact whereabouts of the baby. The baby was not found at the point designated. Several days were permitted to elapse to give the kidnappers every opportunity to keep their agreement."

How Col. Lindbergh "properly identified" the person or persons to whom he gave the $50,000 was thus officially explained: "At the time the baby was kidnapped a means was offered in the ransom note of positive identification of the kidnappers thereafter. Subsequent notes received were identified by this means and at the time that the ransom was paid the kidnappers used this same means to positively identify themselves as the ones who had carried off the baby. This is the only means by which Col. Lindbergh can know for a fact that he is dealing with the kidnappers."

Identified last week as Col. Lindbergh's intermediary with the kidnappers was Dr. John F. Condon, an elderly lecturer at Fordham University in The Bronx. Dr. Condon it was who inserted 13 "personal" advertisements in New York newspapers signed "Jafsie" (J.F.C.) whereby communication was maintained with the baby-snatchers. On April 2 Dr. Condon delivered the ransom money to the kidnappers' agent with whom contact was first made at Woodlawn Cemetery. Pre-

Charles Lindbergh Jr. with Nurse Betty Gow, who saw him last. *"Jafsie" Condon pays off the ransom but does not get the child.*

sumably he was then informed when and where the baby would be returned. When it was not, the following "Jafsie" advertisement appeared last week: "What is wrong? Have you crossed me? Better directions, please."

After it got out that he had sought Federal aid in tracing the ransom money, Col. Lindbergh reiterated his promise not to "try to injure" the criminals if only they would return the child. A spokesman admitted that "he feared that his action in calling upon Federal officials might be interpreted by the kidnappers as an effort to double-cross them."

"A HARD CASE": "What newspapers! What police! And what MAY 2 a country!!"—Montreal *Herald.*

Such was the tenor of worldwide comment on the disappearance of Charles Augustus Lindbergh Jr. Last week the case passed into its third month with the child still missing, the abductors still uncaught. If many people realized that the Lindbergh kidnapping of 1932 must surely loom as a social and criminal milestone, no one but foreign editors and a few vigilant U.S. patriots were saying or doing much about it. Among the vigilant patriots were some American Legionnaires in California who stirred Connecticut's Hiram Bingham to suggest on the floor of the Senate last week that the kidnapping of the country's most celebrated baby was a colossal plot to get the country's most celebrated criminal, Alphonse Capone, out of jail.

Last week Col. Lindbergh made a two-day journey from his lonely estate. He was seen at Milford and Bridgeport, Conn. The "Jafsie" notes disappeared from the newspapers and John F. ("Jafsie") Condon, the retired schoolmaster who paid $50,000 of Col. Lindbergh's money to someone who said he was the kidnappers' agent, went boating in Pelham Bay, capsized, got an icy ducking, went home to recover.

The Lindbergh family's movements during the several hours preceding the kidnapping could be nailed down finally. The Lindberghs ate dinner and within a very few minutes of 9 p.m. Col. Lindbergh sat down at a desk in his living room facing a window. This window was directly under the one through which the kidnappers entered the nursery upstairs. Their ladder had been in direct view of the chair in which Col. Lindbergh later seated himself. Therefore, it is safe to say that the kidnapping occurred during the brief period between the time when Nurse Betty Gow last saw the child, while the Lindberghs were at dinner, and the time when the child's father sat down at his desk—probably less than an hour. Mrs. Lindbergh, who went upstairs after dinner, was bathing in a bathroom separated by only one wall from her baby's bed, empty but still warm.

Contrary to original report, the female footprints found nearby have never been connected with the crime, might have been made by servants or family on routine missions about the grounds. Two sets of male footprints—sizes No. 8 and No. 10—were found about the ladder and under the nursery window. Those closest to the inquiry believe that one man climbed into the nursery, handed the baby to the other at the top of the ladder. The tracks led off across a field toward the south of the Lindbergh property, in the opposite direction from the main entrance. They stopped at a road where the abductors must have boarded their automobile. That roadside spot was as far as any known person had definitely trailed the Lindbergh baby up to last week. But the search fanned out as far as Sweden, Spain, France, Austria, the Pacific Coast. During the search the case leaped dizzily into fantasy. And last week Al Capone promised to return the baby "in two or three days" if Col. Lindbergh could get him free that long.

MAY 16   **MORE SIDESHOW:** In Washington last week another fantastic sideshow in the Lindbergh case was revealed. Principal in this show was a bad actor who first came to fame in the Harding era—Gaston Bullock Means.

Bad Actor Means, 53, a thick-necked, slack-jawed, dimpled-cheeked Southerner, is the author of *The Strange Death of President Harding* in which it is intimated that Mrs. Harding poisoned her husband. The book was written after Means had served three years (1925-28) in Atlanta Penitentiary for bribery and violation of the Prohibition laws. Before the U.S. entered the War, he says, he served with the German spy system in the U.S., once received $1,000,000 from a German agent. At one time or another, Gaston Means, a sleuth by profession, has been indicted for breach of promise, impersonating an officer, fraud, bribery, forgery, murder. He once told a

Gaston Means bilks a rich daughter
with promises to find the baby.

Mrs. McLean. For her $106,000 she
gets 20 promises in 24 hours.

Senate committee that "being indicted" was his business. Last November he was arrested for beating his wife.

It was no great surprise to Gaston Means when a U.S. deputy marshal and a special Department of Justice agent stopped his expensive, chauffeured car on Washington's Massachusetts Avenue one day last week and took him into custody. The charge on which he was apprehended was, however, startling: that he had bilked affluent Mrs. Evelyn Walsh McLean, owner of the Hope Diamond, out of $106,000 on the pretext that he could help her find the Lindbergh baby.

Rich Mrs. McLean, a mining tycoon's daughter much in the Washington limelight, had remembered Gaston Means from the good old Harding days when her husband played poker with the Ohio Gang, decided to hire him to trace the Lindbergh baby.

Means said that he had recently met a man with whom he served in Atlanta Penitentiary. The man had suggested that he and Means abduct the Lindbergh baby. This suggestion, Means said, he had indignantly spurned, but he was willing to find out if the man had carried out the project himself. After a short disappearance Means returned to Washington with the news that, sure enough, his erstwhile jailmate was the one who had done the job. It would take $50,000 ransom, a $50,000 fee for himself and $6,000 for expenses to effect the child's return. Mrs. McLean delivered, without receipt, the $106,000 into Means's hands in unmarked $10 and $20 bills on March 7. Means at once began to give Mrs. McLean her money's worth in detective-story melodrama.

Means had her go to Aiken, S.C., where she was introduced to a sinister character with a gun. Then she made a trip to El Paso, Tex., where the child was to be delivered. For these fruitless expeditions the ever plausible Means had excuses. He made at least 20 promises to deliver the child within 24 hours. Once he swore he had held the baby in his arms.

Finally, the credulity of Mrs. McLean snapped. She went to Chief J. Edgar Hoover of the Department of Justice's Investigation Bureau and swore out a warrant to be served the next time Means stepped inside the District of Columbia. Smiling under arrest, Means had nothing to say to the Press, save that he was sure he would be cleared.

MAY 23 **"NEVER-TO-BE-FORGOTTEN":** If a Negro from Marshall's Corner, N.J. had not decided to get out of his truck and relieve himself in the woods a mile from Hopewell last week, negotiators and police would still be looking for kidnapped Charles Augustus Lindbergh Jr.

At a point 75 ft. from the edge of the concrete Princeton-Hopewell Road, traveled by every official in New Jersey during the 72-day search, William Allen noticed something round and bright protruding from a mound of rubble and leaves. It looked like a human skull. Allen ran back to the truck and summoned his companion, Orville Wilson. It *was* a human skull. On it and nearby were wisps of yellow hair. Wilson hopped in the truck and made for Hopewell, where he found Charley Williams, one of Hopewell's two policemen, in a barber's chair. To him Wilson babbled their discovery of the Lindbergh baby. Policeman Williams notified the State Police and together they went back to the hillside spot, visible on a clear day from the Lindbergh home on Sourland Mountain, five miles away.

Careful examination indicated that the baby had been clubbed to death shortly after being snatched from his crib. The badly decomposed remains, clad only in a flannel stomach band and an undershirt, lay face down in a shallow depression. Nurse Betty Gow identified the body in the Trenton morgue. More positive identification came from the Lindberghs' pediatrician.

The discovery made hushed after-dinner talk for most U.S. citizens, but the child's father did not learn about it until nine hours after the body was found. It came to him by radio. Stirred on by a boat-builder in contact with rum-runners, Col. Lindbergh was groping hopelessly about the dark waters off Cape May, N.J.—still trying to buy his child back from its abductors. Col. Lindbergh was put ashore near Atlantic City, raced homeward by motor.

Now that no amount of secrecy on the part of Press or Police could return the child alive to its parents, the lid of caution abruptly blew off the case. For the first time the text of the original ransom note was unofficially made public:
"Dear Sir,

"Have $50,000 ready, $25,000 in $20 bills, $15,000 in $10 bills and $10,000 in $5 bills. Have them in two packages. Four days we will inform you to redeem the money.

"We warn you for making anything public, or for notifying the police. The child is in gut care.

"Don't publish this letter."

It was 3 o'clock on the morning after the discovery of his child's crumpled body that Col. Lindbergh drove up a Trenton alley and went into the frame morgue building. He asked for a lock of his child's hair. Next afternoon he returned to make an official identification. Then, as mute housewives watched over their back fences, he came out of the building following some men with a small oak box. He accompanied the box to Linden, N.J. In a square, grey building with a straight black smokestack cremation took place. The ashes were removed to Englewood where Mrs. Lindbergh's widowed mother, Mrs. Dwight Whitney Morrow, lives. [The case was solved in 1934 with the arrest of a German-born carpenter named Bruno Hauptmann. He was found guilty of first-degree murder and was electrocuted in 1936.]

FOREIGN NEWS

Germany

As the year began, Germany was suffering severely from the worldwide Depression. Six million Germans were unemployed, and the nation's political affairs were in chaos. So many parties were competing for leadership that Chancellor Heinrich Brüning could not achieve a working majority in the Reichstag and was forced to govern by a series of unpopular decrees. In the wings, waiting to seize power, was Adolf Hitler. His Nazi party had received nearly seven million votes in a 1930 election, and was rapidly emerging as the largest and most violent party in Germany. During 1932 he kept the country in an uproar during two unsuccessful, all-out efforts to win a national election and become Germany's Chancellor.

JAN. 18 **MAY ANTICIPATED:** To most Germans, May is still a long way off. But never for one instant has pale Chancellor Heinrich Brüning forgotten that according to Germany's Constitution Old President Paul von Hindenburg's term of office is up in May. Last week Brüning summoned Adolf Hitler to Berlin and made him a proposition: so that the Fatherland could present a united front to the world in this winter of her greatest trial, would Hitler agree to an extension of President von Hindenburg's term?

Fascist Hitler left in a huff. Canny Brüning had put him in a tight position. Old Paul is Germany's idol. Should he refuse the Brüning request, Fascist Hitler would be accused of repudiating the idol. If he agreed, he would see himself diddled out of his great chance to seize the government legally.

Hitler's Brown Shirts went into a huddle and considered a counterproposal: they would agree provided they were given two posts in the Brüning Cabinet. Correspondents thought it likely that canny Chancellor Brüning would accede. Hitlerites in his Cabinet could not well work for his overthrow.

SILENT ADOLF: Last week Adolf Hitler wrote Chancellor JAN. 25
Brüning a belated letter flatly refusing to help prolong the
President's term by Reichstag action, whereupon the Government set Feb. 28 as election day. On the subject of election
candidates Herr Hitler was glumly silent.

BATTLEFIELD INVESTMENTS: Able Berlin Correspondent Hu- FEB. 15
bert Renfro Knickerbocker has just concluded a series of
reports on conditions in Germany for the New York Evening
Post. Investigator Knickerbocker found 15,000,000 Germans on the dole, wrote touchingly of abject poverty in the
Red quarter of Berlin in striking contrast to gay night life
around the Kurfürsten Damm. In the town of Falkenstein,
Saxony, he found half the population on the dole; in Thu-
ringian villages the specter of starvation. Everywhere Hitler's power was rising. Nearly three-fourths of Heidelberg's
students were Nazis. Germans, facing ruin, were almost unanimous in demanding Reparations cancellation at any cost.
Knickerbocker conclusions:

¶ "Germany can pay no reparations now.

¶ "Germany is determined to re-arm if France does not dis-
arm.

¶ "The German people as a whole have disavowed and repudiated the Versailles Treaty. France considers it her only guarantee of life. French and German differences have grown
worse and they give every evidence of growing still worse in
the future. Whether the development comes to war within
predictable time or not, warlike years lie ahead for Europe.

¶ "American investments on this continent are investments
in a battlefield."

NOMINATIONS: To give his life for his country—such in a FEB. 29
very real sense was the decision calmly made last week by Paul
von Beneckendorff und von Hindenburg. Old Paul is 84. By refusing to run again for President he would doubtless prolong
a life which his big red country house and his rosy-cheeked
grandchildren make pleasant. But, as the President said, the
time in Germany is difficult. Six million unemployed. Four
suicides a day in Berlin alone. Whole industrial regions idle.

"After an earnest scrutiny I have decided," wrote Old Paul
wistfully, "to stand for re-election."

With that, candidate-picking began. First in the field against Old Paul was Communist Ernst Thälmann. His worst enemies, the German Fascists, conceded last week that leather-lunged Comrade Thälmann would get at least 6,000,000 votes. Some 38,000,000 ballots will be cast.

The Hitlerites did a risky thing. They nominated Adolf Hitler. Theoretically, Austrian-born Hitler could gain citizenship, and eligibility for the office of President, by accepting appointment to a public post in Brunswick. With four or more candidates in the field, Old Paul's majority might be forestalled, and on the second round the Opposition votes might be thrown to Hitler. But suppose at the last minute the Reich declares Hitler no real citizen, strikes his name from the lists too late for the Nazis to introduce a new candidate? In such case Old Paul could very well obtain a majority on the first vote.

MARCH 21 **NOBODY WINS:** Nobody won the German election last week. Nobody has ever been elected President of Germany by popular vote on the first ballot. To be so elected a candidate must win 50% of all votes cast plus one vote more.

The returns last week:

Von Hindenburg (Coalitionist) 18,661,736
Hitler (Fascist) 11,328,571
Thälmann (Communist) 4,971,079
Dusterberg (Monarchist) 2,517,876

Since nobody was elected, Germans will vote again Sunday, April 10.

APRIL 18 **HITLER STOPPED?:** No sooner had 19,359,642 German ballots re-elected President von Hindenburg for a second seven-year term last week than audacious Adolf Hitler (who had won 13,417,460 votes) began talking of "My victory!"

Haranguing his brown-breasted Fascists from his "Brown House" in Munich, fiery Herr Hitler exhorted them to win the Prussian Diet election April 24, bade them remember that in national German elections, the Fascist vote is steadily climbing. This major fact—the rising Fascist tide—President von Hindenburg's tremendous personal victory tended to obscure last week. On the basis of last week's presidential returns the Fascist Party is now first in Germany. It cannot, of course, assume first rank in parliament until there is another Reichstag Election—which President von Hindenburg and Chancellor Heinrich Brüning will do their utmost to put off.

PRUSSIAN BRAWL: It started fairly quietly with a debate in the JUNE 6 Diet on the administration of justice in Prussia and the election of Hitlerite Hans Kerri (who likes to refer to Adolf Hitler as "Germany's Jesus Christ") as President of the Diet. Suddenly up sprang Communist Wilhelm Pieck [who would become President of Communist East Germany in 1949.] Shaking his fist at the Fascist benches he screamed: "In your ranks there sit a huge number of murderers!"

That was all that was needed. Spitting on their hands, the Fascists moved in. Inkwells, water bottles, desk drawers, chairs, ledgers, broken table legs went into the fray. Neutral deputies fled for their lives, others marooned on the speakers' dais spent a frantic quarter of an hour ducking missiles and wringing their hands. Safe in their odds of 3 to 1, the Fascists soon drove the last Communist from the Chamber, spent the next half-hour triumphantly roaring old war songs.

It was the worst brawl Prussia's rowdy legislature has ever seen, but violence did not stop with the Deputies. As soon as the story leaked out, Communists and Hitlerites began punching each others' noses all over Germany. In Hamburg a mob

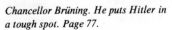

Chancellor Brüning. He puts Hitler in a tough spot. Page 77.　　*President Hindenburg. To block Hitler he runs again at 84. Page 78.*

of Communists swept down the street shouting, "Hunger, Hunger!" A volley of police bullets stopped them. In Berlin a group of Hitlerites was trapped by a surly crowd in a railway tunnel, had to be rescued by police.

Chancellor Brüning was not unduly alarmed. He marched in a religious procession and planned a new legislative program to break up big Junkers' estates in order to provide homes for the jobless and to increase taxes by an emergency decree.

For President von Hindenburg this was too much. Under the influence of a group of German generals who have been intriguing against Chancellor Brüning for months, he abruptly forced the resignation of Brüning's Cabinet. While the President cast about for a new protégé, Herr Brüning was asked to continue in office *ad interim.*

JUNE 13 **CABINET OF MONOCLES:** Brown-shirted Fascists massed and milled last week outside a squat, soldier-guarded mansion on Berlin's famed Wilhelmstrasse, shouted qualified approval of the occupant. They roared not, "Hail Hindenburg!" but, "Hail Hindenburg who ousted Brüning!" To cap the climax President von Hindenburg appointed as Germany's new Chancellor notorious Lieut. Colonel Franz von Papen. English editors promptly splashed out the screamer: EX-SPY BECOMES GERMAN CHANCELLOR!

Intimates of President von Hindenburg advanced a remarkable hypothesis. They suggested that Old Paul had never heard of Military Attaché von Papen's recall from the U.S. in 1915 at the urgent request of President Wilson or of the subsequent indictment charging Von Papen with conspiracy to blow up Canada's Welland Canal. Fortunately the U.S. State Department was able to deny reports last week that the new German Chancellor would be liable to arrest should he enter the U.S. By mere chance the indictment against him which had stood for 16 years was quashed last March, along with a batch of other German spy indictments.

Germans, noting four barons in the new Von Papen Cabinet and that all its members are "high born," promptly nicknamed them the "Cabinet of Monocles."

As he took office, Chancellor von Papen declared that "post-War German Governments have weakened the morale of the people by a system of State Socialism" including the dole, and that "this moral degeneration was enhanced by the class struggle with Bolshevism which, like a corroding poison, threatens to destroy our moral code."

CONTEMPT: Questioned by suave Jewish lawyers in a Munich JUNE 20 court last week, Jew-baiting Adolf Hitler grew hot under his brown collar, egged his brown-shirted henchmen into muttered threats that they would pull the lawyers' noses.

Fascist Hitler had brought the suit. He charged Jewish Journalist Werner Abel with "libel and perjury" in accusing the German Fascist Party of accepting campaign contributions of 2,500,000 lire from Italian Fascists in 1930.

"Didn't you know," softly asked Defense Attorney Kurt Rosenfeld, "that agents of your party negotiated in Italy?"

"What do you mean by 'my party'?" mimicked Herr Hitler, then shouted, "*I* am the party, do you understand? *I* am the party!"

"Perhaps, and perhaps also you took money from the Czechoslovak and French munitions interests," insinuated Lawyer Rosenfeld.

Bounding to his feet Witness Hitler yelled, "That's a lie! Were such things true I'd shoot myself." Clenching his fists, pounding a tattoo on the courtroom table, he wound up screaming: "I won't be insulted! I could not justify myself before my millions of followers if I stood for this! I will no longer answer these Jew lawyers! Not another question, though I will answer anything asked by the Court."

Promptly the Munich judge ruled: "You must answer the lawyer. The Court has no questions." But Witness Hitler kept mum as an owl, sat with arms folded while his brown-shirt followers filled the courtroom with a chant of, "Germany awake! Awake! Awake!!!"

After whispers between the Court and his lawyers, Fascist Hitler submitted to a fine of 800 marks ($190) for contempt of court plus 200 marks ($47) for unruly behavior, then quit the stand snarling, "Those Jewish lawyers were just trying to stage a bit of propaganda."

RADICAL REACTIONARIES: Latins, not Teutons, are supposed JULY 4 to stab each other but there was knife work aplenty in German streets last week as savage riots landed nearly 1,000 Germans in jail, cost eleven lives. Stabbed, a Hamburg policeman died after two nights of agony. Stabbed in the heart at Essen, a young Fascist died on the spot. Meanwhile in Cologne police beat off Fascists who bludgeoned them with iron rods. Street clashes grew so hot at Kiel that German sailors kept prudently in barracks.

The blazing riots sprang, many Germans thought, from smoldering popular resentment at decrees and orders—including new income, sales and nuisance taxes—daily rushed into effect by Germany's new Cabinet.

AUG. 1 **PRESSURE IN PRUSSIA:** In President von Hindenburg's comfortable, unpretentious summer home last week the old Field Marshal reached gravely for a pen and signed a document:

"For the term during which this decree remains in force the Chancellor of the Reich is empowered to assume for himself the official duties of the Prussian Premier and to entrust other persons with the conduct as Commissioners of the other Prussian Ministries."

Next morning the entire Socialist Cabinet of Premier Otto Braun of Prussia was declared deposed. On the surface the Junker dictatorship was a triumph for "Handsome Adolf" Hitler and his followers. For months the Fascists have been demanding the right to parade in uniform. They now have the right. They have also demanded the dissolution of the Prussian Cabinet and the nationalization of the Prussian police. They now have that too.

AUG. 8 **GAIN:** Last week Germany cast nearly 37,000,000 votes for a new Reichstag. Police throughout Germany were kept on 48-hour emergency duty. No mass meetings were allowed. No drink stronger than beer might be sold. Despite these precautions nine people were killed and over 100 wounded in brawls through the country over the weekend.

Hardly had the polls closed when the prime result of the election flashed round the world: once again Adolf Hitler had failed to win legal control of the Government. He piled up the biggest vote in his party's history, but with one Reichstag seat for every 60,000 votes cast he was still 53 seats short of a working majority.

"BE CHIVALROUS": Down the Wilhelmstrasse, into the German Chancellery went bristle-lipped Adolf Hitler last week. AUG. 22 He was led into the former office of the late great Bismarck. Seated at the Iron Chancellor's old desk, his soft white hands folded before him, sat aged President Paul von Hindenburg.

"Herr Hitler," said Old Paul gravely, "are you willing that you or some other qualified persons of the National Socialist movement should enter a government headed by the present Chancellor?"

"I am not willing," answered Handsome Adolf, "nor are my associates. We wish on the contrary to request the President to entrust us with leadership of the government of the Reich and with the entire state apparatus in full measure."

"And what power exactly do you imply in that request?"

"Precisely the same power that Mussolini exercised after the march on Rome!"

Von Hindenburg hoisted his old frame half out of his chair:

"Before my own conscience and in the light of my duty to the Fatherland I will *not* entrust such power to a party which intends to make use of it so one-sidedly! I trust you will oppose in a way that will be chivalrous, and I enjoin you in your future course to keep always in mind your duty to the Fatherland and your responsibility to the German people."

Adolf Hitler made no promise, clicked his heels, bowed, left the room. Old Paul took his cane and walked slowly under the linden trees in the Chancellery garden. Thus ended a week of as tense plotting, bargaining and intrigue as Germany has seen since the War.

GOEBBELS SILENCED: The Hitlerites had their quickest wit, SEPT. 5 their loudest mouth closed up for a week. By government order *Der Angriff,* Nazi organ, was suppressed for "inciting to disobedience and resistance against the State." Editor of *Der Angriff* is Dr. Paul Joseph Goebbels, a gnomelike little man with a tart tongue and a club foot who appeared from nowhere about two years ago, rapidly rose to be Fascist deputy, editor of the party organ and one of the right-hand men of Adolf Hitler. The quotation that caused his muzzling was:

"Never forget it, comrades, and repeat it a hundred times so you will say it in your dreams—THE JEWS ARE TO BLAME! They will never escape the tribunals they deserve."

SEPT. 12 **GÖRING ELECTED:** Only work done by the new Reichstag last week was to organize itself for business. This job, which usually takes days of wrangling, was put through in five hours.

Elected as permanent Speaker was paunchy, polite Fascist Hermann Wilhelm Göring, "the diplomat of his party." Though there are only 230 Fascist Deputies in the new chamber, Col. Göring was elected by a vote of 367 to 216. Famed during the War as a Commander of the late Baron von Richthofen's Flying Squadron, Speaker Göring mounted the tribune with militant jerkiness, replied with a Fascist salute to the salutes of Fascist Deputies who bounded from their chairs shouting, "Hail Hitler!"

YOUNG SPROUT: "I am 43 years old," shouted Leader Hitler at a huge rally of his followers last week in Berlin's Sportspalast, "while my opponent [Hindenburg] is 84. My breath will last longer than my opponent's!"

SEPT. 19 **REICHSTAG IN REVOLT:** In the Speaker's Chair when the new Reichstag met for its first business session this week sat 210 lbs. of Fascism. Not merely fat but broad, Speaker Hermann Göring cut the figure of a squat ogre. But slender and insignificant of mien, Chancellor Franz von Papen was present, carrying ostentatiously under his arm an undated decree dissolving the Reichstag signed by President von Hindenburg.

Everyone knew the Chancellor would use this weapon rather than risk a vote of no confidence (which would force his Cabinet to resign). But most Deputies expected the new Reichstag to live at least long enough for Herr von Papen to explain his scheme of lifting Germany by her own bootstraps. Instead, before the Chancellor could start explaining, up popped Communist Deputy Ernst Torgler, shouting denunciation of President von Hindenburg and demanding a vote of no confidence.

As voting began Germany's welterweight Chancellor von Papen dashed up to her heavyweight Speaker Göring, held out toward him Von Hindenburg's decree dissolving the Reichstag. Brushing this aside, 210-lb. Hermann Göring shouted: "Can't you see that a vote is taking place?"; drew thunderous cheers.

Baffled only for an instant by mighty Göring, Chancellor

von Papen flung the decree of dissolution at the Speaker's desk, stalked from the Reichstag, drew catcalls. Voting continued as though the Reichstag were undissolved. Presently the tellers announced: 513 votes of no confidence, 32 of confidence, five abstentions.

"I consider the dissolution decree invalid," cried Speaker Göring, "because it was presented by a Government which the Reichstag has overthrown!"

TROOPS: As everyone knows the Versailles Treaty limits Germany to 100,000 troops. What kind of troops? In a drastic decree, President von Hindenburg ordered 20 training camps opened at which young German males of every kind (except Communists) will be drilled by ex-officers of the German Army.

Officially the 20 camps will be known as Germany's "National Curatory for the Promotion of Physical Fitness." To avoid too flagrant violation of the Treaty of Versailles, they will function not under the Defense Ministry but under the Ministry of Interior. But German journalists stressed "the absence of sport in the English or American sense" at the National Curatory, wrote that the youths will be instructed in "military sports," such as throwing dummy hand grenades.

"VORWÄRTS MIT GOTT!": Facing President Paul von Hindenburg last week were a properly baked pretzel four feet long, several cases of *Liebfraumilch* sent by an old gentleman and some 22,000 other presents received on the President's 85th birthday. Taking his birthday presents as a touching text, Old Paul broadcast an appeal to Germans, asked them to give him at the general election Nov. 6 one more present: unified support of the Cabinet of Chancellor Franz von Papen. OCT. 17

"Unity of Germans has always been brought about at critical moments," boomed the President, "by the healthy spirit of Germans! Whoever stands with me helps this spirit and gives me the happiest birthday present. Therefore—*Vorwärts mit Gott!"*

Meanwhile at Munich slightly pot-bellied Handsome Adolf Hitler stroked his tuft of brown mustache, took the salutes of his campaign committeemen who cheered themselves hoarse, then gravely launched his campaign: "There are two possibilities: either to give or to deny the Nazis power. The battle can commence now. In four weeks we shall be victorious—victorious! I predict the collapse—the total collapse —of Von Papen's program and of his Government!"

NOV. 28 **HITLER GETS WARM:** Last week a fog of intrigue hung thick over official Berlin as a swarm of airplane-riding Nazis flocked vulture-like to the capital. Their meat was the sudden resignation of Germany's autocratic and aristocratic Cabinet, headed by Lieut. Colonel Franz von Papen, most-hated Chancellor in modern German history.

Caught unawares in Rome, barrel-chested Colonel Hermann Göring, the Nazi Speaker of the Reichstag, instantly chartered a plane, made the longest Nazi flight. Leader Hitler swooped from Munich to Berlin in a thundering tri-motored ship crammed with aides, publicity men and an economist to advise him *à la* Franklin Delano Roosevelt.

At the enormous, detective-watched Berlin residence of Steel Tycoon Fritz Thyssen, Leader Hitler and Colonel Göring ate dinner after their flights. They conferred the same night with Germany's modern Machiavelli, soft-spoken General Kurt von Schleicher, Minister of Defense in the Von Papen Cabinet which continued to function *ad interim*. Germans soon noticed the surprising fact that several Big Business newsorgans had abruptly switched from hostility to support of Adolf Hitler. The *Deutsche Allgemeine Zeitung* urged President von Hindenburg "in the interest of that tranquility required for business revival," to overcome his "strong personal dislike" of Fascist Hitler and appoint him German Chancellor.

President von Hindenburg had shown his strong personal dislike on Aug. 13, 1932 when he received Herr Hitler standing and omitted to invite his guest to sit down. At that time Old Paul is said to have used the words, "If you don't behave, Herr Hitler, I'll rap your fingers!"

Last week, when President von Hindenburg inevitably summoned Adolf Hitler (as the leader of Germany's largest party), the two men understood in advance that they were not going to quarrel but to discuss. Leader Hitler & friends walked through crowds of cheering Nazis to the President's door. The conference lasted, in total secrecy, for more than an hour. Then Leader Hitler stepped forth, close-lipped but with a completely different air than when he left the President on Aug. 13. Handsome Adolf's expression then was hangdog. Last week he radiated smiles, waved his hat, kindled such expectations among several hundred waiting Nazis that they massed around his Mercedes shouting questions, and would not let it move.

President von Hindenburg, according to his entourage, did not entrust Herr Hitler with an official mandate to form a Cabinet as Chancellor, but did authorize him to confer with party leaders and report back to the President whether a Cabinet having a majority in the Reichstag could be formed. This left completely open the question of who should be Chancellor.

Leaks from the Nazi camp indicated that Leader Hitler tried to persuade the President to accept him as Chancellor chiefly by arguing that the Fascist party is now Germany's "sole bulwark against proletarianism." This argument, not mere Hitler claptrap, had strong elements of fact. President von Hindenburg asked Herr Hitler to report to him a day earlier than had been planned. They talked for 15 minutes and the President officially authorized the Fascist leader to try to form a Cabinet as Chancellor, but on "seven conditions" which were not made public. For the first time in his blatant, meteoric career Adolf Hitler was "getting warm." Stocks on the Berlin exchange, which eased when the Von Papen Cabinet resigned, firmed again and began to rise.

"ONLY ONE MAN. . . .": The famed "Iron Man" of German DEC. 5 finance, blunt Dr. Hjalmar Schacht, came out for the first time last week in support of Adolf Hitler. By this abrupt move Dr. Schacht brought a sizeable section of Berlin finance into the Big Business phalanx lined up behind Handsome Adolf by Steel Tycoon Fritz Thyssen.

Leader Hitler was nevertheless unable last week to persuade President von Hindenburg to appoint him Chancellor of the Reich. The Hindenburg-Hitler negotiations continued through an exchange of formal letters which Berlin wits dubbed "the game of questions & answers." With each exchange it became clearer that the President, though he had commissioned Fascist Hitler to try to form a Cabinet with a parliamentary majority, was not anxious that he should succeed.

But Banker Schacht came out with a fighting statement: "There is only one man who can be Chancellor at this period and he is Adolf Hitler! If Hitler does not become Chancellor now, he will within four months. He can afford to wait!"

DEC. 12 **"CHRISTMAS CHANCELLOR":** Last week the Chancellorship fell like a ripe pippin into the calmly outstretched hand of swank, sardonic, intriguing Defense Minister Kurt von Schleicher, who is a general at the age of 50.

Von Schleicher had maneuvered party leaders and the President into an impasse from which the only exit was to make him Chancellor. Beginning three weeks ago with Adolf Hitler, party leaders were forced to admit that none of them could find a majority in the Reichstag on which to base a Cabinet. This they could not do because President von Hindenburg demanded pledges in advance that they carry out his reactionary policies—policies which the 85-year-old President was advised by Defense Minister von Schleicher are essential to the safety of the Reich.

Haste in picking a new Chancellor was urgent because the German crisis had already run 14 days since the resignation of Von Papen's Cabinet; and because last week only four more days remained before the newly elected Reichstag was scheduled to meet.

The thing to do, President von Hindenburg had decided, was to re-appoint his favorite protégé, Franz von Papen. By means best known to himself wily General von Schleicher induced about half the "Cabinet of Monocles" (including Von Papen) to go to the President and tell him that German public opinion had become so set against Von Papen that no Cabinet could carry on with him as Chancellor. Old Paul yielded with extreme reluctance and announced that he was acting "with a heavy heart."

Leader Hitler, meanwhile, had left his famed "Brown House" headquarters in Munich and gone to bed on a sleeper bound for Berlin. In the dead of night he exchanged telegrams with Dr. Paul Joseph Goebbels and mighty-midriffed Hermann Göring, who induced him to leave his train at dawn, meet them in Weimar. Apparently they told Leader Hitler that the Fascist Party must stick by its announced resolve to fight any Cabinet not headed by Hitler. Soon Fascist headquarters officially announced, "Our Party declines any sort of toleration of the Schleicher Cabinet."

Nevertheless, Chancellor von Schleicher ignored the theoretical odds against him, proceeded calmly to build his Cabinet. Germans called General von Schleicher their "Christmas Chancellor" last week, recalled that his was always the directing mind of the Von Papen Cabinet, assumed that its policies will be continued with as little change as possible. Some Germans also recalled a characteristic *mot* of the witty and cynical new Chancellor:

"If I were Chancellor I would need only one assistant—a hangman."

Chancellor von Papen. He once tried to blow up a Canadian canal. Page 81.   *Chancellor von Schleicher. He's ready to fight with paper shields.*

PAPER SHIELDS: Trying his best to look, act and talk like a civilian, Germany's new Chancellor, General Kurt von Schleicher, has put away his bemedaled uniform, hung up his service cap. Last week he made the program speech of his new Cabinet directly to the *Damen und Herren* of the Fatherland's radio audience. German tuners-in, accustomed to the rasping, imperious radio delivery of former Chancellor Colonel Franz von Papen, were pleasantly surprised as muftified General von Schleicher addressed the microphone in soft, even tones, pitched his program speech to conciliate all classes.   DEC. 26

"I am neither a Capitalist nor a Socialist," straddled the

General. "I cannot be bothered about economic doctrines. My program consists of one single point: the creation of work." Jokingly he said that he was "perfectly willing to equip our army with knives and paper shields, provided only our neighbors do the same." Seriously he promised greater freedom of the press and other pleasant things. "Joyous co-operation on the part of all classes," he declared, would enable him to keep these promises and he warned the Communists not to misbehave.

Even enemies of the smart, soft-soaping Chancellor—Germany's modern Machiavelli—admitted that his program speech was a masterpiece of soap. [But General von Schleicher's soft soap could not stand up to Nazi violence. In January 1933, President von Hindenburg would name Adolf Hitler Chancellor.]

Great Britain

FEB. 29   **CHARLOTTE'S COMPANION:** After a decent period of mourning, His Majesty George V had a new dog last week. Like its predecessor, it is a lively, ginger-colored Cairn terrier. Snip, the previous Cairn, was an affectionate beast who whimpered outside the royal bedroom all the time King George lay gravely ill three years ago, and accompanied His Majesty to almost everything except the state openings of Parliament. Snip died in April. Mourned by the royal household and the nation, he was buried in Sandringham by the side of Edward VII's dog Caesar who had the distinction of preceding the Kaiser at his master's funeral.

All summer King George remained petless except for Charlotte, the parrot, a 40-year-old bird that H.M. bought in Port Said when he was in the navy. In her youth Charlotte had a loud and penetrating voice, knew a variety of nautical terms and a smattering of French, and used to frighten visitors to Buckingham Palace by suddenly screaming "WELL WHAT ABAHT IT?" Lately she has grown morose, likes to sit on the King's shoulder at breakfast time cracking sunflower seeds. It was to find a companion to Charlotte as much as anything else that the new Cairn was ordered.

WALES & PATRICK: Edward of Wales last week left London to   MAY 9
visit the poor of his father's Kingdom. H.R.H. gazed at
wretched mining villages in the Newcastle region, deserted
shipyards along the Tyne. He had the following thoughts to
express at an unemployment center in South Shields:

"Let me wish you the best of luck. My sympathy is with
you all. I sincerely hope the employment that used to be here
will come back and hard times will not continue very much
longer."

If it did nothing else the trip gave a lifelong thrill to a small
boy at a nursery school near Gateshead. Stepping backward
H.R.H. trod on the foot of an urchin named Patrick.

"I'm so sorry, Patrick," said he, "now you can tread on
mine."

Patrick did.

DISLANDED GENTRY: To be listed in Burke's *Landed Gentry*   AUG. 1
one had to possess an estate of at least 1,000 acres and an
authentic coat of arms. Recently Burke's reduced this re-
quirement in view of the sale of so many estates. The new
Burke's *Landed Gentry* includes many a name not up to
the old standard, and, with an eye to the future, Burke's are
printing at the end of their new edition a second section tact-
fully entitled *Dislanded Gentry*. Eventually, as more & more
estates have to be sold, the second section is expected to
eclipse the first.

LAST MINUTE: In Berlin a highly successful revue, *The Very*   OCT. 3
Last Minute, was cut by the police, merely because Edward
of Wales had landed in Hamburg 160 miles away on a visit.

In *The Very Last Minute* actors dressed as British tourists on
a world tour have boasted at the sight of each new marvel that
something better of the same kind exists in the United Kingdom. On reaching Venice the guide exclaimed, "How fairylike
is this Venetian night!" Whereat a Briton stoutly boasted,
"The Prince of Wales is even more so!"

Berliners had guffawed for a week at this slander. His presence in Germany apparently aroused Berlin police to order
it cut out of *The Very Last Minute*. Meanwhile slandered
Edward, who had paused for only an hour in Hamburg, was
winging toward Copenhagen. In his favorite rôle of "Empire

The Prince of Wales. He gravely swaps stomped toes with an urchin.   *"Wal" Hannington. His hunger marchers won't turn the other cheek. Page 94.*

Salesman," H.R.H. opened the largest British fair ever held among Danes. It was also a Swedish trip. But did Edward of Wales go to Sweden looking for a bride? Swedish newspapers persisted in mentioning honey-haired Princess Ingrid, plump, Protestant and 22 (H.R.H. is 38).

That King George and Queen Mary have put their eldest son under heaviest pressure to marry, even doing over Marlborough House at a cost of many thousand pounds to receive the Empire's bride, all England knows.

OCT. 31 **"ROYAL PARASITES!"**: British subjects could scarcely believe sworn testimony in a London court last week that when H.R.H. Prince George went to work in the slummy East End ragged citizens shook their fists and shouted: "Give us food! We don't want royal parasites!"

Unperturbed, H.R.H. pursued his task of inspecting the squalid East End, a job Edward of Wales used to do before passing it on to his younger brother. Last week the mob grew less & less appreciative, finally broke a British law which provides that while Parliament is sitting no demonstration shall take place within one mile of it.

The London mob, swarming up from way down East, broke into Lambeth Borough and crowded even Lambeth Palace Road. The fight lasted seven hours. Twenty times battling bobbies put on a truncheon charge. To defend the Houses of Parliament, to keep the mob from crossing the river, London's brave bobbies (in some cases fighting for their lives) were obliged to rush motor cars up to Thames bridgeheads and park them close together as an impromptu barricade.

Meanwhile a new danger threatened. From industrial centers all over England, Scotland and Wales thousands of jobless men were stubbornly walking toward London, lashed by high winds, whipped by pelting rain. Called "dupes of Moscow" by the London Press, these marchers will try to see the Prime Minister and send a "Committee of Fifty" who will try to reach the Houses of Parliament bearing a petition for relief signed by 500,000 unemployed.

ARMY OF HUNGRY: As the great "hunger march" of jobless NOV. 7 men & women from all over the United Kingdom converged ominously on London, one Scottish detachment had a bagpiper who mournfully skirled the subversive "Internationale."

Most marchers frankly admitted that on their way to London local charity folk gave them more to eat than they have had in many months at home. But London itself was different.

"These people," said His Majesty's Minister of Health Sir Edward Hilton Young, "have been induced by a Communist organization to leave their homes. Very well. It is up to the Communists to take care of them."

The leader of the "Communist organization," which calls itself the National Unemployed Workers' Movement, is secretive Mr. W.A.L. ("Wal") Hannington, a young man who looked last week like an overwrought college student as he dashed about London in an open motor car, marshaling the hungry who called him their "Field Marshal." When newshawks caught up with Red Wal, he gave them this to think about: "We do not advocate violence, but if a society responsible for our present evils cannot be removed otherwise, we are ready to use violent revolutionary measures. If the police use batons on us you can't expect the marchers to turn the other cheek. We are organized like an army and we will act like one."

Inevitably London's bobbies had to use their batons. What else could they do when men and women started throwing stones at limousines? As the truncheons went to work, rioters broke branches from Hyde Park trees, used them as clubs. Surging toward the Admiralty Arch, one section of the mob blundered so hard into a cordon of mounted police that one was knocked from his horse. Screamed a swart, hatless man: "Smash the Palace windows!"

Fighting for King and Country, burly bobbies used their truncheons with just one idea, to crack as many crowns as possible. A second mob, however, had rushed down Whitehall, 5,000 strong, heading for No. 10 Downing St., the residence of Prime Minister MacDonald. Until police reserves could beat it back, this mob was briefly checked by a thin line of ornate, scarlet-coated heroes, the Royal Horse Guards—supposed by tourists to be good for nothing but "changing the guard."

NOV. 14 **CHECK FOR A MILLION:** Not police batons but a stack of paper was what put an end to this year's great hunger march of Britain's unemployed. Most important possession of the hunger marchers was a great bundle of papers, a petition containing more than one million signatures protesting against dole cuts and against the "means test" by which an applicant must prove himself a pauper before he gets the dole. This petition they intended to present to Parliament. The House of Commons could scarcely ignore the signature of one million citizens.

But before their third riot a group of marchers rushed to the Charing Cross railway station and checked their petition in the common parcel room. Detectives promptly removed the document, and when the hunger marchers returned later with their precious parcel check, they found nothing to claim.

Back to Scotland, Wales and the Shires dribbled the discouraged Hunger Army last week. Four British railroads agreed to transport the marchers at a flat rate of 1d for three miles, compared with the normal third-class rate of $1\frac{1}{2}$ d.

France

JAN. 4 **MAN OF THE YEAR:** Twelve months ago Pierre Laval was as obscure—even in France—as Governor Calvin Coolidge before the Boston police strike. The compact little Auvergnat (son of a village butcher in Auvergne, south-central France) was a Senator of no party, an Independent. Worst of all, a good many Frenchmen who had vaguely heard of "The Man in the White Tie" understood that during the War he was a slacker and afterwards a Communist.

But on the morning of Jan. 24, 1931 there was again a French crisis. The Cabinet had fallen following charges that the Minister of Agriculture had speculated in wheat. Importunate telegrams flashed from the President's Palace to Aristide Briand begging him to become Premier for the twelfth time. Surfeited with such honors, Briand wired his courteous but absolute refusal, suggesting his protégé and onetime Justice Minister Pierre Laval.

Straight through 1931 Premier Laval gave month after month the consistent impression that he and his Government were working. In October Laval made the journey to Washington, D.C. that stamped his name upon millions of U.S. minds and swelled his fame throughout the world.

President Hoover is well known to dislike almost all Frenchmen, and he and Premier Laval had high words which they called "free and frank." Smoking U.S. cigarets at the furious rate of 80 per day, the didactic Frenchman in striped trousers, black jacket, white tie and suede-topped buttoned shoes wagged his forefinger at the President, making such points as that France will not stand for having another Moratorium thrust forward from the U.S. "suddenly and brutally."

On Christmas Eve the Chamber gave Premier Laval a straight vote of confidence 315 to 255, then adjourned, leaving the Man of the Year triumphant. How great is his achievement may be measured by the fact that only four French Premiers since the War have been able to remain in power for as much as one year. [Laval was ousted as Premier in February and was succeeded by André Tardieu. He served as Premier again in 1935 and became vice premier of the Vichy government in 1940 after the fall of France. Laval collaborated closely with the Nazis, and after the war he was found guilty of treason and was executed by a firing squad.]

HORNET & PAL: Thundering special trains carried Monsieur André Tardieu back and forth between Paris and Geneva (390 miles) by night last week. The cost was enormous, but not for MARCH 7 a Great Man who is the premier of a Great Power. Busy as a hornet, André Tardieu darted *zip* to make a Cabinet in Paris, darted *zip* back to the Geneva Conference where he arrived as Premier, Foreign Minister and Chief French Delegate, darted *zip* back to Paris and again *zip* to Switzerland. No U.S. traveling salesman travels harder. Frenchmen call their hornet-premier *"Tardieu l'Américain."*

Pals are André Tardieu and Pierre Laval. They may sooner or later cease to be pals, for French politics has a way of rupturing personal friendships. But up to last week Senator Laval and Deputy Tardieu had kept the Premiership of France bouncing back and forth between them for 26 out of the last 28 months. In the new Tardieu Cabinet shrewd Pal Laval, who was himself Premier only three weeks ago, lay low, took the minor post of Minister of Labor.

Lying extremely low in the new post, Pierre Laval was obliged, as his first duty, to report that Frenchmen "totally unemployed" increased 19,000 last week to a grand total of 600,000. Naturally Laval was shrewd enough to sugar-coat this unpleasant pill with a statement that Great Britain has five times more unemployed than France, Germany eleven times more, the U.S. 17 times more.

MARCH 14 **THE GREAT PACIFIER:** In Paris the heart of Aristide Briand, Europe's Great Pacifier, failed last week. A few days before what would have been his 70th birthday he died in his small bachelor home. He had been eleven times Premier of France. Called the Master Parliamentarian of Europe, he was also Europe's foremost orator. To the very end, his famed "cello voice" could rouse the French Chamber or Senate to tempests and transports of emotion—but he knew to a nicety how few were his friends.

The great heart of Aristide Briand broke, so France believes, when the Chamber and Senate in joint session and by secret ballot refused to elect him President of France last year. The President of the Republic, Paul Doumer, whose election broke Aristide Briand's heart, came and stood for a while beside the cheap iron bed in the cheap flat, then, speechless with emotion, went away. Premier André Tardieu came, and simple men and women came. Some of them knelt and kissed the left hand of Aristide Briand.

As a pacifier at the very top of his diplomatic profession, Aristide Briand shot his last bolt in 1929 when he proposed "The United States of Europe." This proposal he made at Geneva and at luncheon, as a gentleman proposes. Rare wines had been sipped and the assembled statesmen were toying with exquisite liqueurs, but Aristide Briand modestly said afterward that he proposed the United States of Europe "between a pear and some cheese."

"EST-CE POSSIBLE?": Long years ago the future President of France, Paul Doumer, attended the wedding of the future dean of Paris news cameramen. Last week it came about that bearded Photographer Louis Piston, the venerable dean, was standing with his flashlight upraised, his camera trained on the patriarchal President at the precise instant when a tall, burly Russian bounded forward and fired point-blank at M. Doumer with a Colt pistol. Instantly dropping his flashlight, Photographer Piston wielded his camera like a club, beating the assassin over the head, stunning him momentarily—and throwing away the chance to make a Picture of the Century. MAY 16

At 2:30 p.m. the 75-year-old President, who lost four of his five sons in the War, had left his Elysée Palace to sponsor a sale of books by French War Veterans. At 3:00 p.m. he had just smilingly agreed to autograph a book when a brawny Russian in dark glasses who was standing nearby whirled, drew his Colt, and with a cry of "Die for the Fatherland!" made for M. Doumer and fired. Amid the crush of 500 people, the President of the Republic could not fall. He slumped slowly to his knees while a gush of blood from the wound in his head dyed his snowy beard suddenly dark red. Twice, as he was losing consciousness President Doumer murmured: *"Est-ce possible?"* (Is it possible?)

More blood, spouting from M. Doumer's shoulder wound, soaked his clothing and formed a pool upon the floor. Women screamed, "The President is dead!" Men battled to overpower the furiously fighting Russian. When he was down women's fingernails gashed his cheeks. Meanwhile the President was carried out feet foremost, rushed in a blood-spattered car to a hospital.

Meanwhile the assassin, who police said had "fought like a devil," was in chains, undergoing a ferocious third degree.

President Paul Doumer and sons. While he is honoring four who died in the war, a Russian shoots him dead.

Shouted he: "I know you will kill me! I am Dr. Paul Gorgulov, the President of the National Fascist Party of Russia. European states and America seem favorable to Bolshevism so I decided to kill the President and cause France to declare war on Russia! I am a great Russian patriot. I admire Hitler and Mussolini! I had no accomplices."

At 4:40 the chief surgeon laboring to save the President's life raised a cheer from hundreds of people gathered around the hospital when he exclaimed: "The ball in the head did not touch the brain. Therefore I refuse to say that the President is lost."

At 11:56 p.m. President Doumer recovered sufficiently to ask: "What happened?"

"You were run over by an automobile," answered his family physician.

"Not purposely?" queried M. Doumer. Then the President sank into alternate coma and delirium, seemingly worried about why anyone should have wished to run him down.

Through the whole night Premier André Tardieu and most of the Cabinet remained at the hospital. At 4:37 a.m. the President quietly expired, without recognizing Mme. Doumer or his daughters. Wrapped in a silken shroud the body was taken in an ambulance to the Elysée where, on the second floor, embalmers went to work.

To gaze upon the waxen face of dead President Doumer, the people of France shuffled slowly to the Elysée, packed closely in a queue eight wide, blocks long. Drenched by fickle showers, flecked by hail, many a citizen waited hours to file by the bier.

As President, Doumer had only one eccentricity—which almost drove the police frantic. Respectfully pressed to accept a secret service guard by former Premier Pierre Laval last year, the President replied with an ancient chuckle:

"My little one, your plain-clothes policemen with their heavy boots, long mustaches and inevitable baggy umbrellas are altogether too conspicuous. If I went about with them I would have no privacy at all. Every one would spot me."

NEW PRESIDENT: Drastic precautions against disaster while France elected her 14th President last week included six fire engines parked close to the Palace of Versailles lest it should ignite, 3,250 infantrymen and 600 cavalrymen massed in the Palace courtyard, mobilization of all nearby military garrisons and a ceaseless roaring patrol of airplanes overhead.

As expected, the National Assembly on the first ballot elected as the 14th President of France the President of the Senate, peasant-born Albert Lebrun, 60, who like President Hoover has been a mining engineer. Comfortably obscure, he is the sort of man Frenchmen like to have as President, for in France the President has few powers, many formal duties.

"MYSTIC FORCE": In his Paris cell Russian Dr. Paul Gorgulov, MAY 30 who killed President Doumer three weeks ago, tried to explain away the crime that is expected to send him to the guillotine.

"I was mistaken," cried Dr. Gorgulov. "I thought it was the President who was responsible for the foreign policy of France—her rapprochement with Soviet Russia. Too late I have learned that it is the Premier who directs French policy."

Told that this explanation made no difference, Dr. Gorgulov tried again. "A mystic force armed my hand," said he. "I had no reason at all to kill President Doumer. On the train to Paris I struggled against my idea of committing the crime. Then I drank an entire bottle of cognac. I was too intoxicated to remember what I did."

JUNE 13 **TABBY CABINET:** In Paris, which plays cat to Berlin's dog, a mild tabby Cabinet was quietly brought forth last week. Distinctly tabbyish is new Premier Edouard Herriot, plump and wavy-haired, whose so-called Radical-Socialist Party is not the least bit radical.

AUG. 8 **MADMAN:** Such a trial as could revolve only around a fanatic vortexed in Paris last week around Dr. Paul Gorgulov.

"Kill me! Kill me!" screamed the Russian, tearing his collar from his neck and wrenching his shirt open. "I am glad to leave this earth!"

Frenchmen are practical. After deliberating for 29 minutes the jury sent the fantastic Russian to the guillotine. His head will be sliced off next month. "I salute you!" cried Dr. Gorgulov on hearing the jury's verdict. "I die a hero. *Vive la France! Vive la Russia!* I love you unto death."

SEPT. 26 **"AH, RUSSIA":** The courteous French way of easing a man to the guillotine is to set excellent meals before him for several days previous, offer him brandy & cigarets at dawn and finally for the ornate Garde Républicaine to salute the condemned as he walks from the police van to death. All these amenities were offered last week to Paul Gorgulov.

Determined to scoop the execution, United Press's Mary Knight dressed herself as a man, boasted afterward that she was the only woman to see Dr. Gorgulov lose his head. She told how Gorgulov, his hands and feet heavily manacled, hobbled forward; how the back of the prisoner's neck was shaved "to better expose his flesh to the sharp knife of 'the widow' [guillotine]." Then "like a flash the neck piece clamped Gorgulov into position and, before he could gasp, the knife, well weighted, fell nine feet. There was no autopsy."

Male correspondents noted that the head fell into a basket, that the body was dumped into a zinc-lined wicker coffin (in which the head was later placed) for delivery to pregnant Mme. Gorgulov, that Executioner Anatole ("Monsieur de Paris") Deibler wore his usual derby hat. When souvenir seekers tried to dash forward and dip their handkerchiefs into the wide, dark pool of blood, police forced them sternly back, hitched a hose to a neighboring hydrant, washed the street scrupulously clean.

Russia

STALIN SPEAKS: Russians pored last week over the magazine JULY 4
Bolshevik, absorbed like eager sponges what Josef Stalin
said to German biographer Emil Ludwig during a recent series
of interviews. Excerpts:

Q.: Do you admit a parallel between yourself and Peter the
Great?

Stalin: Not in the least. Historical parallels are always
risky. This one is senseless.

Q.: But Peter the Great accomplished much for the development of his country, to bring western culture to Russia.

Stalin: Certainly, Peter the Great did much to create and
strengthen a national government of landlords and traders
at the cost of the serf, the peasantry, who were thrice skinned.
As for me, I devote my life to the elevation of quite a different
class—the working class. Peter the Great was a drop in the
sea, while Lenin was a whole ocean.

Q.: They say abroad on the one hand that the Soviet Union
is a land ruled by committees and on the other, that everything is decided by an individual. Which is it?

Stalin: No, it can't be decided by an individual. From the
experience of three revolutions we know that of 100 decisions, not tested and corrected collectively, 90 will be one-
sided. Never, under any conditions, would our workers now
endure the rule of one person.

Q.: It seems to me that to a certain extent the stability
of the Soviet power rests on fear. I should like to know
what your own inner reactions are when you know that in
the interests of strengthening power it is necessary to instill
fear.

Stalin: Of course, there is a certain not very large section
of the population which really fears the Soviet power and
fights against it. I have in mind the remnants of the dying
classes now being liquidated and above all a negligible part of
the peasantry—the *kulaks.* But if you take the laboring population of the Soviet Union, the workers and the toiling peas-
ants, who represent not less than 90% of the people, they are
on the side of the Soviet power and the overwhelming majority of them actively support it. In this lies the stability of the
Soviet power, and not in any so-called policy of terrorizing.

AUG. 29 **POWERFUL RABBITS:** Russian meat is scarce and a long and hungry winter grows nearer. In the face of this Soviet officials have discovered that the rabbit, one of the mainstays of the French bourgeois cuisine, is sadly neglected in Russia. Last week rabbit propaganda was put in motion. A rabbit breeding trust was organized, and in Moscow, the important Hammer-and-Sickle factory started its own rabbit farm as a patriotic example for other factories. A government program was announced: within one year the 1,500,000 rabbits must become 7,000,000 rabbits, or 25,000,000 by 1934, or 750,000 tons of meat.

The Press swept into line. "Eschew those," concluded an *Izvestia* editorial, "who underestimate the rabbit."

Stalin's wife, Nadezhda Alliluieva. Some say she died of peritonitis; others mention appendicitis. But she was seen at a play two nights before.

NOV. 21 **POISON OR PERITONITIS?:**Only the very greatest of the Communist great achieve burial. Normally the highest honor is cremation, followed by insertion of the urn into a hole in the Red Square.

Last week all the Russias were agog not because Dictator Stalin's young wife had died a mysterious death but because she was buried. Scratching their tousled heads, Old Bolsheviks said they could not remember another State burial since that of Lenin in his glass case.

Nadezhda Sergeivna Alliluieva had been plugging through

a three-year course from which she expected to emerge the Director of a Soviet Rayon Trust. There was disagreement last week as to whether she graduated last July or would have graduated this December. She was last seen alive (by foreigners) on Sunday, Nov. 6, enjoying a performance at Moscow's Grand Theatre.

On Wednesday morning *Tass,* the official Soviet news agency, tersely announced: "Death came to Comrade Nadezhda Alliluieva on the night between the 8th and 9th." *Tass* men said they had no idea how Death came. Since hardly one Russian in a million knew the Dictator's wife's name, the *Tass* announcement went almost unnoticed by Russians. Foreign correspondents who fancied themselves in the know expected the Dictator to order a quiet, perhaps secret cremation.

Next day the corpse, in a black crepe dress pinned at the throat with a brooch, was laid out on the third floor of the Soviet Parliament Building. The G.P.U. (secret police) band at one end of the room played a funeral dirge now and then. Five men dressed as workers stood guard around the coffin.

As the day wore on news flew by word of mouth around Moscow that one could see the Dictator's wife, that she was dead. By evening a curious Muscovite queue waited four abreast for their turn. Even then the official Soviet expression of condolence omitted the word "wife," paid tribute only "to the dear memory of our comrade and friend. We will always keep in dearest memory the most faithful Bolshevist woman, the friend and devoted aid of Comrade Stalin."

On Friday morning the red flag on the Kremlin staff was seen to be at half mast. Electric with anticipation, a throng of more than 100,000 Muscovites gathered, waiting in the Red Square and all its approaches for they hardly knew what. They waited all morning. Noon came with 12 brazen strokes from the Kremlin Clock Tower. But not until 3 p.m. did the medium-sized red coffin emerge at last from the mourning hall. Instead of the usual Red Funeral March, the wondering crowd heard Chopin's *Marche Funèbre.* The red coffin was placed on a red hearse. Six spirited black horses with red cloth wrapped around their ankles pranced off with it across the Red Square, snorting and champing their bits.

Not a single journalist managed to get through the double

line of G.P.U. special troops and Red Soldiers who guarded every inch of the five-mile funeral route from the Red Square to—of all places—the Convent of New Virgins. This most historic of Moscow's ancient convents is no longer a convent, but its burial yard is still hallowed ground.

Some say Mme. Stalin died of "peritonitis," some say "appendicitis." "A long illness" was the official Soviet explanation, curious because of Mme. Stalin's cheerful presence at a play two nights before her death. [Rumors persisted for years that Mrs. Stalin had been murdered by her husband. But in 1967 her daughter Svetlana revealed in a book of memoirs that she had committed suicide.]

Japan

In 1931, using the blowing-up of a railroad near Mukden as an excuse, Japan had begun the occupation of Manchuria. China had retaliated with a boycott of Japanese goods, and as 1932 began Japanese troops were landing at Shanghai in an effort to force the Chinese to call off their boycott.

JAN. 18   **PUFF OF SMOKE:** Goose-stepping stiffly across the Yoyogi parade ground in Tokyo, column upon column of Japanese troops passed a reviewing stand upon which stood his owl-eyed Majesty, Emperor Hirohito. After the last ammunition truck and field kitchen had rumbled by, the Son of Heaven stepped down, entered a state coach and, escorted by a squadron of lancers, rolled back to the Imperial Palace. A Mr. James L. Vierhus of Peoria, Ill. was standing on the curb. Afterwards he told what happened:

"As the second carriage passed me I noticed a queer sort of grey object hurtling through the air. Then there was an explosion and a puff of smoke. I did not notice any concussion. It exploded as it touched the pavement under the rear axle of the carriage ahead of the Emperor."

The bomb was strangely ineffective. One horse was scratched by a fragment, the carriage was uninjured. Emperor Hirohito popped his head out in time to see Japanese policemen swarming angrily over the bomb thrower, a tall angular Korean named Li Ho-sho.

All Japanese ministers swear to protect the person of the Emperor. Within an hour or two of the explosion the entire Cabinet of white-bearded Premier Inukai bowed their heads in shame and handed in their resignations. Hirohito refused to accept the resignations and Premier Inukai and his Ministers withdrew them.

There was work for the Cabinet to do. In Manchuria, Japanese lines spread over the frozen land right up to the Great Wall, clinched their hold on all of southern Manchuria. And the Japanese were greatly exercised over China's increasingly effective anti-Japanese boycott. Spokesmen at the Foreign Office talked wildly of blockading Shanghai or Canton in retaliation.

IMPERIAL CARROTS: Fortnight ago a strangely ineffective bomb JAN. 25 left Emperor Hirohito, Son of Heaven, untouched. But it inflicted slight wounds on the rears of two horses of the Imperial Guard. Into their stables last week came two Imperial grooms carrying two baskets brightly bedecked with the Imperial colors. By curious Japanese signs they tried to explain to the horses that these were a gift from the Emperor. Then they watched the two horses appreciatively devour their eight pounds of Imperial carrots.

NO. 1: There was in Tokyo last week an assassination of world MARCH 14 importance. The hour lacked ten minutes of high noon. Down Suraga-cho a twinkling limousine purred toward No. 1, the low, impressive marble citadel of the holding company known as Mitsui Gomei Kaisha. In all the world there is no enterprise at once so vast and so diverse. One of its subsidiaries handles one-fourth of all Japan's foreign trade. Under its flag sails a merchant fleet as large as that of France. In the carriage was the great business empire's prime minister, Baron Dr. Takuma Dan, 73. The House of Mitsui, richest in Japan, paid him $291,000 yearly, largest Japanese salary. He was one of only four Japanese peers created by the Emperor as part of his coronation ceremonies, a pluperfect honor.

Last week, just as the old man alighted, a youth of 21 dashed forward, fired one shot. Mitsui clerks rushed to help the Mitsui doorman carry him into No. 1. Just 30 minutes after the bullet was fired, Takuma Dan died. The assassin, one Goro Hishinuma, did not break down under a police third degree. This was not strange. Now in progress is a series of assassinations about which the Tokyo police undoubtedly do not want to learn too much. One by one Japan's men-of-peace-and-goodwill have fallen. But biggest as a Peace Man was Banker Dan. He had thrown the weight of Mitsui Gomei Kaisha against the militarists and against war, unsuccessfully.

MARCH 28 **"WORTHY COMPEER":** Most cheerful event in Japan's capital last week was the farewell round of banquets to William Cameron Forbes, soon to be succeeded as U.S. Ambassador in Tokyo by Joseph Clark Grew, a cousin by marriage of John P. Morgan.

"Ambassador Forbes is a worthy compeer of George Washington," declared Prince Tokugawa, President of the House of Peers. Finally the Son of Heaven received Mr. Forbes in an unusually long audience. "Nothing has occurred or will occur," declared the Ambassador, "to menace the good feelings between the United States and Japan."

Next day the Japanese Foreign Office learned that the U.S. State Department had absolutely refused to recognize the puppet régime Japan has set up in Manchuria. Hotly the Foreign Office's press spokesman burst out: "The United States cannot rob us of the fruits of our victory by withholding recognition of the new Manchurian State!"

APRIL 11 **BLOODY FLAG:** Japanese schoolgirls, fragile as butterflies, small as pixies, must not faint at the sight of blood. To test their courage seven Tokyo high school girls gathered last week around a white cloth in the center of which they had drawn a circle. After a solemn soprano chant the maidens pricked their fingers, held them over the circle until it grew red and the cloth became the flag of Japan. This flag the seven schoolgirls dispatched to Crown Prince Chichibu's crack 3rd Regiment which is part of the Imperial forces still holding Shanghai.

MAY 23 **ASSASSINATION:** The day had been warm, sunny, peaceful. Just before sunset Tokyo was terrified by the sudden dashing through her streets of four or five motor cars (one a commandeered taxicab) from which uniformed Japanese petty officers and cadets flung bundles of leaflets and hurled bombs.

"Down with the disloyalists!" read the leaflets. "Up with the Emperor! End the old corrupt political leaders! Down with privilege! We are Nationalists. We want restoration of the imperial power. Direct action is necessary to save the country!"

Small, weak but exceedingly loud bombs were hurled at the Bank of Japan, the Mitsubishi Bank, the residence of Emperor Hirohito's Grand Chamberlain, the Central Police Station opposite the Imperial Palace.

Meanwhile ancient Premier Ki Inukai, 77, was quietly puffing a cigaret in his official residence. With him were his daughter-in-law, her two children and a family friend. Outside police stood guard.

Suddenly a motor car drew up with screeching brakes. Out leaped two naval lieutenants, an army sergeant and two corporals of Gendarmerie, all pointing pistols which made the guards run. Bursting into the Premier's lobby, the five attackers found it guarded by a policeman. They shot him, forced their way on into the helpless Old Fox's lair. Screamed his daughter-in-law: "Please let us escape!"

"It is useless," said Premier Inukai, calm as he faced Death. "But what do you want, my men?"

"We will shoot you!" cried a navy officer as four more assailants burst in through a back door. Covered by nine pistols, the Premier said: "Let us talk it over before you shoot."

"Fire!" shouted the officer as Premier Inukai pleaded, "Please don't shoot! Maybe we can settle this."

For answer the two young officers seized the ancient statesman, pinioned him while their men put two bullets through his head. Police apparently made no effort to capture the nine killers as they fled. Later 18 young army and navy men came voluntarily to police headquarters, dramatically gave themselves up but confessed nothing, were not subjected to a third-degree.

"FISSIPAROUS TENDENCIES": The Diet and House of Peers SEPT. 5 meet at present in a low, dingy frame building, which "looks like an orphan asylum," according to Japanese correspondents. To this Imperial orphanage went the peers of Japan last week, some in grey silk kimonos, more in frock coats and high button shoes, to sit on stiff benches behind wooden desks and listen to a speech actually addressed to the entire world: an explanation by Foreign Minister Count Yasuya Uchida of his country's foreign policy. Most cautiously, most meticulously was the speech prepared.

Before he had been speaking 60 seconds two facts were glaringly evident: 1) Japan is ready to give formal recognition to her puppet state of Manchoukuo immediately, and 2) she will take no back talk from the League of Nations. These prime points were made with all the suavity of which Count Uchida is capable and the introduction of a word new to newspaper headlines: *fissiparous* (by fission: reproduction by spontaneous division of a cell into two parts, each of which grows into a complete organism). Said Japan's Foreign Minister: "The independence of Manchoukuo has been achieved through the spontaneous will of Manchurians and should be regarded as a consequence of a fissiparous movement in China, and that recognition by Japan of the new State thus created cannot violate the stipulations of the Nine-Power Treaty."

China

JAN. 25 **JEWEL RAIDED:** In red-roofed Tsingtao, chief port of famed Shantung Province, China, the biggest newspaper came out one day last week describing the attempt to assassinate Emperor Hirohito of Japan as "an unfortunate failure." A mob swept out of the Japanese quarter of the city and methodically kicked the offices of the Min Kuo *Daily News* apart. Then they burned the local headquarters of the Kuomintang (Nationalist) Party. Thousands of Chinese gathered up their belongings and fled the city.

Suddenly at nightfall the windows and roof of the Japanese consulate bristled with machine guns. Japanese ships were in the harbor. Their turrets swung toward the city. Boatloads of marines chugged ashore. For 24 hours the city was completely in Japanese hands.

To thoughtful observers of Far Eastern affairs the brief seizure of Tsingtao was a hair raiser. Tsingtao is not in Manchuria, has nothing to do with Manchuria. It is in China proper.

TERROR IN SHANGHAI: First it was Manchuria, then Tsing- FEB. 1
tao, and last week Shanghai. It seemed as though Japan was
deliberately asking for trouble. The raid on Tsingtao fortnight ago was apparently a feeler to see how a world busy
with its own problems would react to the invasion of Chinese
territory. Results were apparently satisfactory. Last week Japan repeated exactly the same formula in Shanghai.

It had to start with a riot. The excuse was a series of anti-
Japanese editorials in the Chinese *Republican Daily News,*
and the tousling of five Japanese monks by a gang of coolies.
Rear Admiral Koichi Shiosawa, commander of the Japanese
fleet anchored off Shanghai, issued an ultimatum: all anti-
Japanese organizations in the foreign settlement as well as in
the native cities must be suppressed "on pain of drastic naval
action." Tokyo backed him up by sending an aircraft carrier
and four destroyers.

This was a threat the rest of the world could not ignore, and
British, French, U.S. officials in Shanghai itself lost no time
replying to Admiral Shiosawa. A delegation of them boarded a
launch, chugged out to the Japanese flagship and demanded a
statement. Hissing politely through his teeth, Admiral Shiosawa replied that he was merely obeying orders from Tokyo.

The Japanese did stay out of the International Settlement,
but they did not stay out of Shanghai. By next nightfall 1,300
Japanese had landed with field pieces and machine guns. Ten
warships were spotted at even intervals all up and down the
river with their guns trained on the city. Admiral Shiosawa
threatened to occupy all the Chinese forts and barracks in the
Shanghai district unless a full apology for the tousling of the
monks, one of whom had died, was made, an indemnity paid,
and the anti-Japanese boycott called off.

FIRE: Japanese Admiral Shiosawa had issued his demands to FEB. 8
Shanghai's Mayor Wu. Frantic, the Mayor and the tycoons of
the city had agreed to accept them. But then Admiral Shiosawa received new instructions. Said he: "In our experience
Chinese promises are never carried out. That is all."

On Thursday night at 11:15 p.m. he began the systematic
occupation of Chapei, the Chinese city stretching north of
Shanghai's rich International Settlement. He had in all about
3,000 troops. Armored cars with searchlights led the way.

Crash! Crash! went the rifles shooting out the street lights as the columns advanced. A few airplanes zoomed overhead. One accidentally dropped a bomb in the foreign quarter.

But woeful Mayor Wu and his Chinese allies had not been idle. China had few planes or tanks or ships to pit against Japan but she had plenty of men. There were over 30,000 of them gathered behind the Chapei district. When Japan reached the North Railway Station the 30,000 struck back hard. Before dawn Admiral Shiosawa learned that ten-to-one were more than he could handle. Japanese suffered losses. Withdrawal would mean a loss of "face." So the Admiral ordered 60 planes from the aircraft carrier *Kaza* to come, bomb.

Friday morning the roof of every tall building in the International Settlement was black with gaping Chinese and foreigners watching the show. Every 20 minutes a Japanese squadron swooped over and dropped a dozen whistling bombs. Flames began to leap from roofs. Chapei was on fire.

NOW NANKING: Nanking, the Nationalist capital, lies 210 miles up the Yangtze from Shanghai. A river patrol of seven Japanese destroyers is stationed there. On Tuesday, without warning, their commander began bombarding the city. Under cover of the bombardment, Japanese bluejackets landed five miles outside the city and engaged in sporadic hostilities with Chinese detachments. Meanwhile, the Drum watchtower, which has warned Nanking citizens of danger since the Ming dynasty, sounded its strident alarm.

FEB. 15 **HOLDING ON:** For all Japan's warships, all her guns, for all her planes, for all her soldiers and sailors, Shanghai's Chinese defenders were doggedly holding on. Day after day Japanese warships in the river blasted away at Chinese batteries (pausing politely to let U.S. and British steamers and warships pass). Three thousand Japanese bluejackets went ashore. No sooner did they move out against the forts than the battered trenches came to life with such a withering rifle and machine-gun fire that the Japanese were forced back.

Ferocious Rear Admiral Koichi Shiosawa was under a cloud last week. Word came from Tokyo that he had been superseded by Vice Admiral Kichisaburo Nomura. Pleasant, grey-haired Admiral Nomura, with many a friend in the U.S., was Japanese naval attaché at Washington during the War, and brought a Japanese squadron to New York in 1929. [In 1941 Admiral Nomura would be one of two Japanese peace envoys negotiating in Washington as the Japanese planes struck at Pearl Harbor.] His arrival at Shanghai was quite a social occasion. U.S. Vice Admiral Taylor's aide, Lieut. Henri H. Smith-Hutton, paid a call. Admiral Nomura stepped into his barge and returned it. British Vice Admiral Kelly popped over for a chat. Chapei's cannon rattled the teacups.

JAPAN SHANGHAIED: Japan's "Big Drive" into China began at FEB. 29 Shanghai last week and Japanese soldiers fought with mounting ferocity which presently became "frightfulness." White witnesses reported with horror how Chinese civilians were shot down, how Chinese property in the form of houses, barns, hay and grain was ignited by the Japanese.

At one point, the Chinese Commander-in-Chief made friendly representations to Col. R. S. Hooker, commanding the local contingent of U.S. Marines, and pointed out to him that Japanese planes were being guided and Japanese gunfire directed by a group of Japanese, operating out of Japanese cotton mills in Col. Hooker's territory.

Suddenly, in the dead of night, Col. Hooker's men entered the Japanese mills, seized two truckloads of signaling apparatus and an arsenal of small weapons. To the terrified Japanese the U.S. Marines left enough small arms and ammunition to enable the mills to stand off any possible attacks by Chinese mobs. Strong protest was lodged by the Government of His Majesty the Emperor of Japan, the Japanese contention being that a search warrant should have been secured by Col. Hooker from the Japanese Consul General.

FISTS: Glasses perched on his nose, U.S. Trade Commissioner MARCH 14 Harold D. Robison saw clearly that the Japanese Naval truck which suddenly sideswiped and dented his car in Shanghai last week was No. 16460. Vexed, Mr. Robison stepped on his starter, chased the truck to Japanese Naval Headquarters. Japanese in the truck jeered Mr. Robison all the way.

Alighting at Naval Headquarters extremely vexed, Mr. Robison tried to lodge complaint, was pushed in the chest by a Japanese civilian wearing a police armband who shouted: "I am a Japanese. Don't!" Previously the Japanese Consul General had given official assurances that there were now no more Japanese "armband police" in Shanghai, but four of them set upon Mr. Robison, striking him with their fists while Japanese bluejackets laughed.

Most vexed, Mr. Robison removed his glasses, prepared to use his fists. But uniformed Japanese policeman No. 73 shouted: "Hold your head and go away!" Mr. Robison got out his glasses again, put them on, entered his car, let in his clutch. Pantherlike, one of the armbanded Japanese sprang upon the running board, hit Mr. Robison a smashing blow in the face as he drove away amid Japanese guffaws.

Fourteen other Occidentals (male and female) also took fist blows from armbanded Japanese in Shanghai last week. Escorted by the Rev. W. H. Tipton of Jefferson City, Tenn., Teacher Rose Marlowe of Williamsburg, Ky. went to inspect the partly destroyed Shanghai Southern Baptist Mission School. Seated in a parked car while the Rev. Tipton was walking among the ruins, Miss Marlowe, who does not speak Japanese, was addressed by two Japanese armbanders.

They accused Miss Marlowe (as she later learned) of stopping the flow of water through a nearby hose. When Miss Marlowe made no reply to their jabber they pitched into her with their fists, also whanged across her face and body with sticks.

MAY 9 **BIRTHDAY SURPRISE:** In Shanghai last week 10,000 Japanese troops celebrated the Emperor's 32nd birthday with a grand military review. Battalions of Japanese infantry goose-stepped across the parade ground, each with its fluttering sunburst guidon. In the front of the reviewing stand were many of the highest officers in the Japanese Army & Navy. Behind them loomed the big foreign military attachés of Britain, France, Italy, the U.S. These officials left the stand as soon as the review was over. The crowd pressed round to listen to speeches.

A Korean on the edge of the crowd threw a narrow tin box high in the air. In an ear-splitting roar, the grandstand flew apart like a mechanical toy. Japanese Minister to China Mamoru Shigemitsu was blown into the air like a jack-in-the-box, his feet flung wide. Consul General Murai's face was un-

Baron Dan. An uncommunicative   *Admiral Nomura. A Korean bomb*
killer shoots him down. Page 106.   *blows out his right eye.*

recognizable with blood and torn flesh. Admiral Nomura's eye was blown out, General Shirakawa lost all his teeth. General Uyeda lost three toes. Kim Fung-kee, the Korean bomb-thrower, was beaten unconscious by Japanese soldiers.

PAX BRITANNICA: Inside the British Consulate at Shanghai MAY 16 last week, closely guarded by His Majesty's Marines in full war regalia, sat an aristocratic Old Etonian, Sir Miles Wedder-burn Lampson. On his desk lay an agreement ready to be initialed by the plenipotentiaries of China, Japan and the Great Powers providing for Japanese evacuation. Picking up a pen, Sir Miles initialed the agreement first himself, then sent it to the hospitals where three of the Oriental signers lay painfully in beds as a result of the bombing fortnight ago.

A Japanese surgeon had just cut out the right eyeball of Vice Admiral Nomura. Another surgeon was waiting to cut off the right leg of Japanese Minister Mamoru Shigemitsu. Propped up in bed, Shigemitsu smiled with heroic Japanese courtesy at Director of Intelligence Samuel Chang, whom the Chinese Government had sent to witness his signature.

"Tell your people—tell the Chinese people," said the ashen-lipped Japanese Minister, "I dearly wish that we shall be at peace!"

Samuel Chang approached the bed, made as though to

shake Ministerr Shigemitsu's right hand, drew back when he saw it was bandaged.

"Here, shake my left hand!" cried the game little Japanese, and as they shook he patted Samuel Chang's hand with his bandaged right. At 1:14 p.m. Minister Shigemitsu signed the agreement, lost his leg two hours later, received a blood transfusion, was described by his Japanese surgeon as "in a condition not quite hopeless." [Shigemitsu hobbled aboard the *U.S.S. Missouri* in 1945 to sign the Japanese surrender ending World War II.]

SEPT. 19 **SPY STORY:** Privately foreigners are telling friends about fun they have constantly had with Japanese spies, even in China.

In Peiping Mrs. Frances Judson McCoy, wife of a U.S. general, entered her hotel bedroom, caught a servant red-handed in the act of "dusting."

"Splendid!" cried Mrs. McCoy. "The room *is* dirty, isn't it? I am so glad you are dusting! Now get a mop and mop the floor."

For two long hours the Japanese spy scrubbed, kept up the pretense that he was a Chinese "boy" (servant).

"Now that everything is clean," brightly observed Mrs. McCoy, "I want you to move all the furniture. Bring that bed here. Move that bureau over there. And then you might scrub the ceiling."

Sweating and grunting the spy obeyed until it was time for Mrs. McCoy to dress for dinner.

"You can go now," she sweetly told him. "Thank you so much, Captain Kitakawa."

International

FEB. 8 **PROMISE TO THE DEAD:** Ever since the last disarmament conference two years ago peace-lovers throughout the world have looked forward hopefully to this week at Geneva. There at last the League of Nations in a major world conference was to come to grips with the explosive question of armies and their limitation.

Thirteen years ago the League of Nations Covenant solemnly promised a reduction of armament in the name of peace. According to most of the greatest orators of Europe, it was a promise made to 8,000,000 slaughtered men, mostly young. Since 1921 the League has been almost continuously mulling and stewing over this matter, trying to devise a method of carrying out the solemn promise at Versailles. The present conference, to which 59 powers, large and small, sent representatives, was to be a climax of its endeavors.

A prime tenet in President Hoover's international credo is limitation of armaments. He has hammered relentlessly away at the thesis that Armies now overburden the world, that the quickest way out of the Depression is to reduce war forces and the taxes which support them. Though the U.S. has no sizeable army to cut (138,000 officers & men), the President consented to join the Geneva Conference in the earnest hope that the U.S. could somehow help other great powers agree to limit their soldiery.

Eight months ago the Study Conference on Disarmament announced: "The approaching Disarmament Conference marks the most important crisis in world history since Versailles." But the world, unfortunately, has had other things to think about. Japan is at China's throat. Japan had agreed unofficially to an investigation of its actions in China, but this was followed almost immediately by a veiled threat from Tokyo that Japan was about ready to quit the League entirely, would do so if the League became too meddlesome.

ARMS FOR DISARMAMENT: *No law except the Sword, un-* FEB. 15
sheathed and uncontrolled! —Rudyard Kipling.

Great primeval monsters, each his own judge of right and wrong, and all ready to fight separately or in combination the moment there was anything to be gained by fighting—such were the Great Powers not long ago. That this shall be so no longer men have now met in Geneva. Last week they worked. Fundamental to their problem are these facts:

1) So-called "International Law," contrary to popular belief, does not necessarily bind a sovereign state.

2) The League of Nations is today no bar to war, as Japan is proving daily.

3) Neither the World Court nor the Hague Court is en-

dowed with an authority over sovereign states in any way remotely comparable to what men mean when they say "a court."

Therefore last week the men in Geneva, the statesmen of 57 nations, had to build almost anew, or fail and leave their Conference a mockery. Up stood a go-getter, France's M. André Tardieu, before the Conference was quite ready to hear him, and dynamically proposed to build anew.

Not new, the plan he proposed merely gave a semblance of creation to the old, calm, logical French argument that only a *real* International Law, only a *real* League of Nations and only a *real* World Court can make sovereign states toe the line of International Decency.

Specifically M. Tardieu offered, subject to similar offers and approval all round, to place at the disposal of the League of Nations upon demand:

1) All the world's long-range artillery.

2) All the world's warships exceeding 10,000 tons each or armed with guns of a caliber above 8 in.

3) All the world's large submarines.

4) All the world's civil airplanes capable of military use, plus an air armada of heavy bombers created exclusively for the League.

5) An International Police Force (ultimate name unimportant) to swing the above nightsticks and crack them over the heads of sovereign states which do not toe the mark of International Decency.

Instantly the French Plan was damned and doomed—though, of course, everyone had to be infinitely polite to M. Tardieu. With fine Roman cynicism the Italian delegation whispered around a witticism to the effect that M. Tardieu, facing 57 armed states, had proposed to create a 58th.

JULY 18 **"PEACE ON EARTH"**: Most credit for inducing the Lausanne Conference on reparations to come to some sort of an agreement last week belonged to snowy-haired, silver-tongued James Ramsay MacDonald, who suffered agonizing headaches from overworking his weak eyes. When the long grind of 24 days ended, climaxed by 60 hours of almost ceaseless negotiation, statesmen and correspondents gave way completely to their emotions.

The motives and emotions of the statesmen at Lausanne last week did them credit. So many conferences since the War have ended in nothing at all. It was an historic moment when the Chancellor of Germany, Franz von Papen, having battled the whole night for a clause wiping out what his people call the "War guilt lie," finally gave in at 3 p.m. saying:

"You have won a great victory, my French friend."

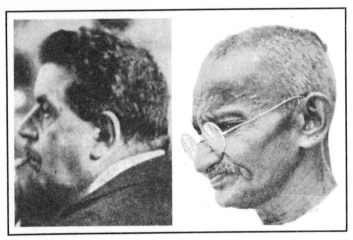

French Premier Herriot wishes the German people "Peace on Earth."

Mahatma Gandhi: "Discard violence! Withdraw cooperation!" Page 124.

It was an inspiring moment when Premier Herriot, warmly clasping Chancellor von Papen's hand, exclaimed:

"We French have listened with emotion to the story of the sufferings of the German people. The Frenchman who is speaking to you desires that we be united in a common thought, in those noblest of words, *Peace on Earth, good will to men!*" [The Geneva Conference on disarmament ended without reaching any agreement; the Lausanne Conference agreed to set aside Germany's reparations, but the U.S. refused to accept the decision.]

WARS OF THE WEEK: Biggest war of last week was the Chinese OCT. 3 conflict along 80 miles of brand new No Man's Land in Shantung, but men were fighting many another war:

¶ Brazil—On at least three fronts "the bloodiest civil war in South American history" neared the end of its third month, ferociously fought by more than 125,000 Brazilians behind a nearly air-tight censorship. Travelers emerging from the United States of Brazil estimated that between 8,000 and 12,000 Brazilians have been killed, had no idea how many have been wounded since São Paulo State, "The Heart of Brazil," raised her gory standard against Brazil's faintly perfumed but sufficiently ruthless Provisional President Getulio Vargas.

¶ Bolivia *v.* Paraguay—In the sweltering, swampy, mosquito-infested Gran Chaco between Brazil and Paraguay a total of 1,250 soldiers of those nations have died in the recent war, according to Bolivian official estimates last week. While Paraguayan soldiers captured one-sixteenth of a mile of Bolivian trenches last week, Bolivian "atrocity stories" began to appear accusing Paraguayans of firing on Red Cross units.

DEC. 19 **BIG v. LITTLE:** In Geneva last week Spain, Czechoslovakia, Sweden and the Irish Free State led an effort to arouse the conscience of the Great Powers. Each of the "Little Four" rejected Japan's excuse that she seized Manchuria in "self defense"; all scored Japan for setting up in Manchuria the puppet state of "Manchukuo"; all pledged their Governments never to recognize Manchukuo, and all accused Japan of violating both the Nine-Power Treaty and the Covenant of the League. The attempt drew cheers and a burst of handclaps—ordinarily banned in the Assembly. Even louder applause rang out when Dr. Eduard Benes, perpetual Foreign Minister of Czechoslovakia, said, "Is the League aware that this is a great test case which will establish precedents for future disputes? Any policy of compromise as regards principles will lead to failure and ultimate death for the League."

The heavy, thankless job of squelching the minor nations—who required squelching because otherwise Japan itself would have withdrawn from the League—was left to two of Europe's highest priced lawyers, Maître Joseph Paul-Boncour, the sonorous, theatrical War Minister of France, and Sir John Simon, icy, meticulous British Foreign Secretary.

Neither of these special pleaders so much as mentioned the issues—whether Japan acted in self defense; whether she broke treaties; whether League states should recognize Manchukuo. Instead both pressed for delay and Sir John Simon devoted most of his speech to stressing "the need of being practical" and rebuking the Chinese Government for not having suppressed Communism in its central provinces—1,000 mi. from Manchukuo.

Bounding to his feet after Sir John sat down, Spain's Salvador de Madariaga cried: "Practical men, whose political shortsightedness is incurable, would like to limit our efforts by saying, 'Provided we can reach a practical solution, let us pass a sponge over the rest.' To this madness, Spain desires to say 'No!' The League Covenant will perish if we permit Chinese Manchuria to become Japanese Manchukuo."

Next morning Japan's Chief Delegate, swart, smart Yosuke Matsuoka, prepared for a showdown by telling newsreel men to get their cameras ready "in case I am historically obliged to withdraw from the Assembly."

This proved unnecessary. To an Assembly which had blown off its conscientious steam, Mr. Matsuoka delivered with crushing effect a speech in which he declared, "the whole Japanese nation is solidly behind our military leaders, who have acted as they should. Sixty-five million Japanese stand together as one man! Do you think all of them have gone mad?

"Even if world public opinion be against us, Japan will persist forever! Humanity crucified Jesus of Nazareth 2,000 years ago. We are prepared to be crucified, but we do believe that in a very few years world public opinion will have changed and that we, also, shall be understood by the world as Jesus of Nazareth now is!"

Overnight the effect of Mr. Matsuoka's speech, plus pressure from the Great Powers, squelched the "Little Four" so completely that the League Assembly, when it met, took just three minutes to put the Manchurian question on ice.

Canada

DEATH ON PORCUPINE RIVER: It took seven weeks, a dozen straining dog teams, an airplane, the life of one constable and the wounding of two others, but last week Mad Albert Johnson toppled forward in the snow and bled to death. The reputation of the Royal Canadian Mounted Police was saved.

FEB. 29

Nobody knew much about Albert Johnson. A quiet, stocky fellow about 40 years old, he appeared in Aklavik, North West Territories, about a year ago, said he had walked in from Alaska. He seemed to have plenty of money. He built himself a little cabin about 100 miles south of Aklavik, shut himself up in it and was notably cool to strangers.

In December Indian trappers complained at the Mounted Police Headquarters in Aklavik that somebody was interfering with their trap lines. Robbing trap lines is a crime, but these traps were not robbed. Somebody was smashing snares and deadfalls, scattering the bait so hungry animals could eat it in safety. Tracks of the trap-smasher were followed to Johnson's cabin. Indians raised the alarm, said the man was "mad."

Constables King and McDowell went out to ask Albert Johnson a few questions. They knocked on the cabin door, but Albert Johnson did not answer. Three bullets splintered the door and smashed into Constable King's chest. McDowell did not wait. He dragged his friend to their sledge and cracked his snake whip as loud as Hermit Johnson's rifle. Tongues out, the husky dogs plunged forward. They made the 100 miles back to Aklavik in 20 hours. It was a record and it saved Constable King's life.

Ten days later a new patrol mushed out to Rat River to avenge Constable King. Albert Johnson had used the interval to turn his hut into a blockhouse. He had dug the dirt floor out to a depth of four feet, cut loopholes at the floor level. For 15 hours Albert Johnson held off the Mounties. Hand grenades blew the roof off his hut. Albert Johnson retired, like an angry woodchuck, into a dugout, kept fighting. The police retired, disgruntled.

For the third time a police patrol set out from Aklavik, but this time Albert Johnson had fled from Rat River, was trying to beat his way through the arctic winter to Alaska and safety. Followed the north country's greatest man hunt. Trappers rushed their wives to trading posts for safety, then joined the posse. Thirty miles further in the wilderness the posse tracked him down. Mad Albert had built a fort of ice and snow. There was another battle. In it, Constable E. Millen died. Police ammunition ran out and the posse withdrew for supplies, leaving three men to watch the fort. In the middle of the night Mad Albert Johnson slipped away again in a blizzard that covered his snowshoe tracks.

Then one of Canada's best known War aces, Capt. W. R. ("Wop") May, a survivor of the epic battle which ended in the death of Germany's famed Baron Manfred von Richthofen, loaded a bomb rack, took off in an army plane in pursuit of Johnson.

The blizzard could not hide Johnson from the eyes of Capt. May. Fortnight later he reported that Johnson had crossed the Yukon River, was tracking west from Pierre House trading post, only 175 miles from the Alaska border. The man hunt resumed, full cry.

Last week they cornered him in the upper Yukon. Sergeant E. F. Hersey and Trapper Noel Verville were driving the lead sledge when they saw Mad Albert Johnson wearily retracing his track along Porcupine River. Johnson saw them too. He jumped off the trail, took cover. Sergeant Hersey and Trapper Verville followed fast. "Wop" May roared in circles trying to drop a bomb without injuring the pursuers. Before he could do so, Albert Johnson sent a bullet through Sergeant Hersey's knee that ranged along his thigh and into his chest. The rest of the posse ran up just in time to riddle Albert Johnson with one crashing volley.

Sergeant Hersey, gravely wounded, was rushed back to Aklavik in "Wop" May's plane. Albert Johnson came back on a police sledge, dead, frozen stiff.

Finland

MARTINI & MANHATTAN: Finland, which lately went Wet, JULY 18 seethed with complaint against the State Alcohol Monopoly Co. last week. For one thing the company's stores are closed on Saturday, Sunday, Monday, holidays, on days preceding and following holidays, and every day from 3 p.m. until the following 10 a.m. For another thing the Government, firmly believing that mixed drinks are bad for the stomach, has issued stringent regulations providing that, without special permission, only two kinds of mixed drinks may be sold, the Martini Cocktail and the Manhattan Cocktail.

India

JAN. 11 **VICEROY v. GANDHI:** Last week Mahatma Gandhi begged audience to discuss the Viceroy's, Lord Willingdon's, recent ordinance suppressing free speech, freedom of assembly and virtually all civil rights in Bengal. He received from the Viceregal court the telegraphic answer:

"His Excellency feels bound to emphasize that he will not be prepared to discuss with you the measures which the Government of India have found it necessary to adopt."

In Bombay the telegram was called "insulting" by President Vallabhai Patel of the Gandhite Indian National Congress. Other Gandhites shouted: "This means war!" Squatting in his little tent pitched atop a Bombay tenement house, the Mahatma meditated half the night. Then loyal followers heard the scratch, scratch of his pen as he wrote to the Viceroy: "You demand co-operation from the Congress without returning any on behalf of the Government. I can read in no other way your peremptory refusal to discuss the ordinances. The Congress must resist with its prescribed creed of nonviolence such measures of legalized terrorism as have been imposed in various provinces."

Next morning a disciple hastily washed all the Mahatma's loincloths, so that he might not lack fresh ones in jail. Meanwhile leading British and Indian merchants and businessmen reminded Lord Willingdon that Mahatma Gandhi's arrest would mean a trade loss of millions of dollars to the Empire, since it would unquestionably provoke a fresh Indian boycott of British goods.

The Viceroy then ordered the Government of Bombay to arrest Mr. Gandhi in the dead of night and lodge him before dawn in Yerovda Jail near Poona, where the Mahatma had twice before been imprisoned (1926, 1930). At 3 a.m. Police Commissioner Wilson, Inspector Hirst and two strapping Indian policemen climbed the tenement stairs, approached the tent within which Mr. Gandhi was sleeping, bearing a warrant for the arrest of the Mahatma "for good and sufficient reasons." Prisoner Gandhi was to be lodged in jail for an indefinite term "during the pleasure of the Government."

"Bapoo, Bapoo!" a disciple cried softly, awakening the Mahatma by his pet name. "The police are here."

As it was Bapoo's day of silence, he received the warrant of arrest with a nod and smile, scribbled with a pencil his obedience to the Viceregal will. "Mr. Gandhi," said Police Commissioner Wilson, "you have half an hour to dress and pack."

Thousands of Indians had massed outside the tenement house, stood silent. With fresh water the Mahatma washed his hands and face, brushed his teeth. "Arrest me, too!" suddenly screamed Mrs. Gandhi, but even the need of comforting her did not cause Mr. Gandhi to break his silence. As she flung herself at his feet sobbing, he patted her encouragingly on the back, then scribbled: "Don't grieve or worry about me. The British will be my warders, but God will be my protector. May the Father of us all keep you in His infinite mercy."

Softly Mrs. Gandhi and other Indian women who had crowded near began to chant the Mahatma's favorite prayer, "The Perfect Believer": "The perfect believer bears no ill will or malice toward any man. He looks upon every woman as his mother. He wishes well to all living creatures and he would cut out his tongue rather than lie."

Immobile, non-resistant, the thousands of Indians who had waited all night around the tenement house made no move to interfere as the four police officers bundled Mr. Gandhi into a touring car, drove off into the night while the crowd chanted like a litany *Victory! Victory! Victory!*

At Yerovda Jail the British warders greeted Mr. Gandhi with extreme kindness, made him welcome in his old quarters. Soon his spinning wheel was whirring. In his last hours of freedom Mr. Gandhi wrote two messages—one to all Christians urging them to boycott British goods, strive for Indian freedom; another to his fellow Indians:

"India, awaken from your sleep! Discard foreign cloth. Spin and weave your own. Discard violence! Protect Englishmen, English women and children, even if they are provocative. Withdraw from the Government all co-operation."

FULL RESOURCES: Last week a detachment of 400 officers and JAN. 18 men from the Welsh Regiment and the Royal Scots sailed for duty in India. The men knew, the world knew that Britain was preparing for serious trouble. The India Office issued a bulletin:

"Mr. Gandhi has stated as part of his creed that civil disobedience is not only a natural right of the people but that it is also an effective substitute for violence or armed rebellion. Experience has proven time and time again that in India civil disobedience cannot be carried on without violence."

India is a country of 318,000,000 souls. To keep it safe for Britain there is at the present time a British force of about 60,000 men and 165,000 native troops commanded by British and Indian officers. Last week the Viceroy stiffened his repressive ordinances still further. Picketing British shops was already a crime. Last week special judges were empowered to pass any sentence including sentence of death on persons convicted of violating the emergency ordinances. At Karachi police charged a crowd after a public meeting, injured 28. At Allahabad the sub-postmaster and two others were killed in a riot. At Srinagar a mob of 12,000 stormed a police station, freed three prisoners. Police found five live bombs in a first-class compartment of the Darjeeling express.

Meanwhile St. Gandhi squatted quietly in jail, spinning 500 yards of yarn a day, sipping goat's milk, walking round & round the prison compound.

JAN. 25 **KRISHNA KANT:** A British magistrate made a mistake in Bombay last week. Outside a store a small, impertinent child shrilly shouted to purchasers to buy nothing but Indian goods. Policemen swooped down, arrested the child as a picketer and hauled him off to court where a short-tempered magistrate sentenced him to four years imprisonment. The child's name was Krishna Kant. He was nine years old. Snapped the magistrate:

"If you disobey orders in the reformatory you will be whipped."

"I am ready to die for Gandhi," said Krishna Kant.

Half of India had heard of Krishna Kant next day. Nationalist agitators thanked their stars for an easy martyr. Wholesale arrests continued. Crowds searched houses for British cloth, built bonfires of it in the streets. Bengal police fired into a crowd, killed one, wounded two.

FEB. 8 **OUTSTARING A COBRA:** At Yerovda Jail near Poona, in a cell not far from the one which houses the sainted person of Mahatma Gandhi, one day last week sat another Nationalist leader named L. B. Bhopatkar. Suddenly he heard a warning shout, saw before him a large, ugly cobra. The warden who had shouted ran off for a club while Prisoner Bhopatkar was left alone with his cobra. Regarded as sacred by most Indians, the cobra must be avoided, not slain.

But Prisoner Bhopatkar, locked in his cell, could not avoid this one. Unarmed, neither could he kill it. As the cobra fixed him with its jeweled eyes, he sat cross-legged, giving back stare for stare. For ten minutes neither moved a muscle. Then the warden returned, clubbed the cobra to death. "That was wrong," said St. Gandhi severely. "The cobra's visit was a good omen."

MAKING ROOM: Throughout India the British Raj pardoned   MAY 2
and released from jail last week numerous pickpockets and minor criminals, thus making room for more followers of Mahatma Gandhi. The Raj was trying to prevent the Gandhite Indian National Congress from holding its 49th session at New Delhi. Fifteen minutes after she left Bombay, the Congress President, famed Indian Poetess Mrs. Sarojini Naidu, was arrested. Her successor, India's revered Pandit Mohan Malavija, was arrested as he reached New Delhi along with 369 delegates to the Congress.

These arrests placed under lock & key in various parts of India some 50,000 followers of the Mahatma, "including all who are nationally known."

SARCASM & SAINT: Last week correspondents learned that   SEPT. 26
Mr. Gandhi had decided to begin "a fast unto Death" to protest the condition of India's untouchables.

British efforts to discredit the Mahatma on the eve of his fast ranged from official announcements that he was being fitted with a new set of false teeth to the instinctive act of a British showman who cabled Mr. Gandhi a cash offer to come to England and starve unto Death as a sideshow freak. "Your case, right or wrong," cabled sarcastic Showman Luke Gannon, "will then be understood by the people of England."

In his cell, meanwhile, the Mahatma appeared cheerful. "There is every cause for rejoicing!" he cried. "This is a God-given opportunity that has come to me—to offer my life as a final sacrifice to the downtrodden."

OCT. 3 **SOUL FORCE WINS:** The Mahatma or Great Soul seemed to twist around his scrawny finger last week the United Kingdom Government, some 220,000,000 Hindus of all castes. Death still hovered over the fragile body (which had lost a pound a day for six days) when Mr. Gandhi ended his hunger strike by saying a prayer, quavering a hymn of joy, sipping an ounce or two of orange juice and exclaiming weakly, "*Satyagraha* [Soul Force] has triumphed."

Eight doctors shook their heads. The Mahatma, they said, had "begun his fast with little fat and lived on muscle." After breaking his fast he was "still in the danger zone and might suffer a stroke of paralysis." Several times the Mahatma showed extreme nausea. Whenever he fainted, Mrs. Gandhi vigorously rubbed his head with olive oil.

What agreement was reached in final frantic haste, His Majesty's Government left unclear, stressing instead the great fact that it had satisfied Mahatma Gandhi. Observers could assume no more than that Mr. Gandhi had received convincing assurances that the caste barriers (which he has fought so long to break down) will not be strengthened by the form which India's electoral laws finally take.

Irish Free State

When Southern Ireland was given Dominion status in 1921 and was established as the Irish Free State, one of the strongest opponents of the new government was Eamon de Valera, who had long fought for Irish independence. He organized his own party, the Republican Society, and refused to let its members sit in Parliament because of a law requiring representatives to sign an oath of loyalty to the King of England. In 1927 the Republicans finally agreed to sign the oath. Then, having been elected President, De Valera once more challenged his country's ties with Britain.

MARCH 21 **MERE FORMALITY:** In order to become President, tall, stoop-shouldered, teacherish Mr. de Valera had to take, in writing, this oath: "I, Eamon de Valera, do solemnly swear true faith

Ireland's De Valera. He was born where the Chrysler Building stands.   *Mussolini. His biography is written—30 times in six years. Page 131.*

and allegiance to the Constitution of the Irish Free State as by law established, and that I will be faithful to H.M. King George V, his heirs and successors by law in virtue of the common citizenship of Ireland with Great Britain and her adherence to and membership of the group of nations forming the British Commonwealth of Nations."

As he has before when inscribing this oath (required of all Irish Free State Deputies), Mr. de Valera said severely to the oath-clerk, "I am not taking any oath or giving any promise of faithfulness to the King of England. I am putting my name here as a mere formality."

In Rochester, N.Y. a quiet old lady who dresses mostly in black was told that her son had become President. "I am very happy to hear the news," said Mrs. Catherine Wheelwright. She bore Eamon de Valera where Manhattan's Chrysler Building stands today. The President's father (a Spaniard) is dead and so is his stepfather, Mr. Wheelwright.

"IRELAND HER OWN": Long, lean Eamon de Valera caught APRIL 11 only snatches of troubled sleep last week, had a bed lugged into his office. Toiling and arguing with his Cabinet Ministers, Ireland's "Messiah of Freedom" faced an invisible and potent foe: the collective opposition of British statesmen throughout the Empire.

The President was trying to draft a white-hot Irish reply to the damp reminder he received fortnight ago from Secretary for the Dominions James Henry ("Jim") Thomas that His Majesty's Government "stands on" the Anglo-Irish Treaty of 1921 and stickles for the oath of fealty to George V. Before sitting down to write, Mr. de Valera had shouted to a Dublin throng, "Britain cannot frighten us!" These words were received with such enthusiasm that the President was swept in a friendly Irish way by the crowd through a picket fence.

"The Irish people," he resumed amid lusty cheers, "have learned the fallacy of surrendering their rights when threatened!"

But Irishmen themselves made their new President's life even more miserable last week than did the British statesmen.

"Damn your concessions to England!" headlined a Dublin newspaper before Mr. de Valera had done or conceded anything. "The Anglo-Irish Treaty, lock, stock & barrel, must go! Ireland wants no connection with England. The Imperial link must be severed."

President de Valera, only a fortnight earlier, had already summed up "the aims of the new Government" thus:

"Ireland her own—and all therein, from the sod to the sky. The soil of Ireland for the people of Ireland, to have and to hold from God alone who gave it—to have and to hold to them and to their heirs forever, without suit or service, rent or render, faith or fealty to any power under heaven."

"IF WE WERE FREE": Pushed by British pressure out of the picture last week was Eamon de Valera's hope and plan that on becoming President he could negotiate for a union of the two Irelands, North & South, Protestant & Catholic. Instead, in a sober, lucid interview with a French journalist, the President said:

"We are united to England by our geographical position and active economic relations. If we were entirely free, if Ireland were an independent democracy, entirely mistress of her destiny within her natural frontiers, I, for my part, would favor a very friendly political understanding with Great Britain. But as long as there exists against us a menacing fortress on our own soil, and we must live, so to speak, in a state of suspicion, true friendship can never be born between the two nations."

ECONOMIC CIVIL WAR: The quarrel of His Majesty's Government in the Irish Free State with His Majesty's Government in Great Britain passed from ominous threats to ominous action last week. At 6 p.m. the King-Emperor gave royal assent to a bill passed by his Lords & Commons empowering the Government to levy an import tax up to 100% on Free State products entering Great Britain. Promptly in Dublin the Free State Cabinet began drafting retaliatory taxes on goods from Great Britain, of which the Free State buys somewhat more than the Mother Country buys from her. The situation thus drifted toward a state of economic civil war. JULY 25

"If England wants a fight, England can have a fight!" cried a De Valera deputy. "Ireland is no longer going to be the kitchen garden of England!"

Previously President de Valera, by no means spoiling for a fight, had exclaimed, "I appeal once more to the British, asking them to state unequivocally that the people of Ireland would not be interfered with by hostile British action should they declare their independence!"

Deputy Macdermott: "Does the President mean war?"

President de Valera: "I mean the kind of action one person takes against another when one feels that the other has done him wrong. I hold that we should be doing no wrong to Great Britain by declaring our absolute independence tomorrow!"

Of course the Free State did not declare its independence next day. Instead President de Valera consented to meet British Prime Minister Ramsay MacDonald again face to face, traveling for this purpose to London last week. Again the two leaders flatly disagreed, an event which so upset old George Lansbury, leader of the Labor Opposition in the House of Commons, that he cried: "I call upon the Pope and the Archbishop of Canterbury to intervene! We have started a fight with Ireland the end of which no man can see." [The Dail abolished the oath to the King in 1933, and an economic war began with England that ended in 1938 with a compromise agreement on tariffs. De Valera remained in office until 1948, then served as President again in 1951-1954 and 1957-1959.]

Italy

MARCH 28 **BENITO SPEAKS:** Excited citizens of Brescia started a run on their Unione Bancaria Nazionale which, in desperation, appealed to *Il Duce* last week. Soon the Mayor of Brescia received this telegram from Rome:

INFORM THE CITIZENS OF BRESCIA THAT I HAVE EVERY CONFIDENCE IN THE STABILITY OF THE UNIONE BANCARIA NAZIONALE.

BENITO MUSSOLINI

Instantly the run stopped. All the rest of that day depositors who had withdrawn their money stood in line to redeposit.

MAY 9 **"THOSE EYES":** Last week Italians were reading the latest biography of *Il Duce* (the 30th within six years), written by his Under Secretary of Interior Giuseppe Cavaciocchi.

"He talks little," declares Cavaciocchi, "often indicating to his associates what he wants done by a single word, a wave of the hand or a roll of the eyes. He has reduced to an absolute minimum the use of his voice. Anyone who stands before him must know how to read those eyes."

JUNE 27 **"THERE ARE NO SAVIORS":** "I can sum up the United States in two words," declared Premier Benito Mussolini last week: "Prohibition and Lindbergh! Dry America will never find herself. She must go Wet to find herself! In the meantime Europe is drifting toward disaster and Bolshevization.

"Democracy is nothing!" the Dictator went on. "The people are nothing and can do nothing. In every country they are weary of talk. They need men of action. They cannot save themselves—they need saviors!"

"Where are those saviors?" the Dictator was asked. Scowling *Il Duce* shot back: "There are no saviors!"

"What then of the future?"

"I foresee a long series of political, economic and military wars," answered Italy's Fascist savior darkly. "There is war now."

"What of America's policy?"

Slowly, bitterly Benito Mussolini answered: "America has no policy."

Presumably this black fit of pessimism was induced in Italy's normally optimistic Premier by his Government's inability to balance its budget coupled with the refusal of the U.S. Congress to sanction cancellation of the War Debts of Italy and her Allies.

"The era of Reparations is ended," was *Il Duce*'s parting shot. "All that belongs to the dead and buried past."

OF WAR & VEGETABLES: Last week, in an amazing contribu- OCT. 17 tion to the *Enciclopedia Italiana,* Signor Mussolini tried to define the "Political and Social Doctrine of Fascism," succeeded in defining himself, exposing some of his innermost mental processes. Excerpts:

¶ Peace—"Above all," wrote *Il Duce,* "Fascism does not believe in the possibility or advisability of perpetual peace. It therefore rejects pacifism. Only war leads to the maximum tension of all human energies and sets the seal of nobility on people who have the virtue to face it."

¶ Christianity—"The Fascist loves his neighbor," *Il Duce* continued, "but love of his neighbor does not prevent the necessary educational severity, much less differences and distances. Fascism rejects universal brotherhood."

¶ Economics—"Fascism rejects the conception of economic 'happiness.' Fascism denies the equation that well-being equals happiness. Such an equation would convert men into animals thinking of only one thing—of being fed and fattened; reduced, therefore, to a pure and simple vegetable life."

¶ Democracy—"Democratic regimes can be defined as those in which, from time to time, the people are given the illusion of being sovereign. Fascism rejects in democracy the absurd, conventional lie of political equality."

PEOPLE

"Names make news." In 1932 the following names made the following news:

In a fire which damaged the Eden Musee, famed waxworks at Coney Island (N.Y.) funpark, figures of CHARLES AUGUSTUS LINDBERGH, LEON TROTSKY, JOHN JOSEPH PERSHING, GAIUS JULIUS CAESAR, HENRY VIII, MR. & MRS. TOM THUMB were melted out of existence. Others who suffered: GEORGE WASHINGTON (broken nose), MARIE ANTOINETTE (decapitated).

Said HENRY FORD: "We are here to work out something, and we go on from where we leave off. That's my religion, though I was brought up an Episcopalian. I'm certain that I have lived before, that I stored up considerable experience before the present stage, and that I will proceed to the next stage when this is finished. It's all trial-and-error."

DANIEL BOONE JR., Kansas City insurance executive, great-great-grandson of the heroic frontiersman, was held up and robbed by a gunman whom he described as "very hard and very drunk."

While bathing, POPE PIUS XI smelled gas, rang for his chamberlain, had the windows opened, himself escorted to another room. An electric water heater was ordered for the papal bathing chamber.

Named Athlete-of-the-Year by 52 votes of U.S. sportswriters in an associated Press poll was Golfer GENE SARAZEN, U.S. and British Open champion. Second with 36 votes was Tennist ELLSWORTH VINES.

SPORT

NEW MILE RECORD: Last week Gene Venzke, a 23-year-old FEB. 15 German-American of Boyerstown, Pa., who was unknown two years ago and no better than a steady pace-setter last year, beat a crack field in a mile race for the Wanamaker Memorial Trophy. His time, 4 min. 11 $^1/_5$ sec., became the new world's record.

GOOD SKATE: At last week's Winter Olympic Games at Lake FEB. 22 Placid, N.Y., there was no doubt that the best girl figure skater in the world was still 19-year-old Sonja Henie of Oslo, Norway. Behind her, on the stand, sat her immense, red-faced father, Wilhelm Henie. He said nothing. Mrs. Henie, however, told their daughter what part of the ice to use, instructed her to keep her beady toque straight on her head. Attached to her dress, Sonja had a rabbit's foot which she did not need. Her performance—a Paulsen, a spreadeagle, a Lutz jump, a Jackson Haynes spin, a backward sweep to the finish—was less original than polished and assured, but it caused 8,000 spectators to agree with the judges when she won the championship.

LONDOS: Christopher Theophilus ("Jim Londos"), who con- MAY 2 siders himself the world's champion wrestler and has a gold belt to prove it, last week advanced across a Manhattan ring and seized the left arm of Joe De Vito, a rubbery Italian with a pork-barrel torso and a door-knob ear. He gave the arm a vicious twist. De Vito, grunting with unreasonable surprise, retaliated by trying to pluck off one of Londos' toes. For 21 min. 42 sec. the two groveled, grunted, snorted, glowered, slapped, twisted and oozed. Finally Londos whirled De Vito around his head in an "airplane spin," threw him down with a loud thud, sat on top of his chest until old fat Ernest Roeber, who used to be a professional wrestler and now referees, patted Londos' back for winning.

Now 34, Champion Londos is one of 13 offspring of a Greek olive picker. He wrestles three times a week, makes about $250,000 a year. This season he has defended his title 207 times. He lives in St. Louis, eats enormously, maintains a library of 1,200 volumes, takes singing lessons, smokes a corncob pipe.

JUNE 13 **LAST OF A GIANT:** A solid, squatty Irishman with a bull neck, John Joseph McGraw looks very much like what he was until last week—manager of one of the most famous baseball teams in history, the New York Giants. He has a gruff, arrogant way of speaking. There was only a touch of his hardness in a type-written message which Manager McGraw last week gave out to the Press in the grimy club offices of the Giants above Manhattan's Polo Grounds: "My doctor advises me, because of my sinus condition, that it would be inadvisable to attempt any road trips with the club this season, so I suggested to Mr. Stoneham that another manager be appointed. We therefore agreed on Bill Terry [Giant first baseman, whom Owner Charles A. Stoneham last spring threatened to 'drive out of baseball' when he refused the $15,000 salary offered him]. I want it fully understood that Terry will have full and complete charge of the team and will have to assume entire responsibility therefor."

When Manager McGraw resigned last week, the Giants were eighth in the National League standing, exactly where they had been when Manager McGraw took charge in the summer of 1902. McGraw's teams in other years had won ten pennants, finished second eleven times, third four times, fourth twice, fifth once. They won three World Series, four pennants in a row from 1921 to 1924. Famed as a strategist, Manager McGraw assumed responsibility for every play. Once he fined a batter, ordered to bunt, for hitting a home run.

First act of Manager Terry last week was to "give the boys a break." Said he: "They won't have to report to the park at 10 in the morning or go to bed at any certain hour. All I'm to ask is that they play good ball."

JUNE 20 **SARAZEN AT SANDWICH:** Gene Sarazen did this spring what few professional golfers think is worth the trouble: he went

*Wrestler Jim Londos. An opponent
tries to pluck off his toe. Page 134.*

*Golfer Gene Sarazen. He wins the
British Open (and wears the cup).*

into training. By eating vegetables and drinking water he removed 15 lb. from his stumpy little figure. He was training to win the British Open, so he practiced on windy days at seaside courses because he expected bad weather abroad. When Sarazen went out to qualify at Sandwich last week, there was scarcely a breeze.

At the top of his sure, perfectly rounded game, Sarazen played the championship rounds so well that on his last round he was supposedly eight strokes ahead of the field. Jaunty and gay, he fingered the lucky necktie, decorated by a question mark, which his wife had given him. He had just reached the turn in 35 when a runner from the clubhouse brought him astounding news. Arthur Havers had finished his third round in 68, a new course record, leaving him only four strokes behind. Rattled by the news, Sarazen mistimed his drive and the ball landed in the one clump of grass in an ugly wilderness of hazards called the Himalayas. He recovered for a par and the Prince of Wales watched him sink a 20-ft. putt for a birdie on the 14th. At the 18th he needed a 4 for a 74. He smashed a perfect drive and asked his caddy, Ernest Daniels, "What club?" Caddy Daniels gave him the No. 3 iron. This last crucial shot was straight and safe. Two careful putts gave Sarazen a 72 hole total of 283, two strokes lower than Bobby Jones' record 285 in 1927.

JULY 11 **CALIFORNIA'S YEAR:** This is California's year in sport. While Southern California was beating Stanford 62³/₄ to 33 for the I.C.A.A.A.A. track and field championship last week (with Yale third and California fourth), Helen Wills Moody of San Francisco and Ellsworth Vines Jr. of Pasadena were winning the two most important singles championships in tennis at Wimbledon. A University of California crew had three weeks ago won the intercollegiate championship at Poughkeepsie. Meanwhile at Long Beach, Calif. last week, more track athletes were competing in the semi-final Olympic trials.

To prepare for this year's Olympics in Los Angeles, the state of California appropriated $1,000,000, Los Angeles $1,250,000. Twelve miles southwest of Los Angeles are 550 pink & white two-room bungalows specially designed to house 2,000 men contestants from 58 nations in a 331-acre "Olympic Village" with five miles of streets, a hospital, an amphitheatre, 40 private kitchens equipped to give foreign contestants native rations.

By last week, foreign contestants to the Olympic games were all either on their way to Los Angeles or about to start. When the Japanese competitors arrive at Los Angeles, they will find a tub large enough to hold 15 men, such as Japanese athletes prefer for bathing. French athletes, disgusted by the refusal of the U.S. Government to allow them to have wine with their meals, were still in France. They were planning, while in the U.S., to sip 125 grams of Cuban sugar syrup every day for stimulus.

AT WIMBLEDON: Last week the galleries at Wimbledon, after watching some tennis as great as Wimbledon ever saw, had a new hero, a lanky, lazy-looking California boy who had come over to play in his first "world championship."

He, 20-year-old Ellsworth Vines Jr., slouched about the grounds, sprawled in locker-room chairs, apparently forgetful of the fact that he was the U.S. singles champion and therefore the most exciting entrant in the tournament. When all the other U.S. players had been eliminated, Vines strolled out to play his semi-final match against Jack Crawford of Australia.

A grey drizzle made the court slippery but the bad footing did not bother Vines. His backhand was suddenly a magnificent offensive stroke. His drives lashed the uttermost corners of Crawford's back court. Crawford said afterward that Vines' first serve "seemed to hit the court the same instant it left the racket." Vines followed it to the net and smashed Crawford's returns so hard that the ball kicked up tufts of grass. When Vines had won, 6-2, 6-1, 6-3, he remarked: "I wish I could always hit like that." [He did and won the finals from Bunny Austen of Great Britain, 6-4, 6-2, 6-0.]

THE GAMES: Observers who expected the Xth Olympiad of AUG. 15 the Modern Era to be a failure because of Depression, international hard-feeling or Los Angeles' promotion methods were vastly disappointed last week. The Xth Olympiad was a gorgeous, unprecedented success. More people attended the Games than ever before (510,000 through last week). The athletes (1,740) enjoyed themselves more than hitherto. In actual competition, it began to look last week as though the Xth Olympiad might be too much of a success: in almost every race, runners broke Olympic records.

Of the 140 women contestants in the Xth Olympiad, by far the most spectacular was Mildred ("Babe") Didrikson of Dallas, Tex. The first event she won was the javelin throw with a world's record of 143 ft. 4 in. She explained that she would have thrown it further if it had not slipped out. In the 80-metre hurdles she set another world's record of 11.7 sec.

TENNIS TEACHER: Spectators at Forest Hills last week were SEPT. 12 well aware of Frankie Parker, most amazing tennis phenomenon of the year, who has four times this season beaten the No. 2 U.S. player, George Lott Jr. Most spectators knew that he had been tutored by Mercer Beasley, tennis coach at Tulane University and instructor at the Detroit Tennis Club. Beasley's other pupils—Ellsworth Vines, Carolyn Babcock —have done so well this year and last that Beasley has become the best-known teacher in the history of U.S. tennis. Some Beasleyisms:

❡ Of Beasley Methods: "I rarely change natural grips. We try to have the footwork done ahead of time and then at the moment of hitting, perfect control, no falling over sideways, no off balance. At Tulane we have the boxing instructor come down to the courts with boxing gloves and show the boys how to foot. My players must never grandstand a play, never make the kill, when a soft accurate shot will suffice. Energy must be saved.

¶ Of Frankie Parker: "It was in 1927 that Frankie Parker came into my life. Little shaver, thin, puny, but quiet and attentive. He had the best eye for a moving ball I've ever seen. It took four years of the hardest work to get the boy's title. He is to be the best of the pack."

¶ Of Ellsworth Vines: "I found Ellsworth working in a bakery shop in Pasadena. He had a Western grip and a roundhouse swing, was about six feet tall and his feet wouldn't be friends with each other. But he had the heart and the willingness."

¶ Of Beasley: "I cannot play tennis."

OCT. 3 **AS ADVERTISED:** The toughest little bulldog in the ring is 174 1/2 -lb. Mickey Walker who started his career as a welterweight, won welterweight and middleweight championships, then became a heavyweight and fought Heavyweight Champion Jack Sharkey to a draw a year ago. Matched against Walker last week was amiable, capable Max Siegfried Otto Schmeling, heavyweight champion until Sharkey won the title on a disputed decision last summer.

Walker and Schmeling were brought together before a crowd whose every sympathy was with snapping little bulldog Walker. They got their money's worth. In the second round hulking Max Schmeling, to his pained surprise, received a thunderstorm in the stomach. His eye was cut. It was a clean round for the little bulldog.

So was the third. So was the fourth. For two more rounds Schmeling ducked and dodged. The crowd pleaded tearfully, "Stay with him, Mickey, stay with him boy!" But those whose view of the match was not distorted through the bottom of a pint flask realized that the tide was turning.

In the eighth round Max Schmeling suddenly pulled himself together and went to work. Mickey Walker was smacked to the canvas for a count of nine, then for a count of six. His mouth protector was slapped right into Schmeling's corner. The referee picked it up, awarded the decision to Schmeling, without boos. Even the Walker cheering section had to admit that Max Siegfried Otto Schmeling had fairly proved his claim to a match to regain his championship.

GREAT WORLD SERIES: Last week, when Lou Gehrig went to OCT. 10 bat in the first game of the World Series between the Chicago Cubs and the New York Yankees, the score was 2 to 0 for Chicago. Side-whiskered Guy Bush, who looks like a nervous villain in a melodrama, had been through the Yankee line-up once, pitching carefully, without allowing a hit. At the start of the fourth, Bush walked Earle Combs, made Joseph (Joe) Sewell ground out, frowned darkly when Babe Ruth hit a whistling single to right. Then Gehrig, stamping his feet on the caked dust, waited till the count was two balls and two strikes. His bat met the next pitch, a Bush screwball, squarely. The ball traveled into the screaming right field bleachers for a home run. Final score: New York 12, Chicago 6. New York won the second game 5 to 2.

Babe Ruth takes two and hits to right —for a record Series homer.

Babe Didrikson hates girls who play with dolls, but likes to cook and sew.

The third game was the most dramatic in the series. In the first inning, hulking Babe Ruth knocked a home run into the temporary bleachers beyond the right field fence, scoring three runs. In the third, Gehrig hit his second home run of the series for the Yankees' fourth run. Meanwhile the Cubs had caught up, with a run in the first, two in the third, another in the fourth. Now, in the fifth, with the score tied, Babe Ruth, whom Pitcher Charlie Root had been ordered not to pass, arrived at the plate with three big bats over his shoulder.

The first ball was a strike. The crowd squealed happily. Fat and cocky, Ruth faced the grandstand and held up one finger. After throwing two balls, Pitcher Root got over another strike. Still cocky, Ruth held up two fingers. The next pitch broke over the corner of the plate. Ruth swung at it. There was a crack. Centerfielder Johnny Moore started to run; then he stood still and watched the ball, a dwindling white spot against the blue sky, clear the wire fence and drop 436 ft. from the plate, one of the longest home runs on record. Babe Ruth shambled slowly around the bases, shaking his fat shoulders and making remarks of mockery to each infielder as he passed. In the uproar, no one was paying much attention to what happened next. Lou Gehrig came to bat and hit the first pitch to the right field flag post. This was a home run also. Final score of the game: New York 7, Chicago 5. The Yankees then won the fourth and final game 13 to 6.

DEC. 19 **"WONDER GIRL"**: At the women's track & field championships in Evanston last summer, a lean, rangy, dark-haired girl from Dallas, Tex. won six first places. She amassed for her team—of which she was the only member—a total of 30 points, to 20 points for a team of 22 which finished second. Overnight Mildred ("Babe") Didrikson, a typist for Dallas Employers' Casualty Co., had become a national sports figure.

Sportswriters Grantland Rice, Paul Gallico, Westbrook Pegler *et al.* were sufficiently amazed by Babe Didrikson to investigate her abilities further. She played golf for their benefit, amazed them afresh by averaging more than 200 yd. with her drives, scoring under 90. When it was established that Babe Didrikson is also an expert swimmer, basketball player, baseball pitcher, football halfback, a proficient billiardist, a clever tumbler, a boxer and wrestler, a fencer, weight lifter and adagio dancer, she could only be described by appalled reporters as a "wonder girl."

But last week the Amateur Athletic Union suspended her

from amateur competition in the U.S. For in newspaper advertisements for Dodge automobiles appeared a picture of Miss Didrikson with a testimonial by her, saying: "One look at its trim beauty and you know it has class." A.A.U. officials decided that the advertisement broke a regulation which says that amateur athletes may not give out testimonials, and ordered the "Wonder Girl" suspended from U.S. amateur competition. Miss Didrikson's reply was that she had not been paid for the testimonial, that she had not authorized it. E. Gordon Perry, auto dealer of Dallas, revealed that he had sold a car to Miss Didrikson a year ago, mailed her compliments on it to his home office. A.A.U. officials announced that if Miss Didrikson could prove, by suing the advertisers for causing her to lose her amateur standing, that she had not been paid for the testimonial, she would be reinstated.

A physical freak in her ability to coordinate her actions with her eye, Miss Didrikson is not freakish in appearance. Now 19, she weighs 126 lb., has slim hard wrists and ankles, long spatulate hands. Beyond a tendency to use explicit language and to despise small girls who play with dolls, Wonder Girl Didrikson's demeanor during intervals between her physical exertions is not unfeminine. She likes to cook, dance, sew. [Babe Didrickson was never reinstated to amateur standing by the A.A.U., but she was recognized as an amateur by the U.S. Golf Association. She won the U.S. Women's golf title in 1946, and in 1947 became the first American to win the British Women's amateur title. In 1947 she turned professional and won the U.S. Open in 1948, 1950 and 1954. She died of cancer in 1957.]

MILESTONES

DIED: Rin Tin Tin, 14, famed German shepherd dog actor; of old age; in Hollywood. He was found during the War in Alsace-Lorraine by Lieutenant Lee Duncan. After four years' education in the U.S. he appeared in his first motion picture, *Where the North Begins*. "Rinty" earned over $300,000 for his master. At the time of his death he was to make a "comeback" appearance in *Pride of the Legion*, in which he will now be succeeded by his son, Rin Tin Tin Jr.

MISCELLANY

COMMUTER: In Tarrytown, N.Y. William R. Laudy drove up to the railroad station in a burning automobile just as his train for New York was leaving. Commuter Laudy caught his train, left his automobile in flames.

THE THEATRE

JAN. 4 **"OF THEE I SING"** is the drollest, merriest musical nonsensity to come down the theatrical pike this season. There is good reason for it to be. The book is a product of wry George S. Kaufman *(Once in a Lifetime).* The music is by gifted George Gershwin. (Numbers to try to whistle: "Of Thee I Sing," "Love Is Sweeping the Country.") Brother Ira has packed the lyrics full of foolishness and funny rhymes. Handsome William Gaxton and Lois Moran of the films carry the burden of the story on cheerful shoulders. And that most despondent of comedians, Victor Moore, is made Vice President of the U.S.

Mr. Moore gets the Vice Presidency as a sort of booby prize when John Wintergreen (Mr. Gaxton) is nominated for the Presidency. Nobody ever pays any attention to Mr. Moore, but Librettist Kaufman has provided some stirring campaign slogans for his running mate:

EVEN YOUR DOG LOVES WINTERGREEN

VOTE FOR WINTERGREEN AND THE FULL DINNER JACKET Having no other campaign issue, Mr. Wintergreen hits on Love. An Atlantic City beauty contest is staged, the winner to become Miss White House and the President's wife—if he is elected. As Lyricist Gershwin puts it:

> *If a girl is sexy,*
> *She may be Mrs. Prexy.*

"A NIGHT WITH BARRIE" is really a night with Laurette Taylor, who is currently appearing in two Barrie plays, *Alice Sit-by-the-Fire* and *The Old Lady Shows Her Medals.*

Actress Taylor is very definitely qualified for Barrie work. Her heavy eyelids, fluttering hands and a manner of speaking as though she were slightly awed by the possibility of vocal communication, create an atmosphere of wistfulness and unreality.

Laurette Taylor. For Barrie she is wistful, unreal, perfect. Page 143.

Nazimova. In "The Good Earth," she commands respect, dies with dignity.

"EARL CARROLL'S VANITIES"–Producer Carroll's tenth dur- OCT. 10
bar is not a perpetual triumph, but it reaches zeniths of one
sort and another. At one point the chorus parades around a
dark stage with long glass tubes of rare gases (neon, argon)
exposing them to an electro-magnetic field from time to time
so that they light up in weird pale colors ("first time on any
stage").

Mr. Carroll's shows have long held the record for border-
line humor. In Comedian Milton Berle is to be found the
acme of hysterical vulgarity. While one part of the audience
blushes and the other part guffaws, Comedian Berle proceeds
to imitate a person of uncertain gender, quip about the show
girls' fundaments, shout depraved announcements into a
loud-speaker. He seems to get a great deal of fun out of it.

"THE GOOD EARTH"–Readers of Pearl Sydenstricker Buck's OCT. 24
homely Pulitzer Prizewinning melodrama of Chinese life will
find the Theatre Guild's adaptation a brief paraphrase of the
novel. Wang Lung, the hardy farmer, as greedy for more land
as the soil is greedy for sun and rain, does not die at the conclusion as he does in the book. And it is O-Lan, with a hard
knot in her womb from brutal childbearing and brutal work,
whose death climaxes with dignity this conscientious play.

Even when its stately Oriental pace tires, Actress Alla Nazi-

George S. Kaufman. His deft hand is evident in "Dinner at Eight."

Francis Lederer in "Autumn Crocus." "Is he divine or is he divine?"

mova as O-Lan commands respectful attention. It is her play. She it is who makes Wang Lung (Claude Rains) buy his first bit of land. Although Wang grows rich and soft as she grows sick and old, it is her death which brings Wang back to the good earth of his and her forefathers.

OCT. 31   **"DINNER AT EIGHT"**–In collaboration for the first time since they wrote *The Royal Family,* Playwrights George S. Kaufman & Edna Ferber have turned out a piece in which they should take pleasure and profit, too. *Dinner at Eight* is serio-comic, and it may be inferred that Miss Ferber supplied the serio-element, Mr. Kaufman the comic. The deft Kaufman hand, however, is thoroughly evident in this excellent play's shrewd direction.

NOV. 28   **"AUTUMN CROCUS"**–Fanny saved up her money to take a little trip through the Tyrol in the autumn. She felt sure she would love the mountains. There was a photograph of them on the wall of the kindergarten in which she taught at Manchester. The moment he saw her the strapping young innkeeper knew that he and Fanny would get along together. The reason he spoke English so well was because he once was a waiter in London. He was not a good waiter. His face, "it vas not vooden enough."

Finally he met her in the high meadow just as the sunrise was dancing on the tall white peaks. That was when they fell in love. Then he confessed he was married. She confessed she was 35. So Fanny goes back to Manchester. The innkeeper does not see her off on the bus, but he sends his little daughter with a basket of autumn crocuses.

From the highly successful London production comes curly-headed Francis Lederer to act the innkeeper. He is a Czech. As she left the *première,* Cinemactress Constance Bennett was heard to remark: "Is he divine, is he divine or is he *divine*?"

"TAKE A CHANCE" reverts to the pre-Depression type of mu- DEC. 12 sicomedy, makes no pretense of smartness but loses no entertainment value in a torrent of gags, girls and blues. Cropping out here & there in the proceedings is curvesome, loud-shouting Ethel Merman.

Funniest situation: Cow-eyed Jack Haley & hawk-nosed Sid Silvers finding themselves recuperating from a pair of dreadful hangovers in the same bed. Most amusing lyric, sung by Miss Merman:

> *Eadie was a lady*
> *Though her life was shady.*
> *Eadie had class.*
> *With a cap-i-tul K.*

"LUCRECE"–There never was a play like this one on Broad- DEC. 26 way. But one thing is certain. No one will soon forget Katharine Cornell's *Lucrece.*

The production, a magnificent theatrical achievement, is the product of seven fertile minds and four cultures. André Obey wrote the piece, helping himself to a liberal portion of the Shakespearean poem. Actress Cornell and her husband, Producer Guthrie McClintic, were sent a script following its London appearance. They telegraphed Thornton Niven Wilder asking him to re-English the piece. Composer Deems Taylor said it needed music and he would do it. Robert Edmund Jones went to work dressing and setting *Lucrece.*

A considerable portion of the part of Lucrece (Actress Cornell) is played in pantomime. Result is that all triviality is stripped away from Actress Cornell's part, leaving her to speak for herself only the big dramatic scenes.

Walter Hampden is unquestionably Dean of the U.S. Stage. No such pat kudos indicates the identity of his consort. Who is the U.S. Stage's queen? There are many actresses now playing: Ethel Barrymore, Jane Cowl, Grace George and Alice Brady, Lynn Fontanne, Eva Le Gallienne, Pauline Lord, Alla Nazimova, Helen Hayes, Blanche Yurka, Lenore Ulric. Do any of these fill the stature of queenhood? For many thousands of U.S. playgoers, only one actress does—Katharine Cornell.

MILESTONES

MARRIAGE ANNULLED: Preston Sturges, playwright *(Strictly Dishonorable);* and Eleanor Post Hutton, granddaughter of the late Cereal Tycoon Charles William Post; in Manhattan. The 1930 marriage was declared invalid by Referee John M. Tierney because Mr. Sturges' first wife had gotten a Mexican divorce which "isn't worth a last year's bird nest."

DIED: Frankie McErlane, Chicago gangster, reputed inventor of the "one way ride"; of pneumonia; in Beardstown, Ill. He was officially suspected of the murders of his common law wife Marion Miller, her two pet dogs, and of John ("Dingbat") O'Berta, Sam Malaga, Spot Butcher, George Meighan, William Dickman, James Quigley, Thaddeus Fancher, Frank Cochrane. Famed was his duel with gunmen in a hospital while he lay with his leg in a cast. Called the most vicious killer in Chicago's underworld, he had gone "gun crazy," began returning the fire of imaginary killers on empty streets.

MISCELLANY

OBSERVER: In Coney Island, N.Y., Edward Koren, 23, sat down and wrote until asphyxiated by gas. "I am going to another world and I am afraid to live in this one. Good by. The blood is beginning to pound on my temples. It does not hurt. It is getting warm. I can feel my heart working fast, fast, fast. My head is in trouble now. I am getting a little bit dizzy now. The gas does not smell unpleasantly. It won't be long now. I want to be buried in these clothes. I am going, going, going. Ha! ha!..." The note ended in an undecipherable scrawl.

FABLES: Cartoonist Robert L. Ripley's national "Believe It or Not" contest was won by Brooklyn's Clinton W. Blume with a proved story of losing an initialed scrubbing brush in 1918 near the coast of France, finding it a year later in the surf at Manhattan Beach where he was a lifeguard.

Second place went to E. L. Blystone of Ardara, Pa. who had written 2,871 letters on a grain of rice, a record.

Other provers of the fabulous: Rev. Mark L. Voyles of Little Rock, Ark. who can give the chapter and verse number of any scriptural quotation read to him and recite the preceding and succeeding verses; W. W. Pitman of Wharton, Tex. who disarmed a man by shooting a bullet into one of the chambers of his gun.

MUSIC

MILLS BROTHERS: In Manhattan, a few months ago, four FEB. 22
brothers were hanging around Harlem jobless. Last week, the
four Mills Brothers, their engagement at Manhattan's Palace
Theatre extended for a third time, rolled about town in their
automobile driven by a liveried chauffeur.

Most people know about the Mills Brothers now because
they perform over the radio twice a week. They sing in trick
quartet fashion and when it pleases them they can simulate
perfectly a tuba, a trumpet and a pair of saxophones.

Piqua, Ohio, knew about the Mills boys when they were
ragamuffins drumming up trade for their father's barbershop.
They had no money to buy instruments so they learned to ape
them. John, the oldest, saved enough money tending flow-
ers to buy a guitar—a $6.25 instrument from a mail-order
house. People find it hard to believe, but that same guitar is
the only real instrument the Mills boys use.

FIDDLER GROWING UP: Yehudi Menuhin is now 15. Already
this season his recitals have shown that, unlike many violin
prodigies (Menuhin was a concert sensation at the age of 11),
his genius advances. So far nothing has seemed to spoil the
boy or make his approach to music commonplace. He hates
nothing worse than being called a prodigy, says: "It's not
a question of how young I am." Menuhin demanded long
pants this season, had them made by the tailor to the Italian
Crown Prince. He demanded an automobile license, too, got
it in California by taking a test on San Francisco's busy Market Street. That automobile license is his most treasured possession. It is the only thing he keeps in his pocket when he
gives a recital. After a recital, Menuhin still asks for a straw-
berry ice-cream soda.

RASCAL: Louis Armstrong, maestro of jazz, would be a good JUNE 13
subject for one of his own songs—a rascal raised in a waifs'

The Mills Brothers (Herbert, Don, John and Harry). For simulating a tuba, a trumpet and saxophones, they now ride around with a chauffeur.

home, whose first real job was playing on a Mississippi steamboat. He always bounces out of the wings, a square, bulletheaded man. He brandishes his trumpet. He gives a roguish grin. His eyes roll around in his head like white, three-penny marbles.

"Ladies & Gentlemen, this is the Reverend Satchelmouth Armstrong." His natural voice is almost whisper-small. "Chinatown, My Chinatown. . . ." He rarely has more than a rough idea of the words. "All right, boys, I'll take the next five bars." He throws back his head, raises his trumpet, bleats noisily but marvelously. He has struck 200 high C's in succession, ended on high F. He slides all around a tune as easily as if he were doing it on a saxophone. He triple-tongues it in a way that has earned him the reputation of being one of the world's greatest trumpeters.

The musicians behind Louis Armstrong are carrying the tune, when it can be detected behind his raspy, comical singing, his fancy trumpeting. Their rhythm is flawless, thanks to their leader who realizes perfectly the need for tireless rehearsing. Louis Armstrong is one of the few orchestra leaders whom radio has not overpopularized. Radio, as a matter of fact, is a little wary of his improvisations. Several times he has been switched quickly off the air for getting profane or slipping in sly remarks about his friends' extra-marital escapades.

TUNE DETECTIVE: Radio has figured largely among the ac- AUG. 22 tivities of Dr. Sigmund Spaeth, jack-of-all-trades among U.S. musicians. Since last November Dr. Spaeth has been broadcasting as the "Tune Detective" in a 15-min. program. Last week he added a new one, the "Song Sleuth."

The Tune Detective is expert in tracing down the ancestry of current songs. Some come piecemeal from the classics, like "I'm Always Chasing Rainbows," which is found in Chopin's *Fantasie Impromptu.* Others are scrambled together like "Yes, We Have No Bananas," which contains bits from Handel's Hallelujah Chorus, "My Bonnie," "I Dreamt I Dwelt in Marble Halls," "Aunt Dinah's Quilting Party" and "An Old-Fashioned Garden."

GUEST: Ten years ago a pale young Hungarian violinist play- DEC. 19 ing in the orchestra at Manhattan's Capitol cinemansion applied for the job of assistant concert-master with the New York Philharmonic, was refused. The refusal proved fortunate for young Eugene (English for Jenö) Ormandy. Not long afterwards the sudden illness of the Capitol conductor gave Ormandy a chance to show that he could conduct. Eugene Ormandy was leading a radio orchestra when he was called upon last year to pinch-hit for Conductor Arturo Toscanini, whose glass arm kept him from leading the Philadelphia Orchestra. He did so well that the Minneapolis Symphony engaged him as a substitute, kept him for its permanent conductor.

Last week instead of Conductor Leopold Stokowski, Eugene Ormandy took the Philadelphia Orchestra to Manhattan. His firm, clear beat, his authority over the orchestra, his unmannered way of letting the music speak for itself, suggested to some people the simple, hard-working conductor that Stokowski used to be before he let his pale hair grow.

AERONAUTICS

FEB. 8 **AKRON'S WORTH:** If the *U.S.S. Akron* should some day wrench apart, vanish in a sea storm, two men—E. C. McDonald, a construction supervisor and W. B. Underwood, mechanic—were in a position last week to shout to the country: "I told you so!" They had charged that the great dirigible was structurally deficient. The House Naval Affairs Committee was investigating. If any disaster ever befell the *Akron,* the public, right or wrong, would hark back distrustfully to last week's hearings.

FEB. 29 **"AKRON'S LUCK":** Six members of a Congressional committee investigating charges of faulty construction in the *U.S.S. Akron* were about to board her for an inspection flight at Lakehurst when a terrific gust of wind whipped her tail free of the ground crew, bounced it against the ground. After a five-minute tussle the *Akron* was made fast again. The lower stabilizing fin, containing the after-control car, was smashed; a large expanse of fabric torn from the belly.

MAY 2 **DIRIGIBLE SCENE:** "When I see girders snap off like pretzels, I know something is wrong," carped a Congressman shortly after witnessing the mishap which befell the *U.S.S. Akron* last February and laid her up for nearly two months for repairs. But nothing was wrong. Last week Lakehurst mechanics were stitching the last bit of fabric to the *Akron*'s torn skin, finished tinkering her broken fin. When Lieut. Commander Rosendahl barks "Up ship!" as he sails to join the Fleet in the Pacific next week, his ship will rise as sound and airworthy as ever.

New, steeper-pitched propellers have been mounted, air screws which will take a bigger bite of air, increase the *Akron*'s speed to world's fastest. But more notable is the installation of apparatus in the ship's belly to permit the nesting of five tiny fighting planes in a marsupial hangar, located amidships within the outer envelope. Through a T-shaped trapdoor the planes, hooked to a trapeze, can be discharged or hoisted in. For the past year the Navy has been training special crack pilots to negotiate the ticklish landing, which consists of threading a large hook atop the plane to the trapeze bar on the mother ship.

THREE MEN ON A ROPE: In a huge circle about the mooring MAY 23 mast at Camp Kearney, near San Diego, Calif., ten thousand people assembled one morning last week to watch the *U.S.S. Akron* dock after a turbulent transcontinental passage. Poking through a gradually lifting fog, the great ship dipped slowly three times, three times was whisked up by rising strata of warm air before the ground crews could grab the spider lines from rings on two dangling cables. The fourth time the crowd cheered as the crew caught hold, started to tug the *Akron*'s tossing silver nose toward the stub mast.

With a loud crack the ring on the starboard cable broke. The *Akron* rolled to port like a porpoise. As the ship lurched, 100 sailors in the port ground crew dragged with all their might. Some even climbed up the grab lines the better to hold down the bouncing ship. A sudden blast of air drove the ship up, jerked the crew into the air. Most of them dropped off, sprawled in a heap on the ground. Soaring rapidly the *Akron* jerked three sailors so high that they dared not let go. On the ground women screamed, men wept, officers shouted. One sailor shot down like a bag of sand, 150 ft. to his death. Two figures still clung to the end of the swinging ropes. One of these soon let go. His body bounced on the hard-packed earth in a little puff of dust.

The crowd watched the *Akron* rise to 2,000 ft. with the one man still dangling beneath her. A yell went up as the lump at the end of the cable showed life. Sailor Charles ("Bud") Cowart had straddled a toggle at the end of the cable, was taking two bowline hitches about his waist. Several times Lieut. Commander Charles E. Rosendahl maneuvered the tossing ship toward earth, but fearing that Sailor Cowart would be bashed to death, soared again. Firemen stretched nets to try to catch him if he fell.

After two hours the lump at the end of the *Akron*'s cable began to rise slowly toward a port in the forward part of the

"Akron" skipper Rosendahl greets rescued sailor "Bud" Cowart. After two hours at the end of a rope, Cowart comments: "Gimme something to eat."

floating ship. As the cable shortened Sailor Cowart's oscillations grew more violent. When he disappeared into the port, the crowd murmured with relief but no one cheered. Aboard the ship Sailor Cowart spurned spirits of ammonia. Said he: "Gimme something to eat." [In April 1933, the *Akron* crashed into the Atlantic during a severe storm. The airship and 73 of her crew were lost.]

AMELIA EARHART: One day four years ago Publisher George Palmer Putnam confided in his friend Capt. Hilton R. Railey that there was a chance for the right young lady to fly the Atlantic. Said Capt. Railey: "You wait," and hastened to Boston. When he returned Publisher Putnam's eyes popped with pleased astonishment.

With the Captain was a lanky young woman of cultured mien. Her tousled blonde mop, high cheekbones and wide, tight mouth made her look remarkably like Charles Augustus Lindbergh, particularly when her hat was off. Her name was Amelia Earhart. She was working in a Boston settlement house but she had learned in California how to fly. She got the job.

Last week Publisher Putnam was fidgeting and fretting in a hotel room. Somewhere out over the Atlantic was Miss Earhart, alone in a red & gold Lockheed. In the four years since her first flight Putnam had backed her flying and nurtured her fame. Two years ago he married her. Now she was flying toward Paris on the fifth anniversary of Lindbergh's flight.

Word came that she had landed safely near Londonderry, Ireland, somewhat north of her course. Exulted Publisher Putnam: "Whoops, my Dear!"

By her courageous flight Miss Earhart not only became the first woman to fly solo across the Atlantic but also set a speed record of 14 hr. 56 min. Advance reports of good weather she found "100% wrong." Ice on the wings forced her down into rain, fog and gusty squalls, perilously close to the water. Her altimeter failed. A broken exhaust ring spurted flame. Gasoline from a leaky gauge dripped down her neck. But still she flew low because "I'd rather drown than burn up." Pushed north by beam winds she met the shore of Northern Ireland, set her ship down on a farm field.

SENTIMENTAL JOURNEY: To frail, spindly, gentle Auguste AUG. 29 Piccard, the stratosphere is not merely a remote layer of the atmosphere. It is an environment, a kingdom, a marvelous sea in which to swim; an Olympus from which to survey Earth's glories.

Last week for the second time Professor Piccard penetrated the stratosphere in a balloon. His purpose, as last year, was to study cosmic rays. But his spirit was that of a voyager revisiting a world which only he had explored.

Within the aluminum globule Professor Piccard was almost grudging about the occasional attention he must give to his instruments. He wanted to be at one of the nine window ports, watching the earth drop away, watching the heavens embrace him. He found time to jot eloquent notes of what he saw. Excerpts:

"*5:43 a.m.* We have soared to a height of 5,248 ft. Lucerne stretches magically beneath us, remote and beautiful in the radiance of this perfect day. We are perspiring profusely.

"*6:15 a.m.* The view is grandiose. It is almost beyond our conception. Below us are the Eastern Alps which I, as a young mountaineer, climbed 15 years ago. Never, then, did I dream of this.

"11:50 a.m. We have only 20 sacks of ballast left. We decide the time has come to descend. We shall make our landing in Italy.

"12:12 p.m. We have attained an altitude of 54,120 ft. All human records broken! It is very cold—5° below zero. We are suffering intensely."

For the next four hours the balloon drifted slowly downward. An Italian pilot circled his seaplane around & around the balloon. Professor Piccard thrust open a port, joyfully waved his handkerchief. For a moment it looked as if the balloon would land in the water but it cleared the southern shore. Then it plunked down into a field. Professor Piccard and his assistant stepped out. Dizzied by the sudden change from freezing to blistering temperature, they staggered. Then they sat down, opened a can of peaches, munched bananas proffered by villagers.

OCT. 10 **BALLOON RACE:** Swaying foolishly in a strong southeast wind, 16 swollen gas bags floated up from Basle, Switzerland, one day last week. It was the 21st James Gordon Bennett International Balloon Race. Last to come to earth was the U.S. Navy's entry, piloted by Lieuts. Thomas G. W. Settle and Wilfred Bushnell, winners of last year's U.S. meet. After 40 hr. in the air they were forced down with a defective valve near the Polish-Latvian frontier—about 921 mi. from Basle. Near Warsaw the Navy bag drifted so low that laborers seized a drag rope, were hauling the ship down until angry Pilot Settle threw a sand bag at their heads. Contrary to experience in nearly all balloon races held in the U.S., no balloons were shot at by the peasantry.

DEC. 19 **EMPTY SEATS:** Most transport planes on U.S. airlines accommodate twelve passengers. In the past year such planes flew each trip with an average of seven seats empty, according to figures published last week by the Department of Commerce.

ART

IOWA DETAIL: Like most hardworking people, Iowans like de- SEPT. 5
tail. Rich in sharp, exact detail was Phil Stong's novel, *State
Fair,* laid in Des Moines. But Phil Stong omitted one detail
of the Iowa State Fair—the art contest for a sweepstakes prize.
Last week as the 1932 Fair began, this year's sweepstakes
was won again, as it has been every year since 1929, by Paint-
er Grant Wood of Cedar Rapids, Iowa, an even more pas-
sionate detail-monger than Author Stong.

Grant Wood, 40, was born at Anamosa, Iowa. His Iowa
landscapes look like photographs of landscapes modelled out
of hard candy. The man-made detail—houses, pumps, fence-

*Grant Wood's "American Gothic." Says a noted author: "Sad and fanatical
faces," reflecting "both what is right and what is wrong with America."*

palings—are mathematically meticulous. The natural detail is stylized, as in a treetop indicated by a score of leaf-shapes that look as though turned out by a cookie-mold. His people have pioneer faces, gimlet eyes, snapping turtle-mouths, long vertical furrows down their faces.

Iowans like Grant Wood's hard, varnished paintings of themselves and conscientiously bought his early pictures. Trained at the Art Institute of Chicago and the Paris Julian Academie, Grant Wood worked for 15 years under the influence of various French schools. Several years ago, returning from Munich to Cedar Rapids, remembering German primitives, he suddenly saw Iowa and Iowans as hard, rich primitives. At once his painting crystallized.

Of his famed *American Gothic,* portraits of a Midwestern preacher-farmer and his daughter, Christopher Morley wrote: "In those sad and fanatical faces may be read much, both of what is Right and what is Wrong with America." Most Iowans saw on the canvas only the hard, exact details of Iowa. They were flattered that Iowa's boy chose to paint Iowa.

WRIGHT APPRENTICES: Whenever Architect Frank Lloyd Wright has a good idea, he does something about it. The best idea he ever had was Frank Lloyd Wright. He has been doing things about that for 63 years. His latest idea is to found a practical architect's school to educate architects in Frank Lloyd Wright's image. The school would be across the valley from "Taliesin," his studio-estate in the dairy country near Spring Green, Wis. He would be the chief faculty member, teaching pupils his basic architectural law: that the architect must integrate his building with its surroundings (function, terrain, climate), make plain its structural elements and if possible develop them as ornamentation. He would teach them the feel of materials by having them blast stone, hew timber, dig soil, work in a machine shop. They would study, sweat, play and brood in unison. They would be called, not "students" as in other colleges, but by the fine old medieval guild word, "apprentice."

The permanently startled look on Architect Wright's face is rightly come by. His *Autobiography* was a naïve exhibition of martyrdom, rage, scarifying tragedy and adolescent yammering. One time he was stabbed eleven times in the back. Soon afterward he was married, had six children, left them and moved in with another man's wife and two children, until August 1914 when a disapproving Negro butler killed the woman and children and four neighbors and burned down the house.

In his working hours Wright had developed steel & glass city buildings, windows covering two sides of a corner, houses made as nearly as possible of one material, the cantilever foundation principle (Tokyo's Imperial Hotel, floated on a mud base to rock with earthquakes), and the unit cement block system of construction chiefly used in California. His great reputation is that of a revolutionist, based on his long campaign against traditional architecture and architects. Once considered in Europe the greatest U.S. architect, he was conspicuously omitted last year from the staff of architects for Chicago's Century of Progress Exposition for 1933.

MILESTONES

BORN: To Col. & Mrs. Charles Augustus Lindbergh; a son; at the home of Mrs. Lindbergh's mother, Mrs. Dwight Morrow, in Englewood, N.J., where two years and two months ago her first baby, Charles Augustus Jr. was born and whither she retired after his death this year by kidnapping.

SUED FOR DIVORCE: By Jane Thurston Harris, 21, daughter of Conjurer Howard Thurston; Harry Harris, 29, Pittsburgh theatre scion; in Pittsburgh. Charges: because she refused his backgammon advice, he hurled backgammon board, glasses and a ginger ale bottle, tore off her clothes before guests. Not mentioned: the 1931 fight in a Detroit hotel between Defendant Harris & Father-in-law Thurston, leaving Harris nearly blinded by a volley from Thurston's tear gas fountain pen.

DIED: Margaret Tobin Brown ("Unsinkable Mrs. Brown"), 65, relict of Denver's famed Miner James Brown, heroine of the S.S. *Titanic* disaster; of apoplexy; in Manhattan. After meeting "Leadville John" Brown at the bottom of a mine shaft, marrying him in three weeks, she tried to spend his $10,000,000 fortune in philanthropy, bizarre clothes and crashing Newport and European society. In a *Titanic* lifeboat she took her turn at the oars before rescue.

MISCELLANY

BEATER: In Oregon, one Charles Morse was sentenced to twelve and a half days for beating his wife, 60 days for beating his horses.

FAINTER: In Chicago, one James Webb earned a good living by fainting on street cars, elevated trains, platforms, sidewalks, etc., until kind-hearted bystanders took up collections for him. "I made an average of twelve faints a day," James Webb told Judge John Sbarbaro. Judge Sbarbaro fined him $200. James Webb fainted.

$$\boxed{\textbf{SCIENCE}}$$

Professor Albert Einstein had been making scientific news ever since 1905 when, while working in the patent office in Bern, Switzerland, he propounded his revolutionary theory of relativity. As a world-renowned figure, he made his first visit to the U.S. in 1921 to raise money for Palestine. He returned in 1931 and again in early 1932 to serve as a visiting professor at the California Institute of Technology in Pasadena. Though only a few Americans understood the intricacies of his work, the great German scientist's name was a household word, and he was treated as a celebrity wherever he went.

JAN. 11 **VISITOR:** All the way from Germany by steamer through the Panama Canal, Professor Albert Einstein reached Pasadena last week. He declined to cross the U.S. by rail for fear of raucous rabble, pesky newshawks. Frau Einstein was with him to worry over his comforts. He will study at prim, red-roofed California Institute of Technology and the Mount Wilson Observatory for the next two months.

FEB. 1 **MILLIKAN'S RAYS:** Last week while 100 guests (including Professor Albert Einstein) listened, Dr. Millikan presented latest evidence for his theory of where cosmic rays come from.

There is a very powerful, very penetrating ray which reaches earth from space. Dr. Millikan recognized this ray ten years ago and called it the cosmic ray. He found that it penetrated 50 ft. of lead, 200 ft. of water. Last year Professor Auguste Piccard, cruising into the stratosphere ten miles above earth, found evidence of the same ray. Also last year Professor Arthur Holly Compton found traces of it atop the Rocky Mountains and the Alps.

Size of the rays is nearly infinitesimal. But the energy with which they are propelled is tremendous. Dr. Carl Anderson of Caltech estimates, by observing how cosmic rays shattered certain atoms in his laboratory, that cosmic rays strike earth with 50,000,000 or more volts of power. The effect is analogous to a quill being driven through a plank by a tornado. Dr. Anderson's 50,000,000-volt rays prove him right, reasoned Dr. Millikan last week. He figures that at the interstellar birth of a helium atom 70,000,000 volts would be released; for oxygen 116,000,000 volts; for silicon 216,000,000 volts; for iron 450,000,000. Those are, he is convinced, the only elements floating between the stars in sufficient quantities to produce radiation effective on earth. Radiations from helium, oxygen and silicon do not reach the earth because the atmosphere damps them. It is iron's radiation which Dr. Millikan believes his adherents and opponents have noticed. Iron's 450,000,000 volts would show on earth at about Dr. Anderson's findings.

EINSTEIN FAREWELL: Albert Einstein ended two studious MARCH 14 months at California Institute of Technology last week. At San Pedro, Los Angeles' harbor, he boarded the Hamburg-American *San Francisco* with Mrs. Einstein, put his pipe and violin in his stateroom with the luggage, and sought out the dining salon for "a German meal cooked as only Germans know how to cook it."

For farewell he gave—in good English—an interview to the Press. Excerpts:

"It is scarcely possible to think that life on other planets does not exist.

"There is some danger of civilization breaking down, but I am too optimistic to believe disintegration will occur.

"American youth has the good fortune not to have its outlook troubled by outworn traditions, or by any imposed development which they resist.

"Taken as a whole the machine age has not been detrimental to the world; but just at the present moment it appears so. The problems of the moment may lead to their solutions.

"Freedom from the necessity of servants due to mechanical household aids is the best feature of American life."

Reporter—"Aren't you finding it easier to talk to reporters?"

Dr. Einstein—"There is a German proverb which says that any one can get used to being hanged."

Another Reporter—"Should Prohibition be modified?"
Dr. Einstein—"That's your trouble, not mine."

JULY 18 **MORE ON COSMIC RAYS:** Last week in Paris Dr. Robert An-
drews Millikan reiterated in a paper read before the International Electrical Congress his belief that cosmic rays are the
"birth cries" of atoms newly born in the cold spaces between
the stars. His paper was written before he heard of a report
published last week in the *Physical Review* by his fellow Nobel
Prizewinner, Dr. Arthur Holly Compton, now in Peru.

What is known is that cosmic rays exist. What is not known
is where they come from and why. They may be photons, the
ultimate unit of light radiations which could not be deflected
by Earth's magnetic field. Or cosmic rays may be electrons,
electrically charged matter which *would* be deflected by
Earth's magnetic field. Since Dr. Millikan's researches showed
that cosmic rays hit the Earth with the same force at different
latitudes, he decided they could not be electrons, must be
photons.

In March Dr. Compton, declining a chance to be president
of Princeton University, set out with a 250-lb. machine to
watch cosmic rays on Pacific mountaintops in Panama, Peru,
New Zealand, Hawaii, Alaska. His preliminary report last
week flatly contradicted Dr. Millikan's findings. Dr. Compton
found "definite differences in the intensity of the cosmic rays
at different latitudes, with a minimum at or near the Equator
and increasing intensity toward the North and South Poles."
These differences made him suspect that cosmic rays were
streams of electrons, particles of electrically charged matter.

SEPT. 5 **DR. EINSTEIN TO NEW JERSEY:** "Nice people, those Americans," commented Dr. Albert Einstein when he landed in
Rotterdam last spring after two months at California Institute of Technology. Last week he let it be known that he was
going to spend five months each year with those "nice people," probably as long as he lives.

He will lecture on theoretical physics at the $5,000,000 In-
stitute for Advanced Study, which Dr. Abraham Flexner is
creating in New Jersey. Money providers were Mrs. Felix Fuld
and her brother, Louis Bamberger, retired owner of Newark's
great Bamberger Store which he sold to Manhattan's Macy's.

COSMIC COMPETITION: Polite and friendly but historic is the SEPT. 12 great dispute between the two foremost U.S. physicists as to what the cosmic rays are made of. Last week, this great dispute progressed a step further.

Dr. Arthur Holly Compton, speeding into the far north after a summer of climbing mountains ibex-wise, reached a point on Hudson Bay only 350 mi. from the North Magnetic Pole in time to take cosmic ray readings during the solar eclipse. His mountain-top observations in many latitudes had led him to suspect that cosmic rays are not pulsations from outer space, but streams of electrons probably originating in Earth's atmosphere. His readings last week on Hudson Bay, he telegraphed Chicago, again confirmed his view.

Dr. Millikan was just leaving Pasadena for Canada when he heard about his friendly rival's telegram. From Winnipeg, he will fly with an electroscope to as close to the North Magnetic Pole as Royal Canadian Air Corps planes can carry him. There, he will make his own cosmic ray readings, then soar eagle-wise southwards to Texas, getting into U.S. Army planes after he crosses the border, making electroscopic observations all along the way.

Dr. Millikan's conception of cosmic rays suits his optimistic temperament. He believes the rays are evidence of the Universe's continual physical regeneration. The Compton view, at first inspection, leaves uncontroverted the evidence that the Universe is blazing to chaos. Interpretations, twinkled Dr. Millikan last week, "will come up later." [Later research indicated that Compton's theory, not Millikan's, was correct.]

LOW BALL: Analogs of Professor Auguste Piccard's flights OCT. 3 toward the stratosphere above Switzerland are Dr. William Beebe's dives toward the bottom of the sea off Bermuda. Dr. Beebe, field agent for the New York Zoological Society, uses a bathysphere, a $4\frac{3}{4}$ ft. quartz-windowed steel ball with walls $1\frac{1}{2}$ in. thick. Its purpose is to withstand the pressure of deep sea water, whereas Professor Piccard's 7-ft. aluminum gondola was constructed to prevent its explosion in rarefied air.

Fortnight ago Dr. Beebe lowered his bathysphere empty to 3,000 ft. at the end of a stout cable. When he hauled it back to the deck of his tug *Freedom*, the bathysphere was full of water under such intense air pressure that it blew the lid's

Dr. Holly Compton climbs mountains ibex-wise to measure cosmic rays.

William Beebe in his bathysphere. At 2,200 ft.: "Rolling like the dickens."

bolt across the deck after it was loosened. There was a tiny leak in a port gasket. Any surface creature inside would have been crushed to jelly.

Dr. Beebe made sure that the bathysphere was water-tight when he and Otis Barton, builder of the diving ball, took a deep ride last week. Dr. Beebe had descended 1,426 ft. two years ago, a record. Last week he broke this record.

An intelligent publicist, he had rigged a telephone line between the bathysphere and the tug *Freedom* to provide the world with a description of his descent:

1,500 ft.—"Black as Hades."

1,550 ft.—"There is plenty of light down here now."

1,650 ft.—"It is absolutely black. Now there are fish about two or three feet away. I can make out their forms from their own light. It is the most amazing thing now, the amount of light down here."

An assistant handling the telephone aboard the *Freedom*, asked: "Can you give the light a color?"

Dr. Beebe, shouting—"It varies from pale blue to pale green. But all on the very pale side. No deep tone. It must be the normal luminescence of the creatures."

2,200 ft.—"Rolling like the dickens."

The water pressure on the bathysphere was about 4,800 tons; the temperature 50° F. within. Dr. Beebe ordered the sphere raised to the *Freedom*'s deck, popped out with: "The scientific results are most satisfactory."

"FOR LIFE": "What the world needs is more light to illumi- OCT. 24 nate what is obscure, more light to enable us to reorganize our intellectual and social and political lives. No one is wise enough to tell the source from which illumination will come."

Thus spoke Dr. Abraham Flexner last week making formal announcement that Dr. Albert Einstein had accepted appointment with the Institute for Advanced Study. Dr. Einstein will be professor of mathematical & theoretical physics "for life." He will be provided a home at Princeton, will work (beginning next autumn) only from Oct. 1 to April 15 for the rest of his active life; will teach only what, when, if and as he pleases; will spend his summers sailing his little boat on Berlin's Wannsee. Exclaimed Dr. Einstein when all this scholastic luxury became certain: "This is Heaven!"

When definite news of the new light at Princeton reached Pasadena, hearts burned among the staff of California Institute of Technology. Brilliant scientists frequent Caltech for work & consultation, among them Albert Einstein. Last week Caltech made sure, and announced that Dr. Einstein would again spend several weeks there, beginning some time in December. His visit is to factualize, by more measurements of nebulae speeds, his present theory that the Universe has been expanding—as he told a Berlin audience last week—for ten billion years, "quite a tidy bit of time." [When Einstein and his wife returned to Europe in 1933, Hitler was already in power, and they went to Belgium instead of to their home in Berlin. Later that year they returned to the U.S. where Einstein took up his post at the Institute of Advanced Study and became a permanent resident of Princeton, N.J. He became a U.S. citizen in 1940, died in 1955.]

RELIGION

APRIL 4 **ZION, TEN YEARS AFTER:** U.S. Jewry was urged last week, as it is annually, to give its mite to rebuild the Jewish National Home in Palestine. Quota this year is $2,500,000, of which one million is to be raised in New York City.

Ten years ago the Lodge-Fish resolution, favoring the Jewish National Home, was introduced in Congress. It was approved by President Harding, became a public resolution. No one could possibly object to the U.S. Government giving official notice to the Zionist program. No one, either, could anticipate much practical result from it. But an anniversary is a good time for a check-up. What are the accomplishments of a decade in Palestine?

World Jewry has sent $220,000,000 there since 1921. Of this the U.S. gave $100,000,000. *Eretz Israel* ("Land of Israel") now has a great Palestine Electric Corp. whose stations in Tel Aviv, Haifa, Tiberias and in the Jordan valley supply all Palestine (except Jerusalem) with power. The clean, white, all-Jewish city of Tel Aviv ("Hill of Spring") more than doubled its population (46,000). In Palestine are now new hotels and resorts for tourists. Palestine's Jewish population has increased from 60,000 to 175,000. There are 328 Jewish schools, 135 agricultural settlements of which 70 are under the supervision of the Jewish Agency. Hadassah (female Zionist organization) looks after 50 hospitals, clinics and dispensaries, which exist for Arabs and Christians as well as Jews. Palestine has its own Hebrew university, founded in 1925.

The Jewish population of Palestine runs its own religious affairs. But it is a minority (16.9%) without political power, save for the advisory powers conferred on the Jewish Agency by the mandate allotted to Great Britain ten years ago.

JUNE 6 **HEAVEN IN SAYVILLE:** One day twelve years ago there arrived in Sayville, L.I., a bald-headed, wizened little Negro with God on his mind. He opened a free employment agency, found many a job for black men and white. Two years later he bought a small frame house at No. 72 Macon St., took in the homeless, fed them, clothed them, black & white. His disciples increased, his house grew, followers came on foot, in limousines, by the busload. Sayville's Board of Supervisors passed an ordinance forbidding parking for more than 30 minutes in Macon Street. Rev. Major J. Divine, the bald little Negro, replied by providing free parking space on all the land surrounding the three big houses into which had spread his thriving cult of "Heaven."

By last winter Heaven had grown too noisy for Sayville. Residents began to move from Macon Street. The village police force grew weary directing traffic. Nevertheless, Preacher Divine continued to feed & clothe a hundred-odd people, to serve six meals a day, each meal enormous. On his wall hung a sign: "PEACE—CIGARS, CIGARETTES AND INTOXICATING LIQUORS NOT ALLOWED—IT'S WONDERFUL."

Sayvillians, estimating that it cost over $30,000 a year to run the Divine establishment, pointed out that the Father had no visible means of support. Suspected as the givers were some of the handsome, well-dressed white "angels" who mixed with the black in Heaven, shrieking of Peace.

Last week, Sayville's patience exhausted, Rev. Major J. Divine was on trial before Supreme Court Justice Lewis J. Smith in Mineola. Said one Believer: "I believe Heaven sends him his money direct." Testified Eva Connelly, non-believer: "When I telephoned him to ask him to stop the noise he said: 'Do you know who you're talking to? This is God Himself.'"

Charged Justice Smith: "There may be those who believe this defendant is God. There are undoubtedly many who believe he is not God. One cannot use religion as a cloak for the commission of a crime." Twelve Mineola jurors declared Sayville's Divine to be a nuisance. [Major Divine, who later became known as Father Divine, was sentenced to a year in prison and a $500 fine; the conviction was then appealed and reversed.]

WASHINGTON'S BAPTISM: Though biographies of George SEPT. 5 Washington have been written in abundance, many details of his life have not been widely known until this year, bicentenary of his birthday. More or less newsworthy have been the revelations that he did not smoke; ordered his wife's dresses; was a shrewd landowner who left an estate of $1,000,000. A George Washington story known to few persons remained to be made public last week as to how George Washington was baptized.

When he was almost two months old, Washington was sprinkled in the "orthodox Episcopal manner." At 33 he took oath to conform to the doctrine of the Church of England "as by law established." Throughout his life he was seen regularly in church though he did not often kneel in prayer or partake of communion. But through his time swept a hot blast of evangelism, chiefly in the Methodist and Baptist faiths. General Washington one day went to Rev. John Gano, chaplain in the Continental Army, and exclaimed: "I have been investigating the Scripture, and I believe immersion to be baptism taught in the Word of God, and I demand it at your hands. I do not wish any parade made or the army called out, but simply a quiet demonstration of the ordinance." In the presence of 42 witnesses George Washington was immersed in the Potomac; but he did not give "personal testimony" which would have made him a member of the Baptist Church.

SEPT. 19 **NEW BISHOP:** "Have you the apostolic mandate?"

"We have."

"Then let it be read!"

So intoning, Eugenio Cardinal Pacelli, tall Papal Secretary of State [later Pope Pius XII], opened last week the first consecration of a U.S. bishop ever to take place in St. Peter's in Rome. In full pontificals the Cardinal sat solemnly on a faldstool before the altar. Before him, bowing low in the cope, biretta and white stole of a priest, was Monsignor Francis Joseph Spellman, 43, onetime grocer's boy and sandlot baseball player in Whitman, Mass., named last month by the Holy See to be Auxiliary Bishop of Boston.

A choir sang. As Monsignor Spellman approached, it hushed; the assistant consecrators bowed slightly. Then Monsignor Spellman was assisted up the steps to the altar, where he kissed the episcopal ring. Now vested in pontifical garments, the Bishop-elect joined the Cardinal in celebrating mass, each at his own altar. Then while the choir chanted the

Bishop Spellman. The onetime gro-
cer's boy goes from Rome to Boston.

Bishop Manning. He helps pick locks
to open up a church in Harlem.

Litany of the Saints, Bishop-elect Spellman lay prostrate on
the floor.

"Receive the Holy Ghost." The Cardinal imposed his
hands, anointed the Bishop-elect's head and hands, thrice
prayed "Whatsoever thou shalt bless, may it be blessed," and
Monsignor Francis Joseph Spellman was a bishop. [Bishop
Spellman became a cardinal in 1946. He served as Archbishop of New York for nearly 29 years, died in office in
1967 at the age of 78.]

BISHOP & LOCKSMITH: All Souls' Protestant Episcopal OCT. 31
Church, at 114th Street and St. Nicholas Avenue in Manhattan, was once all white. The southward spread of Harlem has
turned it Negro by 300 souls to 50. Much vexed were a group
of white vestrymen, led by one Manuel Jesus Roure, who
blamed it all upon the rector, a lank, thin-lipped onetime
curate of Trinity Church named Rev. Rollin Dodd. The vestry ordered Rector Dodd to cease encouraging the Negroes.
When he refused, the vestry asked him to resign, stopped his
salary. When this failed, they had the church closed "for repairs," and the locks changed. Declaring the ceiling might fall
any moment, they had scaffolding put up.

New York's Bishop William Thomas Manning, who is an
extremely formal and frigidly aristocratic little prelate, insists

upon seemliness and order in his diocese. Last week he
jumped to Rector Dodd's defense, announced he would
preach in All Souls'. When Manuel Jesus Roure threatened to
keep him out by "legal means," Bishop Manning said, "I shall
be there."

Sunday morning Bishop Manning put on his biretta, Episcopal vestments, academic hood. When he arrived at All
Souls', he found the rector, the superintendent, twelve policemen and a large crowd waiting. Bishop Manning demanded the keys. The superintendent had none. "Shall we break
in?" asked Rector Dodd. "Yes!" said the Bishop loudly and
firmly, adding that church law and civil law sanctioned him.
Rector Dodd had with him a locksmith. While Bishop Manning waited, they went through the basement, sanctuary and
nave, removing hinges, picking locks, at last smashing the
padlock on the front gates of the church. "You are all welcome," beamed the rector, and all entered. Bishop Manning
stepped through wood shavings and lumber to a footstool
beneath the scaffolding, preached firmly on the rights of the
rector to serve his neighborhood, ending, "I request, and as
Bishop I instruct, that this church shall be open for services
at such times as he shall direct." Then Bishop Manning shook
hands all around, patted the heads of children, said, "God
Bless you" to one small Negro who replied, "All right" and
ran away.

MILESTONES

BORN: To Baron Jozippie Paucci,
vaudeville midget (height 37 in.), and
Margaret Lane, diving beauty (height
5 ft. 8 in.), his estranged wife; a
daughter; in Memphis. Weight: 5 lb.
11 oz. Said Baroness Paucci: "Yes, I
love my husband. We parted because
we were jealous. Women were always
picking him up and telling him how
cute he was."

DIED: Marie Augusta Davey Fiske
(Mrs. Minnie Maddern Fiske), 66,
Grand Dame of the U.S. stage; of
heart disease; in Queens, Long Island, N.Y. A strict vegetarian, a militant antivivisectionist, she was famed
for her fanatical fight against wearing furs.

MISCELLANY

BITER: In Antioch, Ill., convicted by
a jury of having bitten the town marshal, Biter John Brogan dived into
the jury box, rapidly bit eight jurors.

HIT: In Chicago, a southbound elevated train hit Charles Mead, lofted
him over to the northbound tracks
where a northbound train lofted him
back to the southbound tracks where
another train lofted him off the elevated structure to the ground. His
worst injury: a broken leg.

MEDICINE

RADIUM DRINKS: Eben MacBurney Byers, 51, popular Pitts- APRIL 11
burgh sportsman and ironmaster, fell out of an upper berth
five years ago returning from a Yale-Harvard football game
and hurt his arm. His Pittsburgh physiotherapist, Dr. Charles
Clinton Moyar, prescribed a patented drink called "Radithor." It was distilled water containing traces of radium. The
dope eased the arm pain, braced Byers up. He enthusiastically
recommended it to friends, sent them cases of it, even gave
some to one of his horses. Last week Eben Byers died in Manhattan of radium poisoning. A close friend died last autumn
of the same cause. Other of his friends are gravely worried.

Byers' prominence made his death a great scandal. And a
cry went out to investigate "Radithor." An attorney for the
Federal Trade Commission who interviewed Byers at his
Southampton home last September, last week described the
scene: "A more gruesome experience in a more gorgeous setting would be hard to imagine. We went up to Southampton
where Byers had a magnificent home. There we discovered
him in a condition which beggars description. Though men-
tally alert, he could hardly speak. His head was swathed in
bandages. He had undergone two operations in which his
whole upper jaw, excepting two front teeth, and most of his
lower jaw had been removed. All the remaining bone tissue of
his body was slowly disintegrating, and holes were actually
forming in his skull."

The fad for radioactive waters was for a short time valid.
Investigators experimented by activating ordinary water.
Doctors thought that they had evidence that waters so treated
would cure chronic arthritis, gout, neuritis, high blood pressure. But after young New Jersey factory workers who paint-
ed watch dials with radium preparations began dying, experts
denounced the use of radium *internally*. With radium applied
externally and for short periods to destroy cancers they had
no quarrel. But imbibed radium accumulated in the bones. It

was certain death, because, before its ravages could be recognized, it had destroyed a fatal amount of bone.

APRIL 25 **LINDBERGH CENTRIFUGE:** Last week *Science* published a brief paper entitled: "A Method for Washing Corpuscles in Suspension." The paper was signed "C. A. Lindbergh, Division of Experimental Surgery, Rockefeller Institute for Medical Research." Accompanying it was a neat drawing of an improved centrifuge, minutely signed "C. A. Lindbergh 2/15/32."

For several months it has been a Rockefeller Institute secret that Dr. Alexis Carrel, famed Nobel Laureate, had enlisted Col. Charles Augustus Lindbergh's aid in his researches on tissue culture and the transplantation of organs. Although Col. Lindbergh dealt with few at the Institute, peeping typists recognized the tall, fair-haired young man.

In the Lindbergh centrifuge the reservoir for blood is a conical chamber resembling an ocarina. As the machine rotates and produces a centrifugal force up to 650 times gravity, the corpuscles settle out of the blood. Replacement fluid flows into the "ocarina" chamber, dilutes the original fluid which flows off through a vent. In a first test of 15 minutes Col. Lindbergh demonstrated that only a fraction of 1% of the original fluid remained in the "ocarina," that the remaining, washed corpuscles were uninjured and available for Dr. Carrel's study.

The kidnapping of his baby interrupted Col. Lindbergh's efforts to improve a pump which Dr. Carrel uses to drive fluids through vital organs removed from laboratory animals. But close friends of Col. Lindbergh were not surprised by his sally into invention. They realize that he studied mechanical engineering at the University of Wisconsin for a year and a half (1920-Feb. 1922); that he is an active trustee of the Wilmer Foundation (eye research) and has contact with Johns Hopkins University.

BROKEN BONES: Four thousand Yale rats had their legs broken so that Dr. Samuel Clark Harvey, professor of surgery, could learn how broken bones mend. Last week he presented a summary of his study. On a normal diet the rats' legs show some strength the sixth day after the break. Strength increases rapidly until the 15th day, during which time calcium and phosphorus salts are deposited. Then for six days the new bone loses up to 30% of its strength. After the 21st day the bone again grows stronger, healthier, until completely healed. An important observation has to do with diet while broken bones mend. If the diet lacks the necessary salts, the broken bone draws its material from the other bones of the body, weakens them.

KISS v. SHAKE: Because Americans, Englishmen, Germans, JULY 18 Dutchmen, Swedes, Lithuanians, Poles, Danes, Armenians, Serbians, Greeks, Estonians, Syrians, Letts, Icelanders, Norwegians and especially the Japanese think it is effeminate, many a modern Frenchman has abandoned the ancient & honorable Gallic custom of greeting friends with a resounding kiss on the cheek. So widespread has become the custom of shaking hands in France that last week the august *L'Académie de Médecine* was asked for an opinion. Weightily the *Académie* considered, then delivered these decisions: 1) more germs change carriers during a handclasp than during a perfunctory peck of the lips; hence 2) the handshake is more dangerous than the kiss.

MILESTONES

BIRTHDAYS: George Bernard Shaw, 76; Rudyard Kipling, 66; Calvin Coolidge, 60; George M. Cohan, 54; Benito Mussolini, 49; all race horses (Jan. 1).

BORN: To Gloria Swanson, 31, film actress, and Michael Farmer, 29, Irish sportsman, a daughter; in London. Weight: 7 lb. 2 oz. Name: Michele Bridget. Said Actress Swanson: "I'm so excited I can hardly talk. It was all so sudden."

ENGAGED: Marilyn Reynolds Carter Pickford (Marilyn Miller), 32, film & stage actress; and Jose Paige ("Don Alvarado"), 28, film actor; after an involuntary trip together to Southampton on the *S.S. Bremen* when they overstayed at a sailing party in Manhattan; in London.

MISCELLANY

SWEAR: In Illinois, a judge sentenced Mrs. Lee Jordan to 15 days in jail for swearing. Mrs. Jordan swore again. The judge sentenced Mrs. Jordan to 15 more days for swearing. Mrs. Jordan swore more, got 60 days. When she had sworn enough to be sentenced for six months, officers took Mrs. Jordan off to jail, still swearing.

COBBLER: In Reading, Pa., Jacob Rheinheimer, 77, cobbler, died after an operation in which the surgeon found Jacob Rheinheimer's stomach studded with 200 cobbler's nails.

SNORT: In Yarmouth, Minn., walking through the woods, Keith Grey, farmer, blew his nose. A neighbor mistook the sound for a deer's snort, shot Farmer Grey in the neck.

BUSINESS & FINANCE

In 1932 there were an estimated 12 million unemployed in the U.S. Bank failures, which had totaled 642 in 1929, the year the Depression began, had zoomed in 1931 to 2,298. The year 1932 was marked by a Senate investigation into Wall Street practices that would lead to the creation in 1934 of the Securities and Exchange Commission to police the investment business, and by the dramatic collapse of two gigantic financial empires: the Chicago utilities combine of Samuel Insull, and the vast international structure put together—mostly of worthless paper—by the "Swedish Match King," Ivar Kreuger.

MARCH 21 **EXIT THE MATCH KING:** While the Paris Stock Exchange was closed in honor of the deceased Aristide Briand and 500,000 Parisians reverently stood in the Champs Elysées intent upon the funeral, a large pistol went off in a luxurious apartment nearby.

No one heard it except Ivar Kreuger, the "Swedish Match King," the self-made colossus of Scandinavian finance. Matchman Kreuger was putting a bullet into his heart for business reasons and for human reasons. His nerves were drawn so taut (he had suffered a nervous breakdown recently in New York) that to release the strain was welcome, sweet. His physician had warned him the day before that his heart would not stand much more.

Manhattan's Stock Exchange was still open. The French police were instructed by a Cabinet Minister to keep mum. Even when selling of Kreuger & Toll in Wall Street became fast & furious, no U.S. news agency thought to cable Paris for news of the Match King. His friends announced his death after all world markets closed.

Swooping from Stockholm to Paris came a whole planeload of Kreuger relatives. The Match King, who was only 52 and a Grand Officer of the French Legion of Honor, is survived by his father, mother, sisters, brothers. His secretive methods make the estate a question mark. "I don't know how much money I have," this long-nosed Swede often said, "and I don't care! What difference does money make?" Since he was said to control the billion-dollar Kreuger & Toll pyramid with slightly over $250,000 key securities, Titan Kreuger's contempt for personal pelf was natural.

In Stockholm the Royal Government did not of course know that Ivar Kreuger was going to commit suicide, but they had taken precautionary steps. The Royal Government was ready to rush through a bill to stabilize Swedish business by granting a moratorium to Kreuger & Toll. When the news came, the Swedish Parliament put through this bill at a secret session, ordered Swedish stock exchanges to remain closed.

On the morning of his suicide Ivar Kreuger had bought the pistol at a small shop near his apartment. "*Mon Dieu,* how was I to know?" said the shopkeeper. "He seemed perfectly calm, *parfaitement!*" Only the Kreuger concierge noticed anything unusual, noticed that when the Match King came home with a package in his hand he did not smile or reply as he always had to the doorman's greeting. Going upstairs, Titan Kreuger wrote three letters in longhand to relatives, loosened his clothes, pulled the trigger.

KREUGER'S LOANS: Ivar Kreuger, 52, matchmaker and moneylender to many nations, had just been in the U.S., seeking loans for his labyrinth of companies. He had failed to get the loans. How many were his creditors, how much they were owed will not be known for a long time. Ivar Kreuger's business life was known to only a handful of men. In making important transactions he usually revealed only part of the details to any one person.

Principal Kreuger company is Swedish Match—Svenska Tändsticks. It makes 66% of the world's matches, controlling 250 plants in 43 nations. In 1930 its earnings came to $13,000,000. One of the firm's alliances was a sales agreement with Diamond Match Co. to cover safety matches in the U.S. When in 1930 a U.S. tariff was placed on safety matches Kreuger began acquiring factories in the U.S. Last year he bought Federal Match Corp. of Chicago.

Although by the early 1920's Swedish Match had a firm

hold on the world's markets, Matchman Kreuger wished to make it impregnable. He saw an opportunity in the unsettled financial condition of most of the world, realizing that cash-poor nations would grant match monopolies in return for loans. The first loan was to Poland in 1925 and consisted of $6,000,000. Greece followed and then France offered a match monopoly for a loan of $75,000,000. In 1929 the biggest loan of all was made—$125,000,000 to Germany. It was secured not by a direct monopoly but by an agreement to ban all Russian matches. Worry over the safety of this loan was known to be one of the things depressing Ivar Kreuger last week.

Key company to the entire group was the original engineering and real estate firm of Kreuger & Toll, a holding company controlled by Class A shares capitalized at $500,000, the majority of which Ivar Kreuger held himself. This small amount of stock carried control of properties capitalized at over a billion dollars.

Kreuger & Toll has many activities in addition to control of the match companies. It controls financial institutions throughout Europe, including commercial and mortgage banks. It has real estate companies with properties throughout Europe.

While Matchman Kreuger made no matches in the U.S., he

Ivar Kreuger: "What difference does money make?"

Samuel Insull: "I have made many mistakes." Page 176.

raised much cash there. Through his U.S. bankers, the Kreuger companies floated about $200,000,000 worth of securities in the past few years. For some months the Kreuger securities have been weak and on his last visit Ivar Kreuger spent much time consulting with market manipulators. Last week the Kreuger & Toll shares were especially weak. On the day preceding his suicide it was the most active stock on the New York Stock Exchange. This was also true on Saturday when it accounted for 25% of trading although no word of Ivar Kreuger's death had leaked out.

FALLIBLE INSULL: "I do not pose as infallible," said Chicago APRIL 11 utilities executive Samuel Insull last week. "I have made many mistakes and I have erred in judgment, but the same criticism may be leveled at everyone in the business world."

With this attitude Mr. Insull has been answering all current criticism of his management. But U.S. finance was less interested last week in Mr. Insull's attitude than it was in the fate of his vast corporate pyramid, badly in need of cash, indebted to banks. A receivership suit was brought last week against Insull Utility Investments by a Mrs. Helen Samuels of Chicago. She owns four $1,000 notes, now worth about 4% of par.

INSULL'S EMPIRE: Samuel Insull still recalls with pride that APRIL 18 he was born, 72 years ago, in England. From boyhood he had great admiration for Thomas Alva Edison. By a quirk of fate he answered an advertisement for a secretary, found out that the man who had inserted the advertisement was Edison's London representative. Edison was struck with Mr. Insull's weekly reports, sent for him in 1881. For eleven years they worked together, Mr. Insull learning much about the technical side of the young light & power business.

In 1892 Mr. Insull wrote to the capitalists controlling four-year-old Chicago Edison Co., now Commonwealth Edison, suggesting himself for the presidency. He was installed the following year and resigned his post as General Electric vice president in charge of sales. In 1896 the company needed funds. Mr. Insull was unable to get them from Chicago bankers, a fact he has twitted them with on many an occasion. He went to London and obtained a loan of $1,200,000 from London Trust Co.

Although Mr. Insull is considered chiefly a Middle West utilitarian, properties along the Atlantic seaboard now loom in his picture, contribute about one-fifth of total earnings. Insulland has 13 million inhabitants, more than one-fourth of whom are customers. It employs 50,000 men and is a conglomeration of over 150 companies. Before the difficulties of Mr. Insull's position were apparent, the securities of the Insull group had a total market value of over three billion dollars.

Although last week found Mr. Insull 72 years old, he passed through it with his usual quietness and almost autocratic self-assurance. Through his activities in business, in politics, in grand opera, Mr. Insull is one of the best known citizens of Chicago. Last week's problems did not appear to have stripped him of Chicago's respect. His trouble was purely financial. No ice, heat, light or traction service would be interrupted. Criticisms voiced last week were directed against the utility holding company as a financial device rather than against Pyramid Builder Insull himself.

KREUGER'S BOOKS: In one of the most smashing statements ever made by a firm of auditors, Ivar Kreuger was last week pronounced a crook, a swindler, a falsifier of books.

When, in 1928, the famed Boston-born firm of Lee, Higginson prepared to issue millions of Kreuger securities to U.S. investors, it naturally demanded an audit of the Kreuger business. It was persuaded by Ivar Kreuger—one of the most charmingly persuasive men who ever lived—that it was not necessary for a U.S. firm to audit his vast affairs. He had not only one but three great Swedish firms of auditors which over a period of years and throughout the civilized world had learned how to keep track of the globe-girdling assets and liabilities of his huge money-lending match company. So great was Sweden's reputation for honesty that Lee, Higginson decided, as a practical matter, to accept a Swedish audit of the greatest Swede.

When Lee, Higginson discovered last week that it had been gulled, it suffered the most stinging blow to its moral sensibilities in all its 84 years. The truth about Kreuger came from Price, Waterhouse, famed auditors of a large part of all Big Business in Britain and America. Its British partners, called to investigate by the Swedish Government, minced no words in their preliminary report. Their points:

1) "We are able to state that in our opinion without doubt the balance sheet of Kreuger & Toll grossly misrepresented their true financial position."

2) "Under the personal direction of the late Mr. Kreuger entries were made on the books which on the one hand eliminated substantial balances shown to be owing the parent company by him and on the other hand entirely eliminated liabilities to other subsidiary companies."

3) "There are indications that the profits reported for the year 1930 were grossly overstated by means of fictitious entries."

4) "The above statement must be accepted as evidence that gross frauds have been perpetrated by Mr. Kreuger."

The truth, disturbing to man's faith in man, shook financial markets. Estimated losses, largely due to Kreuger fraud, are $300,000,000 throughout the world, of which perhaps $200,-000,000 are in the U.S. And the loss to Sweden is incalculable honor.

BEAR HUNT: If President Richard Whitney of the New York APRIL 25 Stock Exchange was surprised at being suddenly ordered to Washington by the Senate last fortnight, he did not show it. The Exchange's president must be prepared for all sorts of wild stories and charges, especially when the market is in a bad way. The Senate Committee on Banking & Currency wanted Mr. Whitney to get up a complete list of persons on the short side of the market, wanted to quiz Mr. Whitney on bear practices and the Stock Exchange's rules.

Mr. Whitney flatly denied, as he had often denied before, that professional bears had had anything to do with the decline in market prices. "Our investigations," he said, "have disclosed no bear raids." He suggested that the Federal Government itself had put the general public into the market by educating the people to a knowledge of securities through Liberty Loan drives, agreed that public officials had helped to sustain the 1926-29 inflation through bullish statements.

Mr. Whitney pointed out that the Administration's reconstruction measures have given investors an opportunity to get out of the market. Small investors have increased during

Depression, he said. Asked to what cause he attributed the slump in prices, he replied:

"Liquidation by frightened investors who are giving these United States of ours away."

Senator Couzens of Michigan—It has come to my attention that a broker may use his customer's stock to depress the value of that stock.

Mr. Whitney—Senator Couzens, I deny that. No broker may do that.

Senator Couzens—Oh, don't be so innocent.

Senator Brookhart—You brought this country to the greatest panic in history.

Mr. Whitney—We have brought this country, sir, to its standing in the world by speculation. You think you can affect the world by changing the rules of a stock exchange or board of trade?

Senator Brookhart—Yes, we can change them by abolishing the stock exchange and board of trade, so far as speculation is concerned.

Mr. Whitney—And then the people of the United States will go to Canada and Europe to do those very things and pay their taxes there.

INSULL (CONT'D.): Samuel Insull has not bothered to conceal a mild contempt for bankers. Last week the bankers had him, tied and bound, in their hands. But what could they do with him? Perhaps nothing except to let him loose—"Biggest Man" in Chicago.

As market conditions became worse & worse the temporary bank loans Insull had received became fixtures. Last week, the common stocks of his trusts were practically worthless, and the notes and preferred stocks held by the public brought only nominal prices. So the two Insull investment trusts, which had working control of Chicagoland's utilities, went into receivership. That was how the banks, principally the Chicago bankers, had got Insull.

If the bankers desire to put the tsar out of Commonwealth Edison, Peoples Gas and Public Service of Northern Illinois, they can, presumably, do so. But last week, as a "reorganization committee" was being formed, no one suggested that they would. Tsar Insull may have lost his entire personal fortune. But who could take his place as tsar in Chicago? No banker was looking for the job.

KREUGER (CONT'D.): The Kreuger Scandal, already grown into one of the ugliest affairs in business history, last week increased in malignancy with a disclosure which shattered the last vestige of admiration which could have attached itself to the late great maker of matches and showed Kreuger in a scene that might have been taken from a common crook melodrama.

This scene occurred in 1931. Kreuger, failing to get a match monopoly in Italy, needed funds. From an Italian engraver he got copper plates that bore the likeness of an Italian Government bond. On a piece of paper he sketched the way he would like an English-worded statement printed. He furtively took the plates to a Stockholm printer. The printer, knowing Kreuger's affairs were vast, did not become suspicious when he was asked to print 42 bonds, each of £ 500,000 denomination. Kreuger took the counterfeits, forged on them the name of E. Drelli, gave them to his companies in return for good bonds upon which he could borrow. To anyone who became suspicious he would whisper that relations between France and Italy were strained, no mention of his big "loan" to Italy must be made.

Other developments during the week included an opinion that Sweden's high income taxes must be upped another 15% to make up for the loss of Kreuger & Toll's big payments. "Only the beginning" was the gloomy warning of the Government's newspaper, *Svenska Morgonbladet:* "The coming week will be one of the most nerve-wracking ever experienced by the Swedish nation."

BEAR HUNT (CONT'D.): For a long time Congressman Fiorello MAY 9 ("Little Flower") La Guardia of New York had been quietly stuffing a Pandora's Box with woe for Wall Street. Last week the box, a big, brown trunk, was so full of woe that it required two men to lug it into the Senate Committee on Banking & Currency, investigating the stockmarket.

Scouting the previous testimony of President Whitney of the New York Stock Exchange that the public was to blame for its mad scramble to participate in the Coolidge Bull market the burly little Representative from Manhattan charged that brokers and operators always retained a high pressure pressagent to puff stocks selected for manipulation. From his trunk he fished out evidence furnished by one Arthur Newton Plummer, who had "handled" 61 stocks.

Senator Couzens—What do you mean "handled"?

Congressman La Guardia—Ballyhooed—rigged! This one man Plummer paid out $286,271 during the course of his operations. He is a very smart young man.

Given a stock, smart Pressagent Plummer would "proceed to convince these financial newsboys that he had a good story." Handling the ballyhoo for a pool that was bulling Savage Arms in 1924, Pressagent Plummer succeeded in placing favorable stories "605 times in 228 newspapers with a circulation of 11,248,000 in 157 cities with a population of 32,399,000."

For his able puffing of Pure Oil stock in 1925, Pressagent Plummer received a letter from Oscar I. Gubelman, large-scale speculator in oil stocks and director of many a potent U.S. corporation confirming "the arrangement for payment to you of $2,500 in cash for publicity work for one month and an option of 500 shares of Pure Oil at 25, and 500 additional shares at $25\frac{1}{2}$, good for 30 days."

With this cash and profits, Fixer Plummer would pay off the "financial news boys." If they were ticklish about checks, he delivered cash through a pay-off man. Summarized Congressman La Guardia: "Sordid as these facts may seem, I believe that the same sort of story could be told regarding every stock in which there was a pool."

MAY 23 **KREUGER'S NEMESIS:** Who killed Cock Kreuger? What was the final thing which ran him to ground? Last week it became clear that his end was written when Sosthenes Behn, Chairman of International Telephone & Telegraph, with all the deliberateness of a Dane, refused to believe in the sly Swede; and when Gordon Rentschler, astute president of National City Bank, stood by Mr. Behn and asked Ivar Kreuger for facts, more facts, clearer facts.

This final Kreuger chapter started in June 1931, when he sold control of L. M. Ericsson Telephone Co. to I.T. & T. He was given a down payment of $11,000,000 and promised some

I.T. & T. stock as soon as an audit was made. This audit was merely a routine matter so far as I.T. & T. was concerned.

Up to Stockholm went the accountants of Price, Waterhouse & Co. After much investigation they cabled I.T. & T. that Ericsson's cash account had been misrepresented, cheap foreign bonds being carried in the cash account at par value. In Manhattan Ivar Kreuger tried to pass this off. It was a mistake in translation he insisted. Oh yes, the bonds had been placed in lieu of cash but that was just a temporary loan Ericsson Telephone had made to Kreuger & Toll—he would soon put the cash back and take the bonds in return. And did not Sosthenes Behn see that Ivar Kreuger himself had guaranteed the Ericsson accounts? There was nothing to worry about.

But Sosthenes Behn cared little for the guaranty he had been given. And neither, apparently, did his bankers, J. P. Morgan & Co. and National City Bank. Soon Ivar Kreuger was closeted with National City's Rentschler. After ten days of meetings Mr. Rentschler said that Ivar Kreuger would have to cancel the deal, give back the $11,000,000. These dollars I.T. & T. has yet to see.

KREUGER GADGET: In Stockholm Swedes chuckled at an example of Ivar Kreuger's shrewdness which auditors stumbled upon in his private office. On the desk was a concealed button which could be pressed by "accidentally" moving a book with his elbow. It caused a dummy telephone to ring. Herr Kreuger could then ask his visitor to leave or could impress him with imaginary conversations with great bankers and statesmen. JUNE 13

ADIEU: A tremulous smile on his lips, his wrinkled hands shaking, Samuel Insull last week cleaned out his desk. Friends came in to pay their respects. Typical Insullisms on that day: JUNE 20
¶ "I've gone from the bottom to the top and now to the bottom again. I only hope I will be able to keep a roof over my head and care for my wife."
¶ "Here I go, after 50 years of work, a man without a job."
In Chicago it was said that Mr. Insull owes banks $10,000,000 in addition to personal debts. His brother, Martin Insull, was said to be in debt to the extent of $7,000,000. Mrs. Samuel Insull was reported in like straits and so was Samuel Insull Jr. The whole family had loyally "gone down with the ship."

Insull creditors were reported in agreement not to force Samuel Insull through bankruptcy. The three big Insull operating companies last week each voted him $6,000 a year. His friends did not like to call it a "pension," said rather it was payment for "overtime work in the past." Beclouded was the outlook for his expensive hobby, Chicago's Civic Opera.

JUNE 27 **INDEX:** "I believe that we have reached the turning point in the Depression," said General Charles Gates Dawes last week in Chicago. Because he was fresh from the presidency of Reconstruction Finance Corp. his statements commanded attention. "It is the smaller business enterprises with low overhead expense which seem to be showing improvement," he said. "But in time the larger ones must necessarily follow. I would attribute much more importance to the increase in electric power consumption in the country during the last two weeks than to stock or bond quotations."

Only factors tending to discredit this Dawesian cheer last week were his past record and the still-sagging index of business conditions. Included in General Dawes' record is the following utterance:

"People do not realize that conditions are gradually improving."—*June 5, 1930.*

In Chicago, General Dawes will again direct, as chairman, Central Republic Bank & Trust Co. which he founded 30 years ago. A statistic which General Dawes must have pondered last week was bank clearings. After a brief spurt a fortnight ago, they slumped badly last week. And he must have noted with regret the passing of the Sears, Roebuck dividend. Principal grains last week had lost their recent advances and were slumping to new lows.

General Dawes last week could also have heard little but gloom from his steelmaking friends. Ingot production hovered around 18% of capacity. Automobile production, with the exception of Ford, seemed about to slow up last week and *Iron Age* predicted many plants would be idle during the summer. The week's production was 52,560 units, 21% below last year.

KREUGER (CONT'D.): May the thousands of investors who bought Kreuger & Toll and International Match securities obtain redress from the bankers of these companies? Last week an answer to this much-asked question drew closer. In Manhattan one Florence Bramson, owner of five International Match $1,000 debenture bonds (worth $17.50 each last week), brought suit against Guaranty Co. and Lee, Higginson & Co., charging misrepresentation of facts. On the day following Miss Bramson's suit, Lee, Higginson & Co. announced that it planned to liquidate. During its 84 years the house profited from backing the China tea trade, was prominent in the development of U.S. railways, helped reorganize General Motors in 1910 and organized Nash Motors. Its salesmen sold over a billion dollars worth of securities, its distribution system was nationwide.

Meanwhile, the investigation of Herr Kreuger's affairs went on apace. In Stockholm police were searching 150 sacks of waste paper for clues regarding Kreuger transactions. The first actual jail sentence in the case came when Bror Bregberg, one of Kreuger's associates, was fined $162,000 and sent to jail for nine months at hard labor.

LOOP FLURRY: Not all the excitement on the streets of Chicago   JULY 4
last week was caused by the convening of the Democratic National Convention. Some of it was caused by the Chicago banking situation.

At the beginning of the week the city became mildly bank-conscious when Banker John Bain & associates were put on trial as a result of the crash of the twelve Bain banks last October with deposits of $10,000,000, loans of $13,000,000 and only $321,832 on hand in cash. By the end of the week the city was far more bank-conscious. During the preceding three days, 22 outlying banks had closed their doors. Into the Loop, stronghold of Chicago finance, marched a small army of worried depositors, most of them poor, practically all of them owners of small savings accounts. They seemed to select no particular bank for their activities. For two days withdrawals were heavy.

By Saturday withdrawing had subsided. Like all large and sound banking institutions, Chicago's had made plain that the money was there and could be had for the asking. In First National, ruddy, crinkly-faced President Melvin Alvah Traylor made two speeches before crowds of clients, one speech in the savings department, another in the checking department. He explained that his bank had passed through the Chicago Fire (1871) and weathered it; had gone through other Depressions and weathered them; would pass through this Depression. Money was on hand for each & every depositor who wanted his share. The crowds dispersed.

By Monday the Loop was once more quiet. But behind closed doors there was great to-do. Central figure in a long bankers' conference was Charles Gates Dawes. Since his return to Chicago, speculation had run high as to why he had resigned from R.F.C. at what seemed like the peak of the corporation's activities. Toward Monday evening the reason for his return had become more apparent. In the week-end uncertainty, stock in his Central Republic Bank & Trust Co. had slipped badly on over-the-counter quotations—from 46 to 2. Talk of liquidation was in the air. Late in the evening Banker Dawes issued a statement. Said he:

"The demands on the Central Republic Bank & Trust Co. during the past week made necessary recourse to borrowing to meet them. These loans have been completed and place the bank in an impregnable cash position. The loans negotiated are for current requirements and to pay depositors, and are not for the purposes of liquidation."

Observers thought they understood what Banker Dawes meant by this equivocal statement. Everyone was aware that the "borrowing" referred to was made through R.F.C. That fact explained why Banker Dawes had resigned its presidency.

JULY 25 **ANOTHER KREUGER DOUBTER:** Whom did Ivar Kreuger not deceive? Last week another name was added to the small list of bankers and firms which doubted the late felonious match tycoon. It was that of Central Hanover Bank & Trust Co. of Manhattan. In January 1931, the bank lent Kreuger & Toll $1,000,000. Vice President Roger Whittlesey then began to search for more adequate information. He wrote letters abroad, never received convincing answers. In September the loan was called.

Last week a new estimate of Ivar Kreuger's estate showed that he left personal debts of $125,000,000, indirect liabilities of $100,000,000 more, practically no free assets of any sort.

BIG MICK FROM DOWN TOWN:

Mother Machree	$1,000
Kathleen Mavourneen	500
My Wild Irish Rose	400
Where the River Shannon Flows	300
Come Back to Erin	200
A Little Bit of Heaven	200
When Irish Eyes Are Smiling	100

Morton Downey, Rudy Vallée and other high-priced crooners were doubtless astonished last week to learn that comparatively unknown singers in Broadway nightclubs had been paid such prices for the past 13 years for singing the above selections. But Messrs. Downey & Vallée must have been relieved to know that it was not the nightclub proprietors who paid. Exposed as anonymous benefactor to dozens of nightclub crooners was one George D. Phelan, 39-year-old employe of J.S. Bache & Co., Manhattan brokers.

It was the custom of Mr. Phelan to give large dinners at expensive restaurants. Sometimes he entertained 80 or 90 guests. During the course of the evening Mr. Phelan would grow sadder & sadder. He would request the house crooner to sing an Irish song. During the singing Mr. Phelan invariably wept. He then tipped the singer according to the copiousness of his tears. On the basis of these tips was compiled the above wage scale. The beneficiaries, who did not know Mr. Phelan's name, called him simply "The Big Mick from Down Town."

One day George D. Phelan, whose salary was recently cut from $100 to $60 per week, confided to Cashier Alfred L. Goldman of J.S. Bache & Co. that he had stolen $695,000 from the firm's petty cash fund in the past 13 years. He told Cashier Goldman he was confessing "because I know I can't continue these thefts forever."

For a month Embezzler Phelan helped auditors to straighten out his books. Last week he was arraigned on a charge of stealing $1,900, his last speculation. Said he: "I haven't enough money to hire a lawyer, but if I can get out on bail I may be able to find some." A truckman furnished $20,000 bail.

RULING: Because his lease stipulated cancellation if his earnings were impaired by an act of God, Paul G. Forthy of Birmingham, Ala. vacated when the Depression whittled down his income. He was sued by his landlord. Judge Arthur Jenkins last week ruled that the Depression was not an act of God.

SEPT. 26 **DIRTY BACKWASH:** Last week it became quite clear that Samuel Insull, biggest utilitarian in U.S. history and once the biggest businessman west of the Alleghenies, had used the accountant's art to inflate his profits, to hide losses, to make large dividends seem justified. Up to now it has been assumed that Mr. Insull failed with honor. Now this is put in doubt.

This revelation, and a host of others, put a new light on the precipitous departure of Samuel Insull to Paris aboard the *Empress of Britain* and the flight of his brother to Canada. In Chicago the state's legal department opened an office to hear the complaints of investors, and set to examining extradition laws. But no criminal complaint had been filed and Insull loyalists insisted that the brothers expatriated themselves solely to avoid annoyance, petty litigation that would lead nowhere.

The revelations came as the result of a five-month inquest into the books of Insull firms' accountants. In addition to juggled income statements, the backwash included the following facts:

¶ Insull Utility Investments has assets of only $27,473,000 against liabilities of $105,000,000. An $8,000,000 investment in subsidiaries, including Insull, Son & Co., was valued by the auditors at $00000.

¶ Marshall Emmett Sampsell, president of an Insull subsidiary, resigned at the request of the receivers. They found he had "borrowed" 4,000 shares from the firm's treasury, used them as collateral on a joint bank loan with Martin Insull. Two months ago Mr. Sampsell's wife hanged herself.

¶ Among one firm's receivables is 50¢ once borrowed by Martin Insull.

OCT. 3 **FIRE CHIEF & GAG TYCOON:** When Funnyman Ed Wynn's *Laugh Parade* was on Broadway last winter tens of thousands of people saw it, paying top prices of $5.50 at the box office, sometimes three times as much from speculators. One man saw it four times. Each time he bought a seat in a box, turned his back on the stage as soon as the curtain went up. Despite this antic, which seemed eccentric to other spectators, the four-time box-sitter meant much more money in the end to Funnyman Wynn than anyone else in the house. For by keeping his ears open, he decided that Ed Wynn was comical even if people could only hear his lisping voice and silly laugh, could not see his plump figure, his idiotic smile, his fluttering fingers and perpetually rolling eyes, his ridiculous costumes. Because the box-sitter was George W. Vos, chief advertising man in The Texas Co., Ed Wynn received his present position as Texaco Fire Chief, broadcasting every Tuesday night over NBC at $5,000 a performance.

Mrs. Insull. All she wants is to go shopping, but newsmen besiege her.

Fire Chief Ed Wynn: "When you were 8 and I was 9 and we were 17."

Mr. Wynn was reluctant to broadcast at first. He was convinced he could not do it. He finally decided that a studio audience might help, rigged himself up in costume and went ahead. With people in the studio actually laughing so he can hear them, he is able to work. But he has never completely shaken his fear of the "mike," fear that his listeners, estimated at 20 millions now, are not laughing. The Texas Co. is satisfied that Ed Wynn makes everybody laugh.

Mr. Wynn, whose real name is Israel Edwin Leopold, prides himself on being what he calls a "method comedian" rather than a "gag comedian." He writes most of his performances himself, working several hours a day on them. Wynn broadcasts consist of fast dialog between Funnyman Wynn and Graham McNamee. The latter does little talking except to feed cues. The program is punctuated by musical selections. Typical Wynn prattle: "The opera tonight, Graham, is very unusual. The title of it is 'When You Were Eight and I Was Nine and We Were 17.' It's about a boy and a girl. The boy's name is J. Weatherstrip Reilley. He was born during the World War and they called him Weatherstrip because he kept his father out of the draft. So-o-o-o-o."

Mr. Wynn also prides himself on being a good businessman. His plays have been profitable. Last week he increased his stake in the entertainment business by forming an Amalgamated Broadcasting System, Inc., with offices in Manhattan and $1,000,000 worth of business in hand. Its main purpose is to sell programs to advertising agencies and stations.

OCT. 17 **FULL FLIGHT:** Servants in the small Hotel Lincoln, in Paris, were mildly surprised one evening last week to see the short, white-mustached old American who had been stopping at the hotel with his wife for several weeks, making his way furtively out of the house through the dim-lit service entrance. With him was his son, who carried a small handbag. In the street they hailed a taxi, vanished into the night.

The taxi took them to the *Gare de Lyon* where they caught the midnight express for Italy. Early the next day they were across the border. While Samuel Insull and his son were speeding toward Italy, newshawks in Paris flocked to the Hotel Lincoln. Insull had promised them an interview at 10:30 a.m., thus insuring himself a good chance for a clean getaway the night before. The reporters grew impatient. When Mrs. Insull, recently ill and still wan and weak, came out to go shopping they besieged her. "Please let me alone!" she cried hysterically. "I know nothing about my husband's affairs."

Reporters, sensing that sly old Samuel Insull was at last in full flight, took up the hunt. By the time they had followed the trail to Turin, Samuel Insull was safely on his way to Rome. At Rome he took a plane for Albania, then flew on to Salonika. There he changed to a train for Athens. In Greece, his lawyers had told him, he would be safe from extradition.

On his first morning in Athens, Mr. Insull sat on a balcony

sipping a cup of strong Turkish coffee. Finally an Athenian policeman approached Mr. Insull, informed him he was under arrest. The American Legation had asked Athenian police to detain him in order to give the U.S. State Department time to decide whether or not to ask Greece to send Mr. Insull back to face U.S. justice.

INSULL ARRESTED: Once again last week Samuel Insull, fugi- NOV. 14
tive from Illinois justice, slipped out of his hotel's service entrance. But this time it was no prelude to flight. He was accompanied by the chief of the Athenian Security Police. Three days prior, Secretary of State Stimson and Greek Minister Charalambos Simopoulos had met in Washington, D.C. and exchanged extradition treaties, making it possible for the U.S. to demand the arrest and return of Mr. Insull.

Because doctors found Mr. Insull in bad health (diabetes, chills, arteriosclerosis, myocarditis, enlarged liver, high blood pressure, traces of brain congestion), he was well treated and given a special room in the police station.

Next day began the fight in which Samuel Insull hopes to escape at some point from the legal net which might drag him back to the U.S. The first round of the fight started when Mr. Insull's lawyer, Cristos Ladas, went before the Greek Court of Appeals. It was all Greek to Samuel Insull as Lawyer Ladas first flattered Greek law ("The very gods on Olympus were willing to be tried by the ancient Greek judges"), then flattered Greek civilization ("Here is a man who asks to be protected from American liberty under which men are murdered by machine guns in the streets"), then flattered his client ("He is a man who gave light to 43 American cities and who is now accused of petty thefts").

YOUNG ON INSULL: Looking very prim with a black-rib- DEC. 26
boned pince-nez, General Electric Chairman Owen D. Young last week spent five hours in Manhattan explaining his business dealings with Samuel Insull. His questioner was Lewis F. Jacobson, counsel for the owners of $60,000,000 worth of debentures in Insull Utility Investments Inc. who sought "to prove complete knowledge by the officials of the General Electric Co. of the financial structure of the bankrupt and the restrictions against pledging securities."

The first financial relationship between Lawyer Young and Utilitarian Insull was in 1929 when Mr. Insull formed holding companies to retain control of his empire. Mr. Young gladly subscribed for some stock. He never looked at the company's balance sheets "not because I deal carelessly with investments but because it would have made no difference with this particular investment. I could not have sold at any time during that period without incurring Mr. Insull's displeasure."

In December 1931, Mr. Insull asked General Electric for a $2,000,000 loan and received it. "The directors all knew that Mr. Insull had heavy obligations," said Mr. Young. "And I do not think they were surprised when he came to the General Electric. He was a large customer and if he was in need of a million or two, it was not extraordinary that he should come to us." Mr. Young told Counsel Jacobson that no questions were asked because "knowing Mr. Insull as you do and bearing in mind that he had endorsed the note personally, you will understand that I, as chairman of General Electric, would not have asked Mr. Insull what he was going to do with the money."

"Didn't you know by February 1932, that Samuel Insull was financially irresponsible?" asked Counsel Jacobson.

"Yes," said Mr. Young. "I think we all came to that conclusion." But Mr. Young did not inquire into the Insull finances because "it was president of G.E. Mr. Gerard Swope's business rather than mine. We certainly do not duplicate our work more than necessary."

By April Mr. Young was attempting to prevent Mr. Insull's bank creditors from closing in on him. His desire was to keep the Insull structure solvent because a failure "might impair the credit of utilities everywhere, and when you impair the credit of utilities you impair their buying power from the General Electric."

"You did it to save a customer?" prodded Mr. Jacobson.

"To save a customer on one side," answered Mr. Young, "and that was consistent with saving the investors on the other side. Besides I had known Mr. Insull for 20 years, and I respected highly what he had done in the power and light field."

After the testimony Mr. Young asked the newspapermen to listen to a statement "which should be made in fairness to the old man." He pointed out that Mr. Insull's steps "were sound at every point if you assume, as he did, either that the Depression was temporary or that his operating stocks were worth much more than the market price. The most you can say about that old man is that he had too much confidence in his country and in his own companies."

"That old man" was still in Athens last week while the Greek Foreign Office prepared an official translation of the 225 pages of documents covering his indictment in the U.S. When the job is finished Mr. Insull will be formally tried under Greek law. [The case dragged on into 1934 when, ordered by Greece to leave the country, Insull escaped to Turkey on a chartered boat. Turkey turned him over to U.S. custody and he was transported to Chicago to face trial. He was found innocent of all charges and died in Paris of a heart attack in 1938.]

TEA PARTY: Any physical activity in Wall Street, no matter how trivial, is sure to make runners, clerks, bondsalesmen *et al.* stop and gape. Large groups often gather about a man sawing a board. Last week when truckmen began to unload 60-lb. cases, neatly wrapped in matting, before the House of Morgan, the usual crowd swelled to near-riot proportions. Though the cases were plainly labeled "BLACK TEA—Product of China," reports quickly spread that J. P. Morgan & Co. had received a huge shipment of gold from the Orient.

Guards when questioned muttered: "We don't know nothing. Ask him." "Him," a young English clerk, did not know much but he explained: "The bill of lading for the tea came this morning. We could not send it up to Mr. Morgan's house and we could not send it out to his Long Island place, so we are putting it in the vault here."

$$\boxed{\textbf{CINEMA}}$$

JAN. 11   **"MATA HARI"**—One of the legends about Mata Hari, a Parisian cabaret dancer who was executed for espionage during the War, says that she was unable to break herself of the habit of taking off her clothes at crucial moments and was therefore naked when she faced a French firing squad. This episode is omitted from the Greta Garbo version of the affair, which begins with Greta Garbo dancing, very badly indeed, in leggings and something that looks like a pillow on her wiggling rear, and ends as Miss Garbo, majestic in black, is walking down a long corridor between two lines of soldiers. Her lover (Ramon Novarro) is a blind aviator who has said good-by to her under the impression that her prison is a hospital and that she is leaving him to undergo a minor operation. Good shot: two lighted cigarets in a pitch black room, where Garbo and Novarro are talking.

FEB. 15   **"THE HATCHET MAN"**—So convincingly did Edward G. Robinson perform in *Little Caesar* and *Smart Money* that he, rather than Alphonse Capone, has become the prototype of the U.S. gangster. When cinemaddicts read of the doings in the underworld, they form an immediate picture of Edward G. Robinson operating a machine gun in Chicago, a distillery in Manhattan or a poker game in Florida. Shrewdly cast in this melodrama of San Francisco's Chinatown, he needs no make-up to assure you that he is the heathen executioner of the Lem Sing Tong who is forced by the rules of his tong to bury his hatchet in the neck of his best friend.

APRIL 25   **"GRAND HOTEL"** is well filled. In one room lives a ballet dancer (Greta Garbo). Conveniently near, so that he can filch her pearls, is an impoverished Baron (John Barrymore). In a corridor, the Baron makes friends with a pretty stenographer (Joan Crawford). She is waiting to take dictation from a disagreeable textile tycoon (Wallace Beery). One of the tycoon's

Edward G. Robinson, not Capone, is
the prototype gangster. Page 193.

Sidney and March. In their new film
they both take to the bottle.

clerks (Lionel Barrymore) is incurably ill; he has come to the
hotel to finish his last days in one burst of unaccustomed
luxury. Also to be observed are a sententious doctor (Lewis
Stone), a hall-porter (Jean Hersholt) whose wife is having a
baby. The conflicting aims of these people and their proxim-
ity naturally lead to startling readjustments.

CASTING NOTE: When Metro-Goldwyn-Mayer decided to MAY 9
make a picture of Katherine Brush's novel *Red-Headed*
Woman, they thought at once of red-headed Clara Bow,
when and if she ended her retirement. Last week Actress Bow
announced that she would return to the screen, but not in
Red-Headed Woman. Her first role will be that of a half-
caste girl in *Call Her Savage.*

Commentators noted a change in Cinemactress Bow: following the fad begun by Jean Harlow, she had dyed her hair
"platinum" blonde. Likewise startling was Metro-Goldwyn-
Mayer's announcement of who was to play the lead in *Red-*
Headed Woman: Jean Harlow, with head dyed or wigged.

"MERRILY WE GO TO HELL" is about a colyumist (Fredric MAY 30
March) who marries the daughter (Sylvia Sidney) of a packing millionaire. He grieves her by getting drunk inopportune-
ly. He is drunk when they meet, drunk at her announcement

party, slightly addled for their wedding. "Merrily we go to hell," he says on such occasions. Finally Sylvia Sidney sees that there is only one thing to do. She takes to the bottle also.

The picture is brilliantly acted. Sylvia Sidney has an extraordinary way of making audiences believe that she is ecstatically happy. She does it with a thoughtful, crooked smile and a small chuckle. Her pleasant state of mind is credible even when March, who has lost the wedding ring, slips his bottle opener around her finger.

JUNE 27 **"WINNER TAKE ALL"**—James Cagney always does his best sparring against his leading ladies and in this picture he only kicks the one who deserves it (Virginia Bruce).

Like Actor Cagney's previous impersonations, this one is not exactly acting—no one could be taught to say "bhointt up" as Cagney says it without being raised in sight of Brooklyn Bridge—but it is funny. His comment after listening to a piano recital: "That guy has a great left hand."

JULY 25 **"STRANGE INTERLUDE"**—Translated and truncated to cinema form, Eugene O'Neill's cinematized nine-act play retells capably the story of the woman who needed three men to satisfy her comprehensive fixation on her father. The play's famed soliloquies indicating the thoughts of the characters are retained and result in a recurrent trance effect as though an offstage ventriloquist were at work.

Norma Shearer is beautiful as Nina Leeds, particularly toward the end of the picture as the woman of 40. Clark Gable is Ned Darrell, the lover.

AUG. 8 **"WHITE ZOMBIE"** features a zombie factory in Haiti run by Bela Lugosi. The acting of everybody in it suggests that there may be some grounds for believing in zombies.

AUG. 15 **"HORSE FEATHERS"**—It seems that the trustees of Huxley College have been so haphazard as to select Groucho Marx as their school's new president. Harpo Marx is a dog-catcher. He has a large lamp post to attract large dogs, a small lamp post for lap-dogs. Running wildly about the town, he arrives at a speakeasy where Groucho Marx is trying to find a pair of professional football players to improve the Huxley team.

The Marx Brothers (from left: Harpo, Groucho, Chico, Zeppo). Says Groucho to his geography class: "The Lord Alps those that Alps themselves."

Incompetent Groucho Marx hires both Chico and Harpo, gives them each a contract. Presently, all three go to a classroom where Groucho gives a lecture on geography and anatomy. Says he: "The Lord Alps those that Alps themselves." Harpo and Chico stop clawing at pretty female classmates long enough to blow spitballs at Groucho. Groucho dismisses the class, blows spitballs back.

As everyone knows, there are really five Marx brothers: Leonard (Chico), Arthur (Harpo), Milton (Gummo), Julius (Groucho) and Herbert (Zeppo). They are descended from a Hanoverian magician and ventriloquist named Lafe Schoenberg, who toured Germany for 50 years, carrying his scenery, tricks, wife & three children in a roofed wagon.

Gummo now has a prosperous ladies' wear establishment in Manhattan. Zeppo acts straight juvenile rôles, does it poorly enough not to detract from the antics of his confrères.

Chico is differentiated by a certain irrelevant vehemence which makes it seem that he is chagrined by something but has forgotten what it is. Groucho is talkative, cool, depraved.

MONEY MAKERS: *Motion Picture Herald* last week announced the results of its poll of U.S. cinema exhibitors to reveal "The Biggest Money Making Stars of 1931-32." The winners:

1) Marie Dressler
2) Janet Gaynor
3) Joan Crawford
4) Charles Farrell
5) Greta Garbo
6) Norma Shearer
7) Wallace Beery
8) Clark Gable
9) Will Rogers
10) Joe E. Brown

AUG. 22 **"BIRD OF PARADISE"** cost $1,000,000 to make and discloses a volcano spouting lava like Wheatena. When a volcano appears in the cinema it is usually safe to assume that there will be very little else in the way of a story. A boatload of funloving U.S. travelers drops in at Tahiti and one of them (Joel McCrea) stays to make love to a native princess (Dolores Del Rio). He abducts her and builds her, with amazing ease, a native mansion where they live until the volcano begins to regurgitate. Then her tribesmen come to get them, to throw them into the volcano. The schooner with McCrea's friends comes back in time but the princess decides to stay on the island.

AUG. 29 **"LOVE ME TONIGHT"**—In a plot which seems scarcely more than an impromptu play on words and music, the only illogicality is Maurice Chevalier's preferring Jeanette MacDonald to Myrna Loy.

Myrna Loy can scarcely have been surprised at this state of affairs. She has been passed over for leading ladies who are usually her inferior in charm, appearance and ability, in more pictures than any other young actress in Hollywood. Born in Helena, Mont., she went to Los Angeles to go to art school.

The only question in "Love Me Tonight" is why Maurice Chevalier should prefer Jeanette MacDonald (right) to Myrna Loy.

There she fashioned some bits of sculpture that met with the approval of the late Rudolph Valentino and his wife. She became their protégé. When Mrs. Valentino produced *What Price Beauty?*, Myrna Loy had a small part. She has had more than a hundred small parts since then.

"LIFE BEGINS" is *Grand Hotel* in an obstetrical ward—the SEPT. 5 principal members of its cast are seven expectant mothers, one of them equipped with twins. The large lying-in cast of *Life Begins* emphasizes the predicament of its most pathetic member, Grace Sutton. She (Loretta Young) is a young matron who anticipates, in addition to the pangs of a delivery, 20 years in prison because she is a murderess. This causes the physicians who are attending her confinement to make a tragic decision. When her labor pains have lasted for 30 hours, they decide on a Caesarian operation, save the child and let the mother die.

Loretta (real name: Gretchen) Young two years ago helped make a name for herself by eloping to Yuma, Ariz. with Cinemactor Grant Withers, despite protests of her mother who said that, at 17, she was not old enough for matrimony. She refused to try to have her marriage annulled, ended it by divorce after 17 months. Appealing modulation of voice and manner, decorous softness of demeanor are Cinemactress

George Brent and Ruth Chatterton.   *Cooper and Hayes avoid a classic*
Now they can kiss as man and wife.   *botch, produce perfect Hemingway.*

Young's chief characteristics on the screen; she attributes them in part to her schooling in a Los Angeles convent. The fluffiness of her brown mop she attributes to her habit of shampooing it with cleaning fluid.

SEPT. 19 **"THE CRASH"** is a gloomy little survey of hard times in high places. George Brent is Geoffrey Gault, whose system for playing the stock market is to have his wife (Ruth Chatterton) make herself attractive to operators wiser than himself so that they will give her tips.

When George Brent kisses Ruth Chatterton now, he kisses his wife. A month ago Miss Chatterton married tall, dark-eyed Brent who is 28, an Irish newsman's son, born and schooled in Dublin. In several pictures, he played opposite Miss Chatterton, who still enjoys the distinction of being the only famed female stage-star to make an even greater success in talking pictures.

OCT. 3 **"MR. ROBINSON CRUSOE"** presents bouncing Douglas Fairbanks Sr. cheerfully burlesquing Defoe's old story. On his way to Sumatra to shoot tigers when his yacht passes close to a tropic island, he wagers a bet that he is competent to mold jungle into civilization with only bare hands and one toothbrush, and jumps overboard. His dog follows; Fairbanks throws back the toothbrush. Audiences chuckle as he staggers out of the surf with his alert, Boy Scout expression, ready for any emergency.

Having landed June 1, by June 24 he has made saws, jugs, hammocks, hatchet, outhouse with star & crescent. Soon afterward he has made a he-goat run a treadmill to churn the she-goat's milk, trained a turtle to follow food dangled by a stick in a circle, thereby lifting water from a well to run down a chute, over a fire and out of a faucet. And he lives in an impressive four-room house on a platform that must have taken the United Artists carpenter crew months to make.

"FAITHLESS"—Having tried without much success to find a satisfactory vehicle for Talullah Bankhead, whose eyelids have been compared to the fat stomachs of sun-burned babies, Paramount decided to lend her to Metro-Goldwyn-Mayer and see what happened. *Faithless* will probably leave Miss Bankhead about where she was before. She has a better leading man (Robert Montgomery) than in her previous vehicles. Otherwise, the picture is in the Bankhead tradition, a solemn sexual mumbo-jumbo of wealth impoverished and beauty in distress. OCT. 31

"CALL HER SAVAGE"—As the heroine of this opus, Miss Clara Bow is called upon to show the sexual glamour for which she is celebrated by beating a rattlesnake to death with a horsewhip, flaying a half-breed Indian, blacking the eye of her husband's mistress, practicing prostitution, boxing the ears of her second fiancé and punching a horse in the stomach. Confessed Actress Bow when she arrived in Manhattan last week: "I'm getting older, and the old hot-cha doesn't pay."

"A FAREWELL TO ARMS" will disappoint only those pessimists who, hearing about the difficulties that cropped up during the adaptation of Author Ernest Hemingway's novel, expected it to be a classic botch. DEC. 19

The picture emerges as a compelling and beautifully imagined piece of work, acted to perfection by Gary Cooper—whose numb mannerisms are precisely appropriate to his rôle —and by Helen Hayes.

EDUCATION

FEB. 15 **MORNINGSIDE'S MIRACLE:** In the guest's honor some 2,000 Columbia alumni from far & near traveled to Manhattan to gather in the Waldorf-Astoria for the largest dinner they or the hotel had ever given. It was broadcast over 81 U.S. stations and to the rest of the world over two short-wave stations. Similar dinners were also taking place in Paris, London, Berlin, Geneva, Mexico City, Havana, Moscow, Manila.

Every guest to be seated at the head table held honorary degrees from Columbia—except the honor guest himself, the university's president, Nicholas Murray Butler. President Butler has 34 degrees, U.S. and foreign, but Columbia has given him no more than he earned: A.B., M.A., Ph.D. Some day soon the alumni hope to confer upon him a "supreme honorary degree." In the meantime they pay him high personal tribute at the Butler Day banquet which marks Dr. Butler's 30th anniversary as president, 50th as alumnus, and 70th as a very human being.

Publicist as well as university president are the titles Dr. Butler gives himself in his *Who's Who* article, longest of any living U.S. citizen. Often and loudly Dr. Butler trumpets for Peace, the Republican Party and Repeal of the 18th Amendment. For his ardent salesmanship he won half a Nobel Peace Prize last December. [He shared it with social worker Jane Addams.]

"Nicholas Miraculous" was the name Theodore Roosevelt gave to his friend. Few contest the aptness of the title. Dynamic, downright in his "rightness," often sententious and rhetorical in public and private utterances, Dr. Butler serves the U.S. as an unofficial ambassador-at-large. He was the first unofficial foreign visitor ever to be received by the French Academy. He has advised the British Cabinet, lectured the Reichstag in German.

A Wet of Wets, he was one of the first notable persons after Prohibition to come out for repeal. He went as a delegate to his first Republican convention in 1888. Since 1904 he has never missed one. In 1912 as the vice-presidential nominee of his party he went down in defeat with William Howard Taft. In 1920 as the candidate of the New York delegation to the Chicago convention, he got 69½ votes for the presidential nomination that eventually went to Warren Gamaliel Harding. Older now, Dr. Butler has grown faintly supercilious toward public offices and the politicians who fill them. The idea of his seeking the Presidency he brushes aside as altogether unworthy of any man in his position.

COLLEGE BOARDS: At the turn of the century, U.S. headmasters found it a prodigious job to get their students into a college. No uniform requirements existed, each college held its own examinations, to which the candidates were obliged to journey no matter how far. In 1899 a national Entrance Board was suggested by Dr. Nicholas Murray Butler, who already at 37, was a moving spirit in U.S. pedagogy. Many an august college president objected. But Harvard's liberal Dr. Charles William Eliot approved, pointing out that colleges could still admit and reject applicants as they pleased. Colleges throughout the land fell in line, gradually discontinued their separate examinations. Today nearly every U.S. institution accepts, and most big ones require, College Board ratings. JULY 4

Up to Manhattan's Morningside Heights last week journeyed 700 school and college teachers from throughout the land, to mark this year's examination papers. All day long the readers worked. Evenings they talked over papers, swapped "boners" with academic gusto. A biology marker found this one:

Q. "Define and clearly distinguish between a spore and sperm."

A. "A spore grows right straight up into adultery but a sperm does not."

COPEY MOVES OUT: The word goes out: "Copey" will hold his Monday Evening on Wednesday instead of Thursday. Up swarm Harvard undergraduates to No. 15 on the top floor of antique Hollis Hall in the Yard. There is scuffling and grunting as places are found on furniture, window sills and floor. Cigarets and pipes are lit. The small, bald Boylston Professor SEPT. 12

of Rhetoric & Oratory fidgets a bit, adjusts his spectacles. He glares, fidgets some more, waits for silence. Then Charles Townsend Copeland begins to read aloud in a flexible voice, sympathetic with anything from Ring Lardner to Alfred Lord Tennyson.

Last week there was news for all Harvard men who had looked forward this autumn to climbing the creaking stairs to "Copey's" two small bachelor chambers. He announced that he was moving out of Hollis 15, where he had lived for 20 years. The Harvard Corporation had promised him the rooms as long as he should want them. But "Copey" is 72 now, the Yard is noisy, the stairs harder to climb than they used to be. For the past two years his doctor has been urging him to move to an apartment where meals could be prepared for him under his own roof.

Sad as Harvard felt over "Copey's" change of residence, there seemed in it a larger significance. It marked the passing of a style. A newer generation of pedagogs, at Harvard as elsewhere, has eschewed picturesqueness for briskness, practicality and scholarship. Younger savants have degrees aplenty. Charles Townsend Copeland did not bother; the A.B. he earned in 1882 was enough for him. It was fun to be cantankerous and crotchety, teaching Harvard men to write good prose, scaring them when they were late or noisy.

To young fellows "Copey" could be crushing. Two years ago saucy Tom Prideaux, editor of the Yale *Literary Magazine*, went up to look at Harvard. He visited "Copey," who stared at him and said: "Young man, I trust you are not planning to write any sketches." To an impertinent youth who suggested a headline to describe a fire: "Hollis a Holocaust, Copey a Crisp," he countered, "Nonsense! 'Copey Crisper Than Ever.'"

OCT. 3 **RIGHT-MINDED PITTSBURGH:** When General Douglas MacArthur, U.S. Army Chief of Staff, was selected to be commencement speaker at the University of Pittsburgh, 300 students gave tongue against "militarism." Three leaders who planned a pacifist demonstration were arrested, fined. Last week a higher court reversed the conviction. But few days later, every matriculating Pittsburgh student was required to sign an oath of allegiance to the U.S. Constitution, the laws of Pennsylvania and the regulations of the University. Cried University Business Manager John Weber: "We want right-minded students here!"

ANT v. HOUSEFLY: Many a French parent has complained in recent years of the burdensome work put upon his children in school. Some have made protest to the French Parliament. Lately they exhibited the following problem, given to 15-year-olds in the *Lycée* (high school) at Nantes: DEC. 26

On a circular track 25 centimeters in diameter a housefly and an ant ran a race. The stride of the ant was $^5/_{10}$ millimeters in length; three of his strides equaled one of the housefly's. In two minutes the ant made 2,000 strides; the housefly 500.

Given: 1) the race was for 300 meters; 2) after eight hours the housefly began to cheat by flying to the point on the race track diametrically opposite to him, in the space of one second every alternate round, from that minute on; 3) at the same instant the ant sprained one of his ankles so that he could take only 1,200 strides every two minutes.

To find: Which won the race? At the finish, what was the time of each contestant? What was the distance covered while running by the housefly? How many times did the ant run around the track?

The Nantes schoolmaster who set the problem gave his pupils one day for it. None solved it correctly.

The correct answers: The ant won the race in 11 hr. 20 min. The fly's time was 12 hr. 1 min. 16 sec. The fly ran 270 meters. The ant circled the track 382 times.

SEPT. 19 **MORE MERRY-GO-ROUND:** A year ago when *Washington Merry-Go-Round* first appeared in bookstores the *Christian Science Monitor* discharged Robert S. Allen, its capital correspondent, for having been one of the anonymous authors. Lately appeared *More Merry-Go-Round,* another volume of critical chitchat about official Washington. Everyone knew that Drew Pearson, Baltimore *Sun*'s able newshawk at the State and War Departments, was one of the authors. His contribution included a chapter entitled "The Cotillion Leader," which scorched Secretary of War Patrick Jay Hurley. Few days after that appeared, Reporter Pearson lost his job.

In Washington, and among newsmen throughout the land, there was astonishment at the discharge of Pearson, far greater than at the fate of Allen. The *Sun* is liberal, the *Monitor* punctilious. But last week such generalities were forgotten in debate over specific, pungent questions: How much did Secretary Hurley have to do with the firing of Pearson? Whose word should be accepted as truth: "Pat" Hurley's or Drew Pearson's? The Chicago *Tribune* thought the questions important enough for front-page discussion.

Reporter Pearson's story: Just after *More Merry-Go-Round* was published he was summoned by his Managing Editor William Emmet Moore who inquired pleasantly if Pearson were going to write any more books, said the *Sun* would be pleased if every staff member produced a best seller. A day or two later Pearson was summoned to the War Department. He found Secretary Hurley, white-faced, "in a towering rage," pacing up and down his office. Said the Secretary: "This is a terrible thing you have done, Drew. You are trying to ruin my career. . . . Damnable lies. . . . You wrote that I posture before a mirror. Look around my office. There isn't a mirror in it. (The book said: "It became noised around that prior to their big dinners, the Hurleys practiced their exits and entrances before full-length mirrors.") You wrote that I used airplanes at Government expense to make political speeches and that I had smashed up a $70,000 plane. I'm going to put you in your place. I'm going to get your job. You're going to learn that you can't say things like this about me. I won't have it. I'm going to call up Paul Patterson (president of the *Sun*) and tell him about this campaign against me."

Secretary Hurley's story: The Secretary did not ask for Pearson's dismissal.

The *Sun*: Secretary Hurley did complain about news stories filed by Pearson to the *Sun* in recent months, but made no protest about "The Cotillion Leader" chapter in *More Merry-Go-Round*. Of their own volition, *Sun* executives decided that Pearson's part in the book was a "last straw," that his usefulness to the newspaper was ended.

OCHS v. BULLOCK: Manhattanites who do not read Adolph S. SEPT. 26 Ochs' august, authoritative, exhaustive New York *Times,* sometimes give as their excuse that it is "heavy," meaning dull and long-winded. In the literal sense the *Times* is indeed heavy, heavier than any other New York daily. Last Sunday the *Times* weighed 2 lb. $5\frac{1}{2}$ oz.

The *Times* does not, like some provincial papers, extol its mass as a point of glory. But in its 2 lb. $5\frac{1}{2}$ oz. Sunday ediion the *Times* last week carried the following:

COPY OF TIMES FELLS A BULLOCK

AS MARINE PILOT DROPS MAIL

"Managua, Nicaragua, Sept. 17.—

"Captain George L. Maynard of the Marine Corps related that while he was in Jinotega recently an aviator dropped a copy of the New York *Times* from a high altitude and the paper struck a bullock squarely between the eyes, knocking it to the ground. After a short time the bullock arose bewildered and fled into a wood."

$$\boxed{\textbf{BOOKS}}$$

JAN. 4 **"IDYLL IN THE DESERT"**—William Faulkner. If you are collecting Faulkner items, *Idyll in the Desert* would be a good morbid one to get. An unpublished short story by the author of *Sanctuary* and *The Sound and the Fury,* it was limited to 400 copies, each signed by the author, has already been sold out.

The story relates the sad fate of a nameless woman. Married to a rich husband in the East, with two children, she left them to come out to the desert to nurse her "lunger" lover, ten years younger than herself. He recovered and one fine day up & left her. She stayed on in the lonely cabin by herself, waiting for him to come back. He never did. She contracted tuberculosis from him and gradually wasted away. As she was being taken to a California hospital to die, a honeymoon couple passed the open door of the baggage car where she was lying on a stretcher. The man was her lover. He looked at her, did not recognize her, but she knew him. At the next station she was dead.

JAN. 18 **"SWISS FAMILY MANHATTAN"**—Christopher Morley. Beginning in the style of Johann Wyss' classic boy's story, Author Morley's satire purports to be written by a serious-minded, middle-aged little Swiss who leaves his filing clerk's job with the League of Nations to take his wife and two sons on a pleasure cruise in an airliner. Over the Atlantic the airship runs into a frightful storm. Just in time the Robinsons abandon the crippled ship, are whipped away into the night on an air-raft. They come safely to rest on the mooring mast of the Empire State Building, still unfinished, which at first they take to be some kind of gigantic tree. Father Robinson makes several exploratory trips down into the seething jungle below, gradually comes to the conclusion the place is civilized.

Even his criticisms are a left-handed compliment: "The Americans fall into mass hysterias on small provocation; they continually suppose themselves on the verge either of calamity or salvation; everything is exaggerated to a panacea or a menace, so much so that I could not tell, reading the advertising, which was believed the greater peril to the republic: Russian communism or sore gums."

"BRAVE NEW WORLD"—Aldous Huxley. In the Year of Our FEB. 8 Ford 632 the world was a vastly different place. At the Central London Hatchery & Conditioning Centre fertilized human eggs were cultured in bottles, decanted after nine months as lusty infants to be further conditioned by *hypnopaedia* (sleep teaching) into useful, satisfied citizens of Alpha, Beta, Gamma, Delta or Epsilon class. The Betas, Gammas, Deltas and Epsilons did all the work; the Alphas had all the fun. They traveled in helicopters, went to the "feelies," danced to the music of sexophones. In the Year of Our Ford 632 every woman wore a Malthusian belt, blushed with joy if a young man told her she was pneumatic. There was no pain, no disease, no old age, little thought. The words "mother," "baby," "home," were gross obscenities, made so by Our Ford (who sometimes called himself Our Freud).

A page from Swift, a page or two from Jules Verne, Herbert George Wells and Anatole France; put them all together and they spell H-U-X-L-E-Y. Delighted when critics discovered that he was a Thinker, Author Huxley is still unwilling to give up tomfoolery. In *Brave New World* he mixes it so well with sober, cynical conclusions that it is hard to tell where one stops and the other begins.

"1919"—John Dos Passos. When Karl Marx postulated class MARCH 14 struggle as the essence of social history, he meant something subtler than street-riots and strikes. There is also the psychological struggle in which adversity gives the underdog strength and perversity steals the upper-dog's strength away. The War and its aftermath exemplified such a struggle: when the underdogs who did the fighting found out for whom they were fighting and why, there was a revolution in their way of thinking that shed no blood, but shed many of the orthodox ideals that had held society together until then.

In *1919* Author Dos Passos recounts an American history of this mental molt. As in *The 42nd Parallel,* the story sand-

William Faulkner. Only 400 copies of his latest book are printed. Page 207.

John Dos Passos. His "1919" is a story of mental molt in America.

wiches pictorial life-histories between news-clippings, impressionistic sketches, and lives of historical figures written in a kind of prose-libre. The transitions from section to section are artfully casual, abrupt. The all-embracing social transition gives them focus and coherence.

Author Dos Passos closes his book with the burial of the Unknown Soldier in Arlington National Cemetery. "In the tarpaper morgue at Chalons-sur-Marne in the reek of chloride of lime and the dead, they picked out the pine box that held all that was left of—enie menie minie moe." Woodrow Wilson laid on poppies, the orators laid on praise. They did not realize, Author Dos Passos implies, that their civilization was being buried with the dead.

APRIL 4 **"THURSO'S LANDING"**—Robinson Jeffers. Hard by the Pacific surf-line at Carmel, Calif. stands a tower of grey Santa Lucia granite, sea-worn boulders rolled up from the shore and heaved into place by Poet Robinson Jeffers for his own perch. For several years the stones rose in their courses; as they began to invade the upper air, a hawk dropped down to haunt them. Now Hawk Tower stands 30 ft. high.

The building of the tower was urged by Poet Jeffers' wife, who thought the exercise would be good for her husband. Here in the mornings, when his slow pulse beats only 40 times a minute, he slowly writes his poems; in the afternoons, when his pulse speeds up to 60, he plants trees, rolls stones.

Poet Jeffers, though gentle (he has never killed an animal) is not shy; though not shy he is not sociable, seeks neither the companionship of old friends nor acquaintanceship with new. Toward the human species as a whole, he is reserved, cold and the visions, the desires that fool man out of his limits lead Poet Jeffers' tragic heroes & heroines into dark and terrifying ways. "Tamar," "The Tower Beyond Tragedy," "The Women at Point Sur" all tell incestuous tales. "Roan Stallion" tells of a woman's love for a horse. Though critics, with few exceptions, have extolled the splendor and intensity of Poet Jeffers' works, some women think that he spoils his poems with such outrageous themes. Even his wife complained. "Robin," said she after he had finished "Roan Stallion," "when will you quit forbidden themes?" Robin answered with an enigmatic smile. To dignify men's passions, men's predicaments, he had merely motivated his tragedies with themes already given classic sanction by the Greeks.

In *Thurso's Landing,* however, he writes his most native American, least Greekish tragedy, leaving sexual perversion almost entirely out. Its terrors are more Amerindian than Greek—the terrors of a diminishing race under Nature's relentlessly observant eye. The outlines of the American continent and of its troubled inhabitants, grow colder and clearer under Poet Jeffers' western-starry light.

> *The old ocean at the land's foot, the vast*
> *Gray extension beyond the long white*
>   *violence;*
> *A herd of cows and the bull*
> *Far distant, hardly apparent up the dark*
>   *slope;*
> *And the gray air haunted with hawks:*
> *This place is the noblest thing I have*
>   *ever seen.*

"THE STORE"—T. S. Stribling. In *The Forge* Author Stribling gave the first spin to a projected three-novel cycle about the South. *The Store* tells particularly of Col. Miltiades Vaiden and his rise to notoriety in Florence, Ala., about the

JULY 4

time of Grover Cleveland's presidencies. In pitch, scope, execution it is easily the most important U.S. novel of the year.

Col. Vaiden, a vastly human character who should walk straight into the U.S. Pantheon, is more than the central figure of the story. He is the focus in which the town of Florence reflects its earthen realities, its haunting bright potentialities. Left high & dry by the Civil War, the Colonel is now of no particular account in his own eyes, or in anybody else's. In the middle of his middle-aged decay Miltiades looks about Florence for some foothold to begin his climb. A drunken confession on the part of T. Handback, the town's wealthy merchant, gives him his chance. Years ago Handback had cheated Miltiades of his small fortune in cotton; now, when the Colonel learns that the highly respectable Handback keeps a quadroon mistress, he uses the information to pry himself, as a clerk, into Handback's store.

Trusted entirely by the rascally Handback, Miltiades oversees the collection of his crops. Chance brings him the opportunity to settle old scores—he ships 500 bales of Handback cotton to New Orleans, hides the proceeds. The whole town knows of his peculation, accepts it philosophically: "Hit's nachel—hit's nachel. Evahthing what's bad is nachel."

AUG. 29 **"THE PAST RECAPTURED"**—Proustians, whose numbers are growing in all Western lands, say that the late great Marcel Proust was the ranking writer of his time. With U.S. publication of *The Past Recaptured,* seventh and last part of his gigantic "novel," *The Remembrance of Things Past,* U.S. Proustians may now read their Bible from Genesis to Revelations, without benefit of dictionary.

It was not easy to find a publisher for *The Remembrance of Things Past.* André Gide, who later found in Proust "a lake of delights," was at first unimpressed. One publisher was annoyed at Proust's devoting 50 pages to "how he turns over & over in his bed before getting to sleep." Finally the first volume was published at Proust's expense. Critics hardly knew what to say about it, could not make up their minds until the second volume won the Prix Goncourt. From that day on, Proust's reputation, like his ponderous book, slowly gathered strength.

Says Proust: "A part of the book is a part of my life which

I had forgotten, and which I rediscovered eating a little madeleine which I had dipped in tea, a flavor which delighted me before I had recognized it and identified it as one I had once relished almost every morning; immediately all my life at once was resuscitated, and, as I tell it in the book, all the people and gardens of that period of my life came out of a cup of tea."

"VAN LOON'S GEOGRAPHY"—Geography, physical and polit- SEPT. 12 ical, has never been made a very exciting subject in school. Smart Hendrik Willem Van Loon makes it exciting by taking it out of school and glorifying it. Written in Van Loon's familiar, not to say impertinent style, as if he were talking to children but hoped to be overheard by grown-ups, the 525 pages are thickly plummed with sketches and maps, many of them in bright colors. The book's jacket conceals a gaily inaccurate map of the world, "suitable for framing."

Though Nature is the central character, Man is hero of *Van Loon's Geography.* He is shown against an economic and geographic background, his character and achievements modified by the contours of his country, the basis of a mountain race, the tendency of a trade route. The inner workings of the Gulf Stream, the puzzle of which is latitude and which is longitude, are other mysteries brightly revealed.

Hendrik Willem Van Loon. His geography is impertinent and gay.

Ernest Hemingway. As a bullfighter he is hilarious.

SEPT. 26 **"DEATH IN THE AFTERNOON"**—Ernest Hemingway's latest book may alienate many of his disciples, but it is a genuinely Hemingway production.

The bullfight, says Hemingway in this compendious guide, is not really a sport but a tragedy, in which the matador is the literal hero. "Bull-fighting is the only art in which the artist is in danger of death and in which the degree of brilliance in the performance is left to the fighter's honor. The essence of the greatest emotional appeal of bullfighting is the feeling of immortality that the bullfighter gives to the spectators. He is playing with death, bringing it closer, closer, closer, to himself, a death that you know is in the horns because you have the canvas-covered bodies of the horses on the sand to prove it. He gives the feeling of his immortality, and as you watch it, it becomes yours. Then when it belongs to both of you, he proves it with the sword."

The author has done a little amateur bullfighting himself but "was too old, too heavy and too awkward. In the ring I served as little else than target or punching dummy for the bulls. I would fall onto the bull's muzzle, clinging to his horns. This caused great hilarity among the spectators." Husky (200-lb.) Author Hemingway would rather fish than drink tea. At 34 he has become a U.S. legend.

OCT. 17 **"MUTINY ON THE BOUNTY"**—Charles Nordhoff and James Norman Hall. Iron men and wooden ships—South Sea paradise—mutiny—shipwreck—open boats—a trial for piracy—unjust sentence—happy ending—these are the time-honored ingredients of Authors Nordhoff & Hall's surefire seafaring tale. Founded on fact, *Mutiny on the Bounty,* though fictionalized and given a narrator-hero, still reads like an actual account.

OCT. 24 **"THE PRINCESS MARRIES THE PAGE"**—In 1917 Undergraduate Edna St. Vincent Millay, precocious senior at Vassar College, finished a one-act play in verse, *The Princess Marries the Page.* It was her first play. In it a Princess, "the most beautiful Princess you have ever seen," is reading in her tower retreat. A saucy page interrupts her by tootling on his flute. Their little flirtation is doing nicely when he confesses that he is no page but a spy. Soldiers are looking for him. When they enter he hides; the Princess is in process of lying him out of it but he surrenders himself. The King regretfully prepares to do his duty, when the page in time's nick disproves his spydom, proves himself a king's son.

While the rest of the U.S. was buckling into the machine that was to send A.E.F. divisions catapulting into France, seven Vassar girls were whispering and giggling over their parts. On the much-rehearsed night Authoress Millay played the Princess, took many a curtain call. Authoress Millay lost the manuscript of her play. Years later she found it again, among some old papers. Easily most popular poetess of the U.S., Edna St. Vincent Millay could afford now to foist off on her sympathetic public almost any callow piece of juvenilia. But *The Princess Marries the Page* is surprisingly, delightfully neither callow nor juvenile. Her airily unpretentious blank verse succeeds perfectly in cloaking a little masterpiece.

"FAREWELL MISS JULIE LOGAN"—Sir James Matthew Barrie NOV. 14 has certainly done his bit for the world of letters; readers, without actually thinking him dead, may well have thought him finished. But now, after nearly 30 years (in which he has written 14 plays but no stories) comes a little Scottish fairy tale as neat as a pin, bright as a button. Barrie lovers will hail it; it should send readers who do not know him scuttling back to his early works.

Adam Yestreen is pastor of a little hamlet among the hills, still visited (say some) by ghosts of Prince Charlie's men—aye, and women too. When winter sets in in earnest, the manse is isolated from the rest of the village; sometimes the pastor has to preach at his flock from across the brook. He is lonely, but his one neighbor, old Mrs. Lindinnock, always waves goodnight to him by pulling her windowshade up & down.

When one fine night a young and beautiful stranger appears with old Mrs. Lindinnock at a sociable, and even calls on him at the manse, Pastor Yestreen's simple soul is nearly swept from its moorings. Miss Julie Logan is a flirtatious chit, but her heart is kind. Parson Yestreen comes as near as nothing to marrying her outright. The fairy story has a sighing end, as a proper Barrie fairy story should.

Very much of a bygone generation, 72-year-old Sir James Matthew Barrie sets such modern teeth as Aldous Huxley's excruciatingly on edge. If sentimentality be a sin, Author Barrie should fry eternally in hell. But sentimentality has paid him well. From such perennial gold-mines as *Peter Pan* and *The Little Minister,* royalties have rolled him into affluence. Bachelor by divorce, Sir James lives like a grandfatherly pixy in comfortable solitude on London's Adelphi Terrace. He frequently emerges to go to his club (The Athenaeum), to garden parties at Buckingham Palace. With money to burn, he has been generous to other people's fires. He gave some $25,000 to the tragic Scott Antarctic Expedition, some $50,000 more to Scott's widow. He made over the royalty rights of *Peter Pan* to London's Hospital for Sick Children.

DEC. 26 **"MARY LINCOLN"**—In Chicago's big pan, 15 years go, one of the brightest literary flashes was Poet Carl Sandburg. A later day will probably rate his biological work on the Lincolns as his most considerable performance. In *Mary Lincoln*'s 159 pages he telescopes the life of Lincoln's termagant wife as a little companion book to his 604 pages on her husband.

Sandburg's account will not change the picture U.S.-history readers have already formed of Lincoln's chubby, pathologically bad-tempered wife, but may add a few particulars to their knowledge. Sensitive to appearances—especially to the

Edna St. Vincent Millay rediscovers an unpretentious little masterpiece.   *Chubby Mrs. Lincoln never let herself be pictured alone with lanky Abe.*

appearance she and her lanky husband made together—Mary Lincoln would never allow a photograph to be taken of them as a couple. Her three half-brothers all fought in the Confederate army, giving rise to such rumors of her anti-Union sympathies that Lincoln once felt called upon to testify in person, before a Congressional investigating committee, to her loyalty. When she lost her temper, which she did frequently, she completely lost control of herself, regardless of witnesses.

The brain disease to which Biographer Sandburg attributes most of Mary Lincoln's shrewishness finally became too much for her; in 1875 her family had her committed to a sanatorium. Set free a year later, she wandered unhappily abroad, came home, hid in her sister's house in Springfield to wait for a leisurely death.

"AMID THESE STORMS"—Winston S. Churchill. Though Winston Churchill grew up physically long ago (he is 58), he is still and perennially the bad boy of British politics. Bubbling with super-adolescent ideas, he cannot refrain from sounding off on any subject that catches his briskly roving eye. Always refreshing (if you like enthusiasm *per se*), often more humorous than he intends, he apologizes for this collection of outbursts by saying that in an old world one must still amuse oneself like a child.

Aggressively conservative, Winston Churchill's desk-poundings will please many a Fundamentalist in politics. But the next moment, with absent-minded effrontery, he is apt to give away a point to the enemy: "Democratic governments drift along the line of least resistance, taking short views, paying their way with sops and doles and smoothing their way with pleasant-sounding platitudes. Never was there less continuity or design in their affairs, and yet towards them are coming swiftly changes which will revolutionize for good or ill not only the whole economic structure of the world but the social habits and moral outlook of every family. Only the Communists have a plan and a gospel. It is a plan fatal to personal freedom and a gospel founded upon hate."

Optimist Churchill may give other optimists (including himself) food for thought when he admits that if he had a second chance at life, "I have no doubt that I do not wish to live it over again."

Numerals in italics indicate an illustration of subject mentioned.

PICTURE CREDITS

x

PRODUCTION STAFF FOR TIME INCORPORATED
John L. Hallenbeck (Vice President and Director of Production),
Robert E. Foy and Caroline Ferri
Text photocomposed under the direction of Albert J. Dunn and Arthur J. Dunn

QUOTES OF THE YEAR

President Herbert Hoover

> *(to Crooner Rudy Vallée, visiting the White House—p. 12):* "If you can sing a song that would make people forget the Depression, I'll give you a medal."

Dr. Albert Einstein

> *(on being asked by a U.S. reporter for his views on Prohibition—p. 160):* "That's your trouble, not mine."

Italian Dictator Benito Mussolini

> *(p. 131):* "I can sum up the United States in two words—Prohibition and Lindbergh! America must go Wet to find herself."

Richard Whitney, President of the New York Stock Exchange

> *(testifying before a U.S. Senate investigation into Wall Street practices—p. 179):* "We have brought this country to its standing in the world by speculation."

Ernest Hemingway

> *(describing his own attempts at bullfighting—p. 213):* "I was too old, too heavy and too awkward. I would fall onto the bull's muzzle, clinging to his horns. This caused great hilarity among the spectators."

ANSWERS TO PICTURE QUIZ—1: Pierre Laval, Premier of France; 2: Al Smith, Democratic Presidential contender; 3: Emperor Hirohito of Japan; 4: President-Elect Franklin D. Roosevelt; 5: Poet Robinson Jeffers; 6: Charles A. Lindbergh Jr.; 7: Tennis Champion Ellsworth Vines; 8: Britain's King George V; 9: Violinist Yehudi Menuhin; 10: James A. Farley, Chairman, Democratic National Committee; 11: German Chancellor Franz von Papen; 12: Actress Katharine Cornell; 13: Edouard Herriott, Premier of France; 14: Senator Huey Long of Louisiana; 15: Norman Thomas, Socialist Candidate for President; 16: Neville Chamberlain, British Chancellor of the Exchequer.